THE LEADERLESS
REVOLUTION

THE LEADERLESS REVOLUTION

*How Ordinary People Will Take Power
and Change Politics in the 21st Century*

CARNE ROSS

Have the courage to read the truth.

**SIMON &
SCHUSTER**

London · New York · Sydney · Toronto · New Delhi

A CBS COMPANY

First published in Great Britain by Simon & Schuster UK Ltd, 2011
A CBS Company

1 3 5 7 9 10 8 6 4 2

Simon & Schuster UK Ltd
1st Floor
222 Gray's Inn Road
London
WC1X 8HB

www.simonandschuster.co.uk

Simon & Schuster Australia, Sydney
Simon & Schuster India, New Delhi

A CIP catalogue for this book is available
from the British Library.

Hardback ISBN: 978-1-84737-534-6
Trade paperback ISBN: 978-0-85720-901-6

Typeset by Hewer Text UK Ltd, Edinburgh
Printed and bound in Great Britain by CPI Mackays, Chatham ME5 8TD

To I and C

War will be dead, the scaffold will be dead, frontiers will be dead, royalty will be dead, dogmas will be dead, man will begin to live.

Victor Hugo

The revolution will not be televised.

Gil Scott-Heron

CONTENTS

Introduction:
The Sheer Cliff Face

Turning and turning in the widening gyre
The falcon cannot hear the falconer;
Things fall apart; the centre cannot hold;
Mere anarchy is loosed upon the world,
The blood-dimmed tide is loosed, and everywhere
The ceremony of innocence is drowned;
The best lack all conviction, while the worst
Are full of passionate intensity.

"The Second Coming" W.B. Yeats, 1921

Some stories from the young 21st century:

When the H1N1 "swine flu" virus struck Mexico in early 2009, it took only hours and days to spread to every continent in the world except unpopulated Antarctica. Authorities struggled to contain the spread of the disease. Desperate to prevent the import of infection, some governments resorted to aiming remote thermometers at arriving air passengers to measure their body temperature. The World Health Organisation, responsible for global coordination of the fight against disease, admitted some months after the first outbreak that it had been unable to keep up with the vast flow of data from national health bodies. The virus, it later appeared, was spreading out of control.

One Sunday that same year, a preacher from a Sikh sect was attacked during a service in Vienna, Austria. Sant Rama Nand was set upon by six men armed with knives and a pistol and died early the next day. Within a few hours, widespread riots had broken out across the Punjab, where the preacher's sect was based. By night-fall – only six hours after Sant Rama Nand had died – several people had been killed in turmoil that had convulsed Punjabi towns and cities. Thousands of Sikhs took to the streets, clashing with police and setting fire to buildings and vehicles. Major high-ways were blocked by bonfires of tyres and sticks. Trains were attacked in several places. The authorities had little or no warning of the outbreak.

One afternoon in 2010, it took less than thirty minutes for the Dow Jones Industrial Average to fall by nearly 1,000 points – the biggest one-day points decline in the Dow's history. It took five months for regulators to explain what had happened. According to the Securities and Exchange Commission report, the rapid plunge was triggered by a poorly executed sale by one mutual fund company. The firm started to sell $4.1 billion of futures contracts through an algorithmic trade, mistakenly taking account only of volume, not time or price. Buyers, including "high-frequency" traders who make rapid high-volume purchases and sales to exploit tiny price margins in a dynamic market, purchased the contracts. As sales of the contracts accelerated, the seller's algorithm responded to the increase in volume by unloading the contracts faster, pushing prices down further. The liquidity crunch then spread to the equity market. Many traders withdrew from the market. Some reverted to manual systems but could not keep up with the spike in volume. As the market dived, shares in some household-name companies were sold for as little as a cent. The SEC's report was widely criticised for offering no effective prescription on how to prevent such disruption in future[1].

In the summer of 2008, food prices increased dramatically across the globe thanks, it seems, to a sudden surge in oil prices, although the causes of the spike are not fully understood. One factor may have been the introduction of subsidies for ethanol production in the US Congress. Another possibility: speculation. The rocketing prices caused riots and political tension in Cairo and Indonesia and many other countries and reinforced an already-emerging trend that some have called a "food crunch" of static global supply and rising demand[2]. The prices of commodities such as rice and wheat jumped to record highs, triggering food riots from Haiti to Egypt to Bangladesh and Cameroon and prompting UN appeals for food aid for more than thirty countries in sub-Saharan Africa.

In response to this phenomenon, companies and in some cases governments in money-rich but "food-poor" countries, like South Korea and Saudi Arabia, began to buy up land and agricultural rights in money-poor but land-rich countries. The Saudi Star company plans to spend up to $2 billion in the next few years acquiring and developing 500,000 hectares of land in Ethiopia, one of the poorest – and hungriest – countries in the world[3]. Up to fifty million hectares of land – an area more than double the size of Britain – has been bought in the last few years or is under negotiation by governments and wealthy investors, often enjoying state subsidies. The South Korean company Daewoo bought the rights to as much as half of Madagascar's available agricultural land. This deal in turn helped trigger a coup against the Malagasy government that signed the deal. This coup produced political instability in Madagascar that continues to the time of writing.

Earlier in the century, an Egyptian architecture student living in Hamburg was horrified by reports of Russia's brutal campaign against separatists, mostly Muslim, in Chechnya in the Southern Caucasus, a war whose horrors were scarcely reported in the information-overloaded citadels of the West. The Chechnya war confirmed his view of the global oppression of Muslims. Mohamed Atta joined a local mosque where, it was later learned, he was introduced to the concept of *jihad*, a personal struggle for liberation.

Atta made his way to Pakistan, to join a terrorist network called "The Base" or Al Qaeda, which had been founded – and funded – by a middle-aged man who himself had been radicalised by the Soviet Union's occupation of Muslim Afghanistan – as well as America's military domination of his home country, Saudi Arabia. In the Afghan *mujahideen*'s victory over the Soviet occupation forces, Osama bin Laden found his inspiration to seek a global *jihad*. Mohamed Atta was to become the pilot of the American Airlines Boeing 767 which cannoned into the North Tower of New York's World Trade Center. Walking to work that dread morning, I heard his aircraft fly overhead.

The singular act of the 9/11 attacks helped trigger the allied invasions of two countries, and further massive, complex and unforeseeable change. The attacks were brilliantly anatomised in the US Congress 9/11 Report, which took over eight hundred pages to describe the antecedents and chronology of this one single, if remarkable, event: and *that* was concise.

More recently, the defaults of a few "sub-prime" mortgage holders concentrated in just three American states triggered in a very short space of time a global economic meltdown that – amongst many, many other things – brought down several long-established banks in America and necessitated a $700 billion bailout of other banks. When confidence in the ability of US banks to meet their obligations collapsed, the rapid contraction of credit was contagious across the globe, destroying in quick time both over-leveraged banks, and the deposits of their customers. Banks in Iceland fell overnight, eliminating at a stroke the savings of depositors in the UK. The ramifications of that event continue to delay Iceland's entry into the European Union, while in Britain the credit crunch, among other factors, has contributed to the most severe austerity measures and government spending cuts in many decades, including a seventy percent cut to higher-education budgets. In Hong Kong, thousands of small investors and pensioners suddenly lost their Lehman "mini-bonds", worth billions of dollars, when Lehman Brothers, founded in 1850, fell in the US[4].

The origins of the "credit crunch" were manifold and are debated still. Greedy lending by banks, unwise borrowing by house-buyers, loosening legislation from government, enacted with the worthy intention of enabling broader home ownership: perhaps all of them played a part. But some have suggested a more deep-seated cause – the growing inequality in America between the rich and everyone else, which drove the income-stagnant middle classes to borrow ever more to maintain their living standards amidst rising costs.

Another intriguing factor has been barely noted. The statistical models used by the banks to assess the risks of bundled mortgages were out of date: not only did they underestimate the volume and riskiness of the increasingly popular sub-prime mortgages, the banks' models also underestimated interconnectedness within the housing and mortgage markets, regionally and nationally. The preponderance of the "no money down" high debt-to-deposit sub-prime mortgages meant that only a small dip in the economy made huge numbers of mortgages suddenly unaffordable, and the buyers defaulted. The banks had underestimated the degree to which one thing would lead quickly to many others. They underestimated complexity.

Whatever the cause, no government was ready for the crash, which came almost without warning. President George W. Bush declared later that he had been "blindsided" by the crisis, saying that he "assumed any major credit troubles would have been flagged by the regulators or credit agencies"[5]. The cascading and multiple effects of the "credit crunch", many of which have yet to be felt, included the loss of tens of millions of jobs across the globe, and an immeasurable but nonetheless notable shift of power from West to

East, as the US relied ever more heavily upon China to buy up almost a trillion dollars' worth of American government debt to finance the government bailout.

The tortured, twisting paths of cause to effect in these stories of the 21st century are discernible only in retrospect by separating out these threads from the confusing rat's nest of simultaneous events – itself a somewhat artificial and falsifying exercise. But these stories are not extraordinary. They are typical of a vastly interconnected age, where billions of people are interacting constantly, a wholly unprecedented phenomenon which we are only beginning to understand. These events were not predictable by most conventional theories of politics or economics.

Some may see chaos in these episodes, or purely random cause and effect. These events do not suggest the structured order of past experience – of units, be they states or individuals, behaving according to established theories of international relations, or neo-classical economics, predictable for the most part, and comprehensible with our existing models. But neither are they chaos, a random meaningless mess. They are something else. This is a new dispensation – complexity – requiring new tools: the science of complex systems. Pioneers in many fields are using techniques like agent-based modelling and network analysis to begin to offer powerful new insights into this multiplying complexity.

But this new world requires something else beyond new tools of interpretation. This world is defying the ability of existing structures and institutions to understand and arbitrate events effectively. Even senior government officials confess the decline of state power: ". . . we are in a world where governments, as a whole, have less power than they once did" a senior US State Department official recently said, sensibly concluding, "Let's take the world as we now see it."[6] Confidential briefing papers prepared for the UN Secretary-General noted the declining importance not only of the UN itself, but also of governments in managing the world's most pressing

political, economic and environmental problems, observing cheer-
ily that, "Our planet's ability to sustain life, as we know it, is under
enormous strain." [7] As Parag Khanna has commented:

> globalisation is . . . diffusing power away from the west in partic-
> ular, but also from states and towards cities, companies, religious
> groups, humanitarian non-governmental organisations and
> super-empowered individuals, from terrorists to philanthro-
> pists. This force of entropy will not be reversed for decades – if
> not for centuries.[8]

Timothy Garton Ash has called this world "Not a new world order
but a new world disorder. An unstable kaleidoscope world – frac-
tured, overheated, germinating future conflicts."[9] Governments
failed to predict the credit crunch, as they did 9/11. Their blunt
methods to manage both economic volatility and terrorism – as
well as other global problems – are insufficient, and sometimes
counter-productive.

Politicians argue that only if *they* are in power will decisions be
the right ones, and thus we must suffer tedious rounds of facile
political argument over enduring and deep-seated problems, when
closer analysis of these problems leads to the more disturbing
conclusion that no politician and no government, however wise,
however right, is able to solve them. Somehow we know this.
Frustration with conventional politics is rising everywhere, depressing voter turnout and fuelling popular anger. Politicians too can
sense the mood, but are unable to offer any prescription except
more of the same politics, perhaps spiced with a dangerous and
hollow populism.

This new world requires something else beyond more promises, something beyond new theories of interpretation, something
that might, just might, make us feel at last that the tools fit the job.
This new world requires a new politics.

* * *

Climate change, terrorism, ceaseless wars in places that defy understanding or resolution and where victory or defeat both seem far
away*, a perpetual economic volatility. These are now already-
familiar problems of this young and turbulent century. They are
easy problems to define: borderless, a product of the new
"globalised" world. But at the same time they appear intractable:
there seems very little that any individual can do about them.

Taking their allotted rôle, instead governments, and associations of governments – the UN, the EU, international conferences
in Copenhagen or Doha – claim that *they* have these problems in
hand. Every day witnesses a summit, a statement or a resolution
claiming to address these worrying ills. It is a never-ending video-
feed of activity, tedious to watch in detail, but nonetheless
reassuring in its unceasing activity and torrent of verbiage: at
least, that is the intention.

"Trust us", the statements say, we have these problems under
control. But the evidence suggests otherwise, more and more
insistently. Measure the *outputs*, not the promises made. Take two
familiar problems.

At the 2009 Copenhagen climate-change summit, an intensive
two-year international negotiation involving hundreds of delegates
from almost every country, and thousands of pressure groups and
lobbyists, produced, at its end, a short two-page document which,
in hastily drafted and ungrammatical prose, offers only the most
general statements of concern about the problem of climate change
and no binding commitments to limit carbon emissions or to
compensate those most affected by its manifold impacts.

Despite the global membership of the negotiation, encompass-
ing almost every country in the world, the statement was hashed out
in the last few hours of the conference in a closed-room session

---

* The head of the British armed services, Sir David Richards, told the BBC in
November 2010 that Al Qaeda could only be "contained" not defeated, saying
that you cannot defeat "an idea". Source: BBC website, "West cannot defeat Al
Qaeda, says UK forces chief", 14 November 2010.

involving China, Brazil, the US and India. The needs of those most affected by climate change like the low-lying island states or Bangladesh, which are already losing land to rising seas, were ignored.

The Copenhagen process had been formidably complicated, involving multiple "tracks" of negotiation in an attempt to address the many different aspects of the problem of climate change, including forests, technology transfer and protection of oceans as well as the "big picture" questions of carbon emissions and how to finance the costs of adapting to the effects of rising temperatures. Despite the thousands of hours spent negotiating these subsidiary issues over the previous two years, none of them was addressed in the final text.

In Cancún, a year later, delegates successfully agreed that their states wanted to limit global warming to 2°C – the "danger" level, beyond which, a recent paper in the scientific journal *Nature* warned, warming may increase beyond any control. The conference was widely touted as a "success", as the Mexican hosts managed to secure agreement on key issues, including financing for climate adaptation in poorer countries. But there was no agreement on how climate change might be prevented and no concrete agreement on the carbon-emissions targets that scientists concur as necessary. As *The Economist* reported, Cancún was successful in rescuing the UN climate negotiations "process"; its value in rescuing the climate was less clear[10].

Recently, the UN Environment Program reported that even if states fulfilled all of their commitments to reduce carbon emissions, including those made at Copenhagen, the world's temperature would still most likely exceed the 2°C "danger" level. Outside of predictions and commitments, and in the real world of the earth's atmosphere, where success or failure is truly measured, the concentration of carbon in the atmosphere has continued to rise unabated. In 1992, at the time of the first international gathering of governments to address climate change*, the concentration of carbon in the atmosphere was

---

* The so-called "Earth Summit" in Rio de Janeiro

354 parts per million by volume. By 2010, it was nearly ten percent higher, an unprecedentedly rapid increase.

Meanwhile in the global economy, the years that immediately followed the 2008/9 "credit crunch" witnessed innumerable G8, G20, UN and Basel Committee discussions attempting to agree new standards and rules to prevent a recurrence of the devastating crash. But within the confusing barrage of statements and commitments on new taskforces, committees and "watchdogs", nowhere to be found was the one measure – higher capital/debt requirements for banks at a sufficiently high level, a step that almost all disinterested analysts believe would actually prevent a crash happening again. And there was a reason for this absence.

While globalisation intensifies apace, its rigours and stresses ever more evident, its rewards seem to accrue mostly to a minority: the top one percent of the population in the US takes home nearly twenty-five percent of all income, the highest percentage since 1928[11]. Middle-class incomes have stagnated, but living expenses have not. Meanwhile, for many of the poorest, life has actually got worse.

Across the globe, more than one billion still live on less than one dollar per day; two billion live on a pathetic two dollars per day. And while it is easy to ignore the miseries of life in Somalia and Bangladesh, it is more astonishing that in New York City one in five children is dependent on food stamps for survival, while Goldman Sachs bankers enjoy bonuses of some $700,000 each and hedge-fund traders throw parties costing hundreds of thousands. In 2011, as leading bankers declared that the "years of apology" should be over[12], one study showed that seven million of the poorest Britons had seen their living standards decline by a massive ten percent over the previous decade[13]. In 2009, one in seven Americans was living in poverty, the highest proportion of the population for fifty years. In some parts of America, life expectancy is actually declining thanks to poverty, though healthcare spending per capita – averaged across the population – is higher here than anywhere on earth.

As the whole world, except North Korea, adopts the capitalist model, such inequality is rising everywhere both between and within countries. In China, the introduction of free-market economics has freed hundreds of millions from poverty. But at the same time it has created the worst inequality in Asia, apart from Nepal, until very recently an autocratic monarchy: official esti-mates suggest one percent of Chinese households enjoy forty to sixty percent of total household wealth[14]. In India, politicians obsess about headline GDP growth rates, and the richest build billion-dollar skyscraper houses, but hundreds of millions remain in abject poverty and malnourishment – the calorie intake of the poorest has remained stagnant for over a decade and more than half of India's children under five suffer stunting and poor brain development[15]. Even in the supposedly egalitarian Nordic coun-tries, the gap between rich and poor is growing fast. Worldwide, a new trend has emerged, barely noticed: beyond a certain level of development those at the top benefit enormously, those at the bottom often do actually worse, whilst the income of the bulk of the population stays more or less stagnant.

It is little wonder then that this model is so confidently extolled as ideal by those who benefit from it. So often are the virtues of this system avowed that it has taken on the characteris-tics of a *moral* system, where anything done in the name of that system, however gross, is morally justified as part of the necessary mechanics of the market.

The future offers an unsettling vision of ever-greater competi-tion for markets and scarce resources. The ferocious contest of the global marketplace is like being chained to an accelerating tread-mill, under constant pressure to cut costs and invent new products, trapped by a ceaseless desperation to attract customers who them-selves are ever less satisfied, hopping from product to product (as surveys reveal) craving a satiation – a fulfilment – they can never find. As billions join the global labour force, no job is secure; no industry is stable; no profession may not one day face destruction.

While economic insecurity is on the rise, so too is a more

insidious and equally permanent anxiety – political insecurity and violence. As US officials with great candour admitted after 9/11, we are in a "Long War" with global terrorists, and it seems to be getting longer. The war with Al Qaeda is spreading across the world's geography, as its affiliates metastasise. The invasion of Afghanistan, whose rationale I delivered to the UN one winter morning*, wholly justified to remove the government brazenly hosting our attackers, has succeeded not only in perpetuating civil war in Afghanistan but has also triggered the spread of instability and extreme violence to the border areas and across Pakistan, where now every major city has seen repeated suicide attacks of horrific violence.

In the "homeland", violent jihadists may be found not only among immigrants and visitors, but from the ranks of our own population: "Jihad Jane" who was radicalised in her Philadelphia suburb; the US army doctor who killed thirteen and wounded thirty at Fort Hood. A third of all charged US terror suspects are American citizens[16]. Contrary to the received wisdom that economic under-development is the fount of terrorism, former CIA case officer Marc Sageman found in a study of 172 Al Qaeda terrorists that the majority were middle- to upper-class, well-educated, married with children, and occupied professional or semi-professional positions, often as engineers, architects, scientists and doctors. In Britain, suicide attackers who killed fifty-six and injured several hundred on the London Underground and buses on 7 July 2005 came not from Saudi Arabia but from Dewsbury and Leeds. The would-be murderers who tried to detonate a nail bomb at a London nightclub in 2007 included a highly trained and British-born National Health Service doctor.

Thanks to the spread of technology – which can be as simple as cell phones and fertiliser – and information on the internet, it is now straightforward for small groups of extremists to kill large

---

* The letter set out the legal justification – self-defence – under Article 51 of the UN Charter for the United Kingdom's participation in the allied invasion.

numbers. In Japan, police discovered that the Aum Shinrikyo sect had the capability to produce the deadly nerve gas sarin in aerosol form. Had they chosen to use this method, the fanatical group could have killed many hundreds. Instead, they chose to deploy the less toxic liquid form of the agent, but still killed scores and horribly injured many more.

In Oklahoma, Terry Nichols and Timothy McVeigh killed five hundred and injured thousands with a truck bomb assembled at a cost of less than $5,000. After mounting attempted attacks in 2010 to detonate package bombs on several airliners, the Yemeni branch of Al Qaeda (AQAP) announced that "Operation Haemorrhage" was part of a new approach eschewing major attacks, and instead setting out to cause "death by a thousand cuts". The group stated that, "To bring down America we do not need to strike big," adding the total bill for the parcel-bomb operation was a mere $4,200, but that it "will with-out a doubt cost America and other Western countries billions of dollars in new security measures. This is what we call leverage."[17]

Some 700,000–800,000 light weapons are produced every year, adding to the vast stock of weapons already in circulation, as many weapons remain in use decades after their manufacture – Taliban fighters carry AK-47s made in the 1960s or earlier[18]. Countries like Austria, Canada, the UK and US join North Korea, China and Russia as the largest producers of these weapons, the primary means of conflict worldwide. The annual authorised trade in such weap-ons exceeds $6 billion a year[19]. The *Small Arms Survey* now reckons that globally there are nearly 900 million light weapons, some of ever-greater sophistication: sniper rifles deadly at two miles' range; man-portable missiles that can down airliners; mines that can sink cruise liners. In Mexico, drug-traffickers have used submarines and anti-tank missiles in their wars with each other and the authorities.

But it is not only the growing ubiquity of weapons and terror-ism – what's in the backpack of that man down the carriage? – that threatens our sense of safety and wellbeing. In Britain, the millions

of CCTV cameras broadcast their own message of our lack of trust in one another. Some cameras now bear loudspeakers to broadcast their correctional message to the "anti-social". In some city centres, authorities deploy noise-making devices whose deterrent screech can be heard only by the young, like dogs or rats already designated as "trouble makers". Police are beginning to deploy unmanned drones with high-resolution cameras to monitor car traffic and the population, as defence companies push for military technology to be adopted in policing. Some of the drones carry loudspeakers with which to relay instructions to the civilian populace[20]. It is reported that the London 2012 Olympics will be monitored by Royal Air Force "Reaper" Unmanned Combat Aerial Vehicles (UCAVs), hitherto deployed in Afghanistan to attack insurgents.

Meanwhile, in the United States, nearly 4,000 federal, state and local counter-terrorism agencies monitor the population, while 30,000 officials are employed solely to monitor telephone and other communications, creating in the words of the *Washington Post* "a new level of government scrutiny" of its citizens. Thousands of Americans are included in a vast database, including many who have never been accused of any wrongdoing[21].

But the intrusiveness of such measures does little to lessen the evident tension in public spaces, nor deter random, almost casual, violence. In 2008, Kevin Tripp had an argument with a stranger in a supermarket check-out queue in South London. The argument escalated. Tripp was punched to the ground, suffering serious head injuries. He died later in hospital. In Baltimore in 2010, one man killed another with a chunk of concrete during an argument over a parking space.

Research data show that community life in Britain, and America, is deteriorating. Measuring the number of people in an area who are single, those who live alone, the numbers in private rented accommodation and those resident for less than a year, researchers found that all communities in Britain were "less rooted" than they were thirty years earlier[22]. Comparing data from a census taken in 1971, researchers at the University of Sheffield found substantially higher levels of "rootlessness" and "anomie" in contemporary communities.

Commenting on this data, the research leader, Professor Daniel Dorling, said, "Even the weakest communities in 1971 were stronger than any community now". Ninety-seven percent of communities studied had become more fragmented over the last three decades. "These trends may be linked to higher likelihoods of fearfulness because we are less likely to see and therefore understand each other's lives."

In the US, over a similar period, the rate at which Americans invite people to their homes has declined by forty-five percent. In his classic study, *Bowling Alone*, Robert Putnam reported indices of discohesion and social fragmentation rising across the board. For instance, membership of chapter-based organisations, where members attend regular meetings and participate in social activities like the Rotary Club, the Masons, the NAACP, Boy and Girl Scouts etc., halved in the last fifty years. Others report that Americans are also – unsurprisingly – lonelier. Between 1985 and 2004, the number of Americans who said they had no close confidants tripled. Single-parent households are on the rise, and the US Census estimates that thirty percent more Americans will live alone in 2010 than did so in 1980[23].

As if these data were not dismal enough, it seems too that the very ground on which we stand is less firm than before. Once conquered, mankind foolishly believed nature would remain quiescent in our plans. Rising sea levels have already required the evacuation – for ever – of several low-lying islands. In Australia and Russia, forest fires rage with a new and terrifying ferocity, consuming whole towns. Even the sceptical notice greater volatility in the weather – everything's hotter and colder, and wetter and windier than it used to be. This too is consistent with science's predictions. The volatility feeds a deeper disconnection between man and his environment. For the first time ever, more people now dwell in cities than the countryside. The urban majority now barely encounter what their forebears took for granted: trees, fresh air, birdsong, *silence*. Lives are lived out in a frantic, noisy hecticness; fulfilment is distant, with peace and escape dreamt of, sometimes purchased, but all too rarely experienced.

This list is so depressing that together these problems offer a sheer and intimidating cliff face upon which there appears no handhold, no purchase at all. The temptation is simply to switch off, tune out, escape.

And indeed advertising offers us a tantalising vision of that escape, a ceaseless promise to leave the burdensome everyday and wander into sunlit uplands: "Go Forth!" says one advert for jeans, with an evocative image of a young man shirtless in a field of waving grass. These messages claim not only to sell us jeans but to solve our all-too-obvious, if never to be admitted, existential crisis: that all this – the modern condition of prosperity, a sort of peace, a sort of freedom, is simply not enough. The yearning for more, for distraction, never quite goes away however much is purchased, however many holidays are taken.

This hunger is all but explicit in the advertising (Go forth! Find yourself! Choose freedom!), but can never be confessed in a culture where our arguments – capitalism, democracy – are supposed to have won, and provide a convincing, empirically justified answer to all objections, except the one we cannot admit to.

But in this existential crisis, the first fragile handhold upon the cliff face of intractable problems is revealed. The answer to both the personal and collective crises is in fact the same. And it is simple. It is embodied in one word: agency. Agency over events – the feeling of control – is a gross absence in the contemporary condition. Capturing it is available through one simple mechanism: action. And this in a nutshell is the simple essence of the philosophy to be offered here. We lack control; we need to take it back.

*   *   *

The incredible and seismic changes of the late 20th and early 21st century have forced dramatic and sometimes revolutionary changes in almost every realm of human activity – finance, technology, culture – save one, politics. In this most crucial forum, the institutions and habits acquired in earlier and different times have endured, even when their effectiveness is less and less evident. On the contrary, the evidence is accumulating that these inherited bodies and rules are less and less able to comprehend and arbitrate the forces now swirling around us.

Something else is desperately needed. That necessity has been articulated by many, but none has offered a solution except more of the same, politics-as-usual: futile calls for more "political will" to address this or that problem, or celebrity-endorsed "single issue" campaigns for the public to pressure their representatives to address one particular crisis over others. Some believe that technology alone will deliver the necessary revolution, but here too it is clear that technology's effects may be as often malign as benign, serving the dictatorial in China as much as the democratic in Tunisia. A more fundamental shift is needed.

One telltale sign is the increasing number of politicians who now promise to "change politics" itself. In 2008, it was Barack Obama; in Britain it was the Conservative/Liberal Democrat coalition of 2010 who promised to change the very nature of the system. In America, the change-the-system sentiment is now expressed by the Tea Party movement, with its demand to "take back our government". And just as surely, the Labour party in Britain, now in opposition after thirteen years in government, will develop a new claim, that it too will "change the system" if only voters give them a chance. The pattern is a clear one. Politicians can smell the frustration, and must respond to it, but are surely doomed. With each electoral cycle, the disillusionment appears greater, data show that voters chop and change parties with greater frequency, while turnout falls steadily in all democracies, with only the occasional upwards "blip", like the sputtering of a dying fire.

This revolution is as profound as it is simple. Evidence and research are now suggesting that the most important agent of change is us ourselves. At a stroke, the prevailing notion that the individual is impotent in the face of the world's complex and manifold problems is turned on its head. Instead, the individual is revealed as a power-ful motor of change, offering the prospect of immense consequences for politics and the world, and, no less, for themselves.

I once believed in the capability and rightness of enlightened government so fervently that I went to work for it. I was a British diplomat, in an institution and a system which was founded on a deep belief that state officials like me could understand and arbi-trate the world effectively, for the benefit of the less informed masses. I no longer believe this. This disillusionment came not from ideological conversion, but experience.

In my work on many of the world's most worrying problems, including climate change, terrorism and the wars in Afghanistan and Iraq (I was responsible for both issues for the UK at the United Nations), it became slowly clear to me that government was unable, by its very nature, to comprehend and manage these forces effec-tively. Why will become clear, but in short I realised, dimly and slowly, a profound and intrinsic deficit of governments: that they are required to take what is complex – reality – and turn it into simplistic pronouncements and policy, the better to convince the population that government has matters in hand. People in govern-ment are not bad or stupid, on the contrary, but the contract between people and government forces them to claim something which no sensible person should claim, that government can under-stand and predict the massive complexity of the contemporary world, and manage it on our behalf. Every politician must claim to voters that they can interpret the world, and produce certain effects, just as the officials working for them must pretend that they can too. I know this because I did it.

I saw how in looking at places like the Middle East, and by extension the whole world, governments were forced to reduce hugely complicated and dynamic situations into simplistic models, us and them, security vs. threat, just as they were required to project the manifold needs of their own diverse peoples into simple, and artificially invented sets of "interests". Such a process is inherently false, requiring governments – and officials like me – to create stories and policies that offer clear, straightforward and therefore often very simplistic solutions. Then, to justify these stories their officials must seek out the facts to suit the policy, the very opposite of a more valid empirical method – where we observe the world, then respond accordingly. Governments have it the wrong way around.

I gladly took part in such processes, writing speeches and talking points, and arguing in vicious negotiation to claim that Saddam's Iraq was a threat, that his regime's overthrow would deliver stability and spread democracy across the Middle East. In Afghanistan, I wrote embassy telegrams from a Kabul freshly liberated from the Taliban, explaining how democracy "Afghan style" would bring peace and prosperity to the Afghan people, conveniently overlooking the reality that much of Afghanistan remained unliberated from the Taliban's grip and that the democratic government we proclaimed was in fact largely our own creation, our own fantasy of what democracy *should* look like, rather than necessarily what the local people really wanted. After fifteen years as a diplomat, I was highly skilled in writing cables and reports and policy submissions that endlessly reaffirmed our version of events, often without the benefit of any knowledge from the ground at all. In five years working on Iraq, not once had I set foot in the country, yet at the UN I was called Britain's Iraq "expert". I was not alone in such ignorance, nor in the arrogance that, despite it, government could declare with confidence what was happening or what might happen in such places.

My own personal crisis with government is described later,

and erupted when my government's stories about Iraq stepped from over-simplification into downright falsehood. But even this took me some time, and much anguish, to realise, and sadly it required the death of a decent and honest man, my colleague David Kelly, for me to see the light as to how far government would go to protect its own false stories. I had ignored earlier signals, all too obvious in my own work as much as in any later analysis, that government permits and indeed encourages its protagonists to become morally detached from the consequences of their own actions, allowing me to become a guiltless architect of much suffering to distant others – in this case, described later, innocent civilians in Iraq. And only after much subsequent slow and sometimes painful reflection did I come to these broader conclusions about the intrinsic amorality, but also incapability, of government.

I watched the dramatic forces at play in the world, and felt the rising frustration at the seeming inability of government, or indeed anyone, to offer meaningful and plausible solutions. As political violence spread, and the credit crunch exploded, I watched desperate politicians, some of them friends, as they argued to pretend that they might understand, might control these forces – terrorism, the stresses of globalisation, the deteriorating natural environment. I watched the growing angry chorus in public gatherings and on the internet, demanding action, change, *something*, with ever more belligerent rhetoric, but never themselves offering solutions beyond rejection of the current cohort of lousy politicians.

And I pondered change itself, how to react to this vastly complex world with a method that might work, that might provide the satisfaction of finding real traction upon the ghastly sheer cliff face of problems. And I realised that perhaps the worst deficit of government was this: in claiming to arbitrate the world's problems, unintentionally it encourages our own inaction and detachment. And in that detachment, rage and frustration have fermented dangerously. In Kosovo, I had seen how depriving people of a voice in their own future can sometimes lead to violence – a story that will come later. And back at home, in the disembodied anonymity of the internet, or the vapid chatter of commentators and news-readers, and in the ceaseless demand for government and politicians to act – do something! – I saw how our opinions have become yet more polarised, an alienation from each other exacerbated by the mobility and rootlessness of modern economies. The problem is always someone else's, never ours, to solve.

And yet it is action – and only action – that changes things. Whether in the history of the battle for civil rights in America's South or the Franco-Russian wars, or in the contemporary research of social scientists and network theorists, the same and ancient truth is repeated: it is the action of individuals which has the most effect on those around them, on their circumstances, and thus the whole world. Whether in Gandhi's salt march to free India from colonial rule, or a group of men trying to stop muggings in their neighbourhood in New York City, it is the expression of conviction through action that has the most powerful impact upon each other, our surroundings, and indeed our own wellbe-ing. The scale of the world's difficulties – the sheer cliff face – and the magnitude of globalisation produce a paralysing sense of impotence and frustration. But, in fact, a world that is more inter-connected than ever before, where each person is only a few links away from anyone else, means that actions in our own microcos-mos can have global consequence.

These stories and ideas will be explored in this book; facts, research and stories that together suggest a radical philosophy of how to create a better world, one that more closely reflects the current reality than the easy but dangerous assumption that we can leave it all to government to fix. This philosophy could fit under the broad school of thought known as anarchism, a term commonly associated with violence and nihilism: more what it is against, than what it is for. And mere opposition to government, authority and hierarchy is clearly insufficient as a solution. This book has a more positive vision, presented in detailed principles to guide action. It is

A Conservative Radical   Center for Opposition
                                          Rethink

not proposing a violent overthrow of government, but a much gentler revolution – in the way we think about the world, and how we – ourselves – might therefore respond to it. Changing our own approach is critical: embodying our political beliefs in every action. Changing the self may change the world. In all the haze and chatter, rediscover what you truly believe in, then *act*. And following that transformation, another necessary shift – negotiating directly with one another, rather than leaving it to distant institutions. In contrast to the paralysis of modern legislatures, too often dominated by the interests of the powerful rather than the mass (as we shall see all too clearly), collective decision-making, whether in New Orleans or Brazil, has emphatically shown the benefits of shared debate and responsibility: respect for one another, for facts, but above all agreement upon better, fairer and more enduring solutions.

co-op

(co op)

In a world where government influence is in inexorable decline, and other transnational forces assert themselves, some beneficent but some malign, there is little choice but to take on the burden of action ourselves. If we do not, others surely will, whether criminal mafias with worldwide reach, global terrorist movements, or multinational companies with no concern but their own profit. This book offers some simple pointers to what that action might comprise – conviction, action, consultation – with some inspiring stories of how these principles have worked before. But this is no historical survey; it is an attempt to look at the world as it actually is, not as we or governments might wish it to be, and design a plan of action to respond. It is above all a manifesto about *how* to act – method – not a prescription of *what* end-state or utopian system to seek. No book can offer solutions to every problem, though there are several suggestions here. But that *how* is the key, for, as we shall see, the method is the point – the means are the ends. For in that method, there are extraordinary prizes to be won – not only the accomplishment of the desired goal, but a greater sense of cooperation, respect and community with our fellow human beings, and a deeper sense of our own satisfaction and purpose, needs that are all but ignored in the current obsession with material wellbeing, status and celebrity. It is a humble and very practical manifesto, though its ideals are transcendent.

In the current crisis there are small but glimmering signals that point the way forward. These signals are but rarely noticed by those who defend the current order, but the lessons of this new philosophy are all around us, if we care to look. You won't find this teaching in the academy, nor in economists' predictions or politicians' speeches. Those demonstrating this new way of doing things are not to be found in university lecture halls, or newspaper columns, but in sports stadiums and on the ill-defined frontlines of the century's many new wars, and they are wearing suicide vests.

1

THE MEXICAN WAVE AND
THE SUICIDE BOMBER

WHEN AMERICAN TROOPS ENTERED IRAQ IN 2003, THEY
were briefed to expect a conventional army consisting, as such armies
do, of tanks, artillery and infantry. Saddam Hussein's army had once
contained more Main Battle Tanks, a primary unit of the conventional army, than all the armies of Western Europe put together*.

The lead elements of the American and British armies, then,
were surprised to find that most of the opposition they faced
comprised not tanks and howitzers, but men in pick-up trucks,
bearing rocket-propelled grenades (RPGs) and machine guns.
These bands would attempt to ambush the advancing allied
columns, launch the RPGs, then flee. They were not often successful. Indeed, so desperate and dangerous to their participants were
these attacks that they resembled nothing so much as the Japanese
kamikaze suicide attacks familiar from the Pacific theatre of the

---

* As an official working during the first "Gulf War" with Iraq in 1991, one of
my duties was to count Saddam's tanks and soldiers in such a way as to affirm
the claim, not strictly true but made by a politician and therefore requiring
some kind of validation, that Iraq had "the third largest army in the world".
This claim could only be "proven" if all of the reserve forces of the Iraqi army
were included in the count, but were ignored in counting the armies of other
competitors for the third-place slot (India, US, Russia).

Second World War. These *fedayeen* fighters, as they came to be known, did not appear to belong to particular Iraqi army units, or if they did, their members had abandoned their uniforms and badges that denoted their unit allegiance.

The allied invasion proceeded with remarkably little substantial opposition. The American tanks at the head of the advance reached Baghdad almost as fast as they could drive. The capital quickly fell, the statues of the hated dictator were toppled, and the allies assumed control of the country, taking possession of the main government buildings abandoned by Saddam's cohorts and thus, they believed, control.

It was only in the days that followed that the real military opposition to the invasion began to assert itself. The first suicide attack had taken place during the march on Baghdad. The attacker – an Iraqi army officer dressed in civilian clothes – drove a taxi to a checkpoint near the central city of Najaf and, as American soldiers approached, detonated the vehicle. Four soldiers were killed[24]. Iraq's then-President, Taha Ramadan, warned that there would be many more such "martyrdom missions": he was right, though the attacks that followed were not under government orders; his government would soon disappear. A few days later, two women suicide bombers killed three coalition soldiers north of Baghdad.

Over the days and months that followed, the number of suicide bombings rose dramatically. In one month in 2004, there were several attacks every day. As Dexter Filkins reported, "in the first five years, more than nine hundred people detonated themselves in Iraq, sometimes several in a single day. That was before you counted the car bombs when the driver got out before it exploded. There were thousands of those."[25]

Suicide bombers used cars, trucks, and motorbikes; often they came on foot; sometimes on bicycles. During the "surge" of American troops in 2008, attackers launched fusillades of massive "lob bombs" – explosive-filled gas cylinders propelled by crude rocket engines – from flatbed trucks parked alongside US bases.

The operators, their intent clearly suicidal, were inevitably annihilated, but only after unleashing hours of bombardment. Such were the ferocity and effectiveness of the attacks, and the allies' inability effectively to stop them, that they began to undermine the will of the US to remain. Even before Barack Obama's election as President in 2008 when during the campaign he had promised to withdraw US troops from Iraq, the administration of George W. Bush had declared a date when the soldiers would leave.

In Afghanistan, allied war planners preparing the 2002 invasion had expected a more irregular resistance. The Taliban who ran the country were more militia than a conventionally organised army, more AK-47 than Main Battle Tank (though they did have a few tanks, at least before the allied airstrikes began). Their tactics had been honed in decades of fighting against other Afghan militias and conventional military forces during the Soviet occupation in the 1980s.

Adept at ambush and hit-and-run attacks, the Taliban fighters were extremely hardy and able to endure long periods without logistical support. After trekking over Afghanistan's harsh terrain, they would launch an attack with RPGs and machine guns, and occasionally a heavier weapon like a mortar or small artillery piece, then melt away into the unforgiving countryside. The Taliban were not known however to use suicide attacks. During the Soviet occupation of Afghanistan, there were no known instances of such tactics, except very occasionally by foreign *mujahideen* fighters, some of whom later became infamous as Al Qaeda.

When I was posted to Afghanistan as a diplomat shortly after the allied invasion, the defences of our embassy reflected this assessment of the Taliban's military capabilities. The embassy was located in a compound surrounded by high, thick walls. Atop the walls was another high fence of sturdy netting, designed to prevent the flight of RPGs into the compound.

In the early days, during and after the allied invasion, this military assessment proved correct. But after a while, as in Iraq, things began to change. The harbinger had taken place on 9 September 2001, an event overshadowed by the attacks shortly afterwards in Washington and New York. Suicide bombers posing as a television film crew assassinated the anti-Taliban *mujahideen* leader, Ahmed Shad Masood. Setting up the camera to film him, the "cameraman" blew himself up, and fatally wounded Masood, who died a few hours later. Indicative of the changing and multinational nature of that conflict, the bombers were Tunisian; the camera had been stolen in Grenoble, France.

There were other antecedents. The Tamil Tigers used suicide attacks extensively against the Sri Lankan army (and, sometimes, civilians) in their fight for a separate Tamil homeland in northern Sri Lanka. Hezbollah cadres used bomb-laden cars and explosive-bearing individuals to attack Israeli army patrols and convoys during Israel's occupation of Southern Lebanon. To those watching elsewhere, the technique appeared crucial in dislodging an enemy which otherwise enjoyed a massive military advantage: Israel's conventional strength in tanks and aircraft was far superior to Hezbollah's. Israel withdrew from Lebanon in 2000, demoralised by the suicide attacks it could not effectively prevent.

But it was the suicide attacks in Iraq that seemed to have the most influence. As such attacks mounted in Iraq and increased the discomfort of the allies, suicide attacks became more frequent in Afghanistan, where before they had barely featured. Allied troops, and even trucks carrying humanitarian supplies, were forced to form convoys, protected by tanks and armoured vehicles. Not a single major road was safe to travel.

In both Iraq and Afghanistan, the use of suicide bombings produced its own consequences. American and allied forces were forced to adopt aggressive defensive tactics to prevent attacks, including challenging, shooting and destroying people or vehicles that approached allied patrols too closely and ignored (or failed to hear or understand) the warnings given them.

The consequences of these tactics can be imagined and were

realised in civilian deaths and growing antipathy to "the occupiers". Eleven members of the same Iraqi family were shot dead in their car approaching coalition troops, just days after the first suicide attack in March 2003[26]. The effects on the troops obliged to adopt these tactics can also be imagined. As in Iraq, debates grew about the wisdom of a long-term allied military presence in Afghanistan. One reason for the spread of the technique of suicide attacks was all too clear: it worked.

This was a new phenomenon. Normally, the deployment of particular military techniques – aerial bombing, mass armoured assault – was a function of hardware: the availability of tanks or aircraft, and carefully constructed strategy. These factors themselves are functions of others: economic development and the degree of organisation within both the military and society as a whole. The spread of suicide bombings was different. They were spreading like a virus. If their appearance was correlated with anything, it was not the degree of economic development or military organisation, but their opposites.

Some analysts suggest that common to suicide attackers is their strategic objective to remove occupiers from desired territory[27]; some that religious ideology, and in particular Salafi jihadism, is the driving force[28]. Whatever the debate about motives, there is agreement that the incidence of suicide attacks has dramatically increased, everywhere, over the last two decades, and particularly the last few years. Suicide attacks were not confined to religiously motivated terrorist groups like Hezbollah, the Taliban or Al Qaeda; in Turkey's Kurdish regions and Sri Lanka, the technique was used by groups driven primarily by secular, and indeed nationalist, ideology[29]. Whatever the motivation, the empirical results – of casualties caused, and political effects in consequence – were demonstrable.

This recent trend had earlier precedents. Japan employed *kamikaze* attacks only during the last stages of the Pacific war, when all chance of strategic victory had evaporated. The Japanese leadership did however encourage the attacks, after initial experiment, for the very same reason: they worked. During battles such as that in Leyte Gulf, the US navy lost scores of vessels to *kamikaze* attacks. A later survey showed that *kamikaze* missions were four to five times more likely than conventional missions to damage or sink their targets[30].

Just as today suicide attackers are often characterised as fanatical and therefore irrational, the *kamikazes* have been similarly dismissed as the product of death-loving *samurai* cult-like thinking that gripped the Japanese military élites. But for them too, there was a logic: the higher the price exacted upon US forces approaching the Japanese homeland, the more, they hoped, America would hesitate to attack the home islands, and would instead sue for a peace more favourable to Japan. Just as in Iraq, Lebanon and now Afghanistan, suicide attacks were permitted by a culture that celebrated death in combat, but also, and above all, because they had a palpable and successful political effect.

By 2005, the use of suicide bombings had spread to Bali and Britain, which suffered major suicide attacks on the London Underground and buses that year. The US of course had already seen such attacks on 11 September, 2001. In Mumbai in 2009, suicide attackers killed nearly two hundred people and wounded more than three hundred in a three-day rampage of shooting and murder. Suicide attacks are now frequent across North Africa and the Middle East, Pakistan and the Horn of Africa and have spread elsewhere including sub-Saharan Africa, Turkey, the Caucasus, Indonesia and the Indian sub-continent and even Iran, where in 2010 suicide bombers killed thirty-nine.

Despicable as some may find it, suicide bombing has been perhaps the most influential political-military technique of the late 20th and early 21st century: in conflicts that are about different ideologies, territories and religions, fighters have adopted the technique without prejudice. In its horror, suicide bombing offers up an insight into something important, something about how change happens, and how we as people work, and thus how things might be changed for the better – but without killing people. Curiously, that lesson is apparent too in the football stadium.

At a football game, it takes one, or a small group, to stand, and raise their arms in an attempt to start a Mexican wave (they may whoop or cheer at that point). Sometimes the attempt is ignored, but at other times it might initiate a coordinated, yet spontaneous motion of tens of thousands of people around the ground. It's frivolous, fun but also oddly moving: "we're in this together".

In his book, *Herd*, marketing guru Mark Earls explains why people buy what they do: or rather how they are influenced by the person sitting – or whooping – next to them. Earls cites the sales phenomenon of the Apple iPod. He describes how the colour of the headphone cable was a crucial factor in the device's dramatic sales success: the unusual white colour of the cords attracted people's attention – and enabled them for once to see the brand choices of their peers even though the product itself remained hidden: the cables made the otherwise private choice visible. The innovative features of the product were of course a vital factor in the ultimate decision to buy the iPod, but it was the white cords that triggered the chain of events that led to the purchase.

Earls suggests that most of our lives are "quotations from the lives of others" as Oscar Wilde put it: a phenomenon evident in the spread of agricultural mechanisation across America's mid-West in the late 19th and early 20th century, when farmers bought tractors when they saw their neighbours had them, or the names we give our children and the music we listen to. All of these trends, Earls asserts, are shaped by social influence first and foremost and not by our own independent decisions or the inherent appeal of the thing being chosen.

Hitherto, economic theory has suggested that rational choice – a weighing-up of the costs and benefits – is the primary basis for decision-making, and particularly purchase decisions. But it turns out that nothing more complicated than mimicry may be a better explanation of why people buy what they do. As one correspondent to the *New Scientist* put it, man should not be named *homo sapiens,* "wise man", but *homo mimicus,* "copying man".

Conventional economic theory claims that humans calculate by numbers, assessing rationally the profit and loss of any transaction. But it appears that even in deciding our finances, like taking on or abandoning a mortgage, the behaviour of others is influential. The herd-like popularity of sub-prime mortgages is already well documented. More recently, the practice of abandoning properties whose mortgages cost more than the value of the house has spread "like a contagion" according to a recent study, as both its economic rationale but also, crucially, its social acceptability have grown: "it's okay to walk away"[31]. Researchers found that borrowers were twenty-three percent more likely to default on their mortgage once their neighbours had done the same.

This mechanism is evident elsewhere. The British government commissioned research to find out how to persuade people to adopt more pro-environment behaviour, for example to limit their carbon emissions. The research found that government was itself an ineffective device to encourage behavioural change: people did not trust government and believed it was using climate arguments as an excuse simply to raise taxes[32]. (Indeed, this distrust is one reason why government may be ineffective in promoting the change necessary to protect the environment.) Instead, the research found, the government would need to recruit more influential agents to persuade people to act. These were not scientists, officials or experts, all of whom were nevertheless more trusted than government. Those with the most potential to influence others' behaviour were, the researchers concluded, our next-door neighbours. Indeed, it appears from another study that people take more notice of each other's actions than they do of formal rules.

Researchers at Groningen University tried to see whether the well-known "broken windows" theory of policing actually worked: the concept that if police aggressively target minor crime, such as littering and vandalism, they will reduce overall lawlessness, including major crime, like assault and mugging[33]. The researchers ran various experiments to find out how context – the environment people encounter – affects behaviour, including law-breaking. The researchers were trying to understand how disorderly behaviour spreads.

In one experiment, they tested whether people took more notice of a clear legal prohibition – a police sign telling people not to lock their bicycles at a particular spot – or of whether other people were violating the rule by locking their own bicycles there. To test this, they ran scenarios with and without the sign, and the presence or absence of other rule-violators: people illegally locking their bikes.

The study's results were clear. People were more inclined to violate the rule and lock their bicycles illegally if they saw others doing the same thing, regardless of what the police sign said. The study's authors suggest that their evidence therefore confirms the so-called "broken windows" theory. As such, the study could be taken as affirmation of an assertive policing model where police act quickly and robustly to deal with minor violations, and thus deter more serious crime. But the study also suggests a more subversive message. The Groningen experiments show that norms are more important than rules: it is the *actions* of other people that have the most influence on what we do.

Earls offers the Mexican wave as a metaphor for this model of change – it is also in its way an example. It takes no instruction or authority to initiate the rolling wave of spectators standing up and lifting their arms at a sports stadium. One or two people might try to start a wave. If others around them follow, the wave can quickly ripple around the stadium, involving tens of thousands of people in an utterly spontaneous yet coordinated act. The point is a clear one: the person most important in influencing change may be the person standing right next to you.

Suicide bombing and Mexican waves thus offer from their different examples strikingly similar lessons in how to affect others.

Intriguingly, both suggest that it is action in the microcosmos, our own little universe, that matters most: what we *do*. This is not the only parallel.

First, neither suicide bomber nor Mexican waver looks to anyone else, let alone their government, to produce the desired effect. Simply, if you want to start a Mexican wave, you do not wait for someone else to stand up. More starkly, the suicide bomber is prepared to sacrifice their own body and existence to attack their enemy. Horrible though it may be, it is truly a politics of personal and direct action.

Secondly, the action is directly linked to the desired effect: in fact, the action *is* that effect. Standing up in your stadium seat, though a small action in a crowd of thousands, in itself constitutes the start of a Mexican wave. In contrast, voting for a Mexican wave to be started most emphatically does *not* constitute the start of a Mexican wave. Detonating a bomb that kills your attackers, as well as yourself as the necessary adjunct, may be viewed by many of us as unconscionable but it does constitute resistance in a very material and – often – effective manner. Action and consequence are connected without intermediation.

Third, both suicide bombing and Mexican waves can plausibly be replicated by others, indeed in the case of the Mexican wave, that is the very point. One reason why suicide bombing has proven so effective is that it requires very little training to undertake and is relatively cheap compared to other military tactics: others can easily imitate the tactic. An uneducated peasant can suicide-bomb as effectively as an experienced infantryman. Indeed it would be a waste of a trained soldier to expend him so.

Fourthly, the action offers the possibility of real and immediate change. The Mexican wave if initiated at all, is initiated *immediately*. This must be very satisfying to the person who stands up to start it (I have never done this). The suicide bomber, if successful, will destroy the enemy vehicle or the people he or she is targeting. Though they will die in the process, the effect they seek is as immediately forthcoming as their own death.

And in one crucial respect, of course, suicide bombers and Mexican wavers are very different. Unless coerced, which they sometimes are, suicide bombers are motivated by a belief (some would call it fanaticism) so great that they are willing to sacrifice their lives. This too helps explain the uniquely persuasive power of suicide bombing. Along with the bomb belts portending the deaths of themselves and their victims, suicide bombers carry something else, undeniably: conviction.

And here is where we must abandon the example of the Mexican wave as too superficial, for however fun, few would be much impressed by the conviction of those participating in a Mexican wave. And it is conviction that convinces.

Suicide bombers illustrate this truth with horrific violence, but others – Gandhi, American civil-rights protesters – have shown the uniquely persuasive force of non-violence. But in either case, it was conviction that propelled the action; it was the action that recruited others to the cause. Thus, an essential first step to produce any lasting influence and change is the discovery of conviction.

This discovery is sometimes a personal realisation; sometimes it is conducted with others. For Gandhi, it began in South Africa when as a "coloured" he was thrown off a whites-only train. In Alabama in 1955, a fifteen-year-old girl decided that she had had enough of the racial segregation that required her to sit at the back of the bus. Claudette Colvin was riding the bus home from school when the driver demanded that she give up her seat for a middle-aged white woman, even though three other seats in the row were empty, one beside Ms. Colvin and two across the aisle. Claudette Colvin refused to budge. As she put it, "If she sat down in the same row as me, it meant I was as good as her."[34]

For this act of transgression, she was arrested. Two police officers, one of them kicking her, dragged her off the bus and handcuffed her. On the way to the police station, they took turns trying to guess her bra size. Colvin's action took place six months before the same was done by Rosa Parks, whose refusal and arrest are the more celebrated. But together their actions triggered a bus boycott. The court case occasioned by the boycott, at which Claudette Colvin testified, effectively ended bus segregation. Colvin's action was only recently celebrated in a book, giving her some of the attention hitherto devoted mostly to Parks[35]. As the biographer of Martin Luther King commented, "It's an important reminder that crucial change is often ignited by very plain, unremarkable people who then disappear."[36]

Interestingly, network researchers have found similar effects. Contrary to some recent popular books, such as *The Tipping Point**, it is not necessarily a few key influencers who create viral trends, such as a fashion for Hush Puppy shoes or the popularity of a particular band, it can be anyone. In fact, Duncan Watts has found that predicting who is influential in starting or shaping any particular trend is more or less impossible[37]. It could be anybody, including ordinary individuals who are not particularly popular or well-connected. This may be bad news for advertisers trying to save money by targeting their campaigns at a few key influencers, but in terms of political change, it is very exciting. It can be anyone who initiates a profound social trend.

Whatever the insights of network theory or marketing gurus, political change is rather different from buying iPods or the latest Lady Gaga single. Our beliefs about right and wrong are powerfully held. To shift the convictions of others requires profound experience or equal if not more powerful conviction, something rather more substantial than clicking "like" on a Facebook page or signing a petition. In a word, action.

These forces are rather harder to measure, though somehow we can tell when such experience strikes or when we are moved by the actions of others: you know it when you see it. Conviction can

---

* In this book, itself influential, Malcolm Gladwell suggests that a few highly connected people influence the choices of everyone else, what he calls the "Law of the Few". Another – *The Influentials* – similarly claims that "one American in 10 tells the other 9 how to vote, where to eat, and what to buy".

be found in myriad different ways, but it can rarely be told: as in all good theatre, it is better *shown.*

To find true political conviction, beliefs that move us and others, they must be tested, lived, embodied, just as the suicide bomber, horribly, embodies theirs. And for this to happen, it's necessary first to confront a painful abandonment.

It is comforting to believe that governments can provide for us, and protect us. Governments want us to believe it; and we want to believe them. Unfortunately, it is ever more evident that this comfortable pact between us rests upon weak foundations indeed.

2

THE PACT

WHEN A CHILD IS BORN IN BRITAIN, AS IN MOST OTHER developed countries, its parents must register its birth. It is not made clear why this is necessary, but it is legally obligatory. At the local-council website, it is politely explained that a new parent is required to register a birth; it is not stated – anywhere – *why*. You are however told that you will receive – free of charge! – a short birth certificate. Failure to register a birth is a criminal offence, and can incur a hefty penalty.

It is an ornate and archaic ritual. The harried parent must put aside nappies and bottles in order to attend the local register office, which can be many miles distant. When the appointment takes place, the registrar will enter parents' and child's details into a thick ledger, a heavy book weighty with portentousness. In my case, the registrar had a bulbous fountain pen with which to inscribe the birth date, location and other minutiae. She took an evident pleasure in wielding this instrument, carefully unscrewing the cap and lovingly poising the pen above the thick vellum page for a second, the better for her, and me, to contemplate the gravity of the registration moment.

In Britain, government first instructed its subject populace to register births, deaths and marriages in 1538. The purpose then, of course, was to monitor the population in order to maximise the collection of tax. Today, if it is stated at all, the implied rationale for such registration is the protection of the citizen.

The presence of government at these cardinal moments of life – its beginning, its end, the entwining of one's life with another in marriage – is rarely questioned, but assumed. In this way, government inserts itself into the very foundation and fabric of our lives. With self-assessed taxes, the individual is required to declare to government almost every significant event of their lives.

Reading the registration form for my children (they are twins), I noticed an odd question: was the child, at birth, alive or dead? I questioned the registrar. She confirmed that indeed parents of still-born children are required to register their births. The deadline – six weeks – is the same as for the births of living children. If the parents of a dead child do not meet that deadline, they too must pay a fine.

"We are the ones we've been waiting for" was a compelling slogan from the Presidential election campaign of Barack Obama. It captured something about his promise of change, but also, more subtly, spoke to our deeper anxieties about the troubled state of democracy today. It yoked these two ideas together to evoke, in eight words, the suggestion that collective mass action by us could change things at last. The problem is however that the slogan contains a profound but unadmitted contradiction: even led by a man as enlightened and sophisticated as Barack Obama, government is *not* about mass collective action; only getting someone elected is.

During the campaign, Barack Obama gave a speech in a sports stadium in Denver. "Invesco Field", named after its corporate sponsor, had been chosen over other smaller venues in anticipation of the enormous demand to hear him. And indeed tickets for the event, Obama's major speech at the Democratic National

Convention, were oversubscribed by over four to one. This was an event almost without precedent. Only John F. Kennedy had managed to fill a stadium at such a moment. This time, over 80,000 people filled Invesco Field, once known rather more appealingly as the "Mile-high" stadium. Thousands of others watched on huge video screens outside the stadium. Millions looked on around the country; many more across the world.

The *New York Times* published an extraordinary panoramic picture of this crowd, composed of several shots taken over a short period[38]. The picture deserves iconic status: it has an almost religious quality, like a fresco on a cathedral ceiling. The photograph shows a vast and diverse crowd, young and old, black and white: an astonishingly vivid snapshot of Americans animated as never before in this generation by the election of one man, the first African-American with a chance of the Presidency, the first Democrat after eight years of George Bush's Republicanism. The picture is moving and awe-inspiring, a visual testament to the political energy and enthusiasm Obama's candidacy unleashed.

During Obama's campaign, reportedly over a million people volunteered to work for his election. This was a larger number than recorded for any previous campaign. Obama raised $650 million for his campaign, the largest amount ever raised. Though records on this point are scarce, it appears that not only was this the largest amount, it was raised, significantly, from the largest number of donors, ranging from pensioners handing over five dollars to billionaires, a fact highlighted by Obama and his team on frequent occasions. They did not however highlight that only a minor proportion of their overall funding came from small individual donors. The vast bulk of the largest donations, as usual with contemporary politics, came from the rich and corporate donors, including banks and corporations like Goldman Sachs, Microsoft, Citigroup and Google[39]. After his election, the Obama administration, following traditional Washington form, appointed over two dozen of the largest donors to the Democratic Presidential campaign to choice overseas ambassadorships.

The Denver crowd and the extraordinary mass effort mobilised by Obama's campaign spoke of a hunger for change and a willingness to contribute to it without precedent in recent history. The enthusiasm did not end with his election. After Obama was elected, and his team was recruited, an astonishing 90,000 people applied for the 3,000 or so political appointments in his administration.

Obama realised the requirement for such mass mobilisation to win the election. Epitomised in the slogan "Yes we can", Obama's campaign played upon people's desire for change as well as, crucially, for *involvement* in politics. Both during the campaign and since, Obama urged people to become involved in their communities, to volunteer and themselves help fulfil the political promise of his election. But in this message there was, unadmitted, a contradiction. For what Obama was asking for, first and foremost, was not for volunteers to improve their communities, but for volunteers to campaign for his election. As if to highlight this awkward fusion of objectives, one group – Obama Works – was set up for people to volunteer for local activities in the name of Obama's campaign. Obama's campaign call to local action was a secondary if necessary moral buttress to his primary appeal for voters' support. The political end of his campaign was not change itself, but for him to be *elected* to deliver change; a subtle but crucial distinction, and the disjunction at the heart of representative democracy.

The night of Obama's election, a great roar could be heard across lower Manhattan when his victory became apparent. A large man strode down Avenue A shouting, joyfully, "Yes we can!" as if it was a party chant, rather than a political party slogan. But the party atmosphere soon dissipated. After Obama's election and the excitement of his inauguration, you could almost sense the air going out of the balloon.

With the government's encouragement, volunteering fairs were held across the country. And while numbers attending were unusually high, it was noted that this enthusiasm was less a function of a new surge of political activism, but more a consequence of the rampant unemployment of the post-election months, which saw the worst recession in America since the 1930s. In Brooklyn, a few hundred turned up to a volunteering fair, where thousands had been hoped for – in a borough numbering millions. Tellingly, the fair was described as seeking to exploit energy "left over" from the campaign[40]. Obama Works went into "hibernation". Since then, there has been no revolution in volunteering and community organising. The conventional model of politics has remained largely unchanged. As usual, attention focuses on the intentions and utterances of a very small group of people in the White House and a slightly larger group in Congress, where the betrayals, party switches and deaths of a small number of Representatives and Senators determine the nature of legislation imposed on a country of three hundred million people. Everyone else is left to rant about their doings on websites or, more commonly, simply get on with their lives with a shrug of the shoulders. It seems like the ones we've been waiting for weren't us after all.

Some attribute this passivity to the inherently idle and feckless nature of ordinary people: some politicians I know are inclined to this supposition. But in truth, the reason is that conventional representative democracy, where the many elect the few, rests on a pact between voters and government: we vote, they act; we get on with our lives, they protect. This is the pact in which the parent must enrol their baby after birth. It endures until death. This pact is rarely examined nor is it anywhere clearly or fully stated; it is rarely admitted to, though its effects are profound.

The pact has several layers. At the most fundamental, the pact implies that government will protect its citizens; it will provide for their security and safety. In return, citizens agree to limit some of their freedom: they accept the rule of law, and with it various restrictions on their behaviour. To government is reserved certain extreme powers and rights, which are denied the rest of us. These include the power to deny freedom to others, to imprison and to punish. In some countries, like the US, this includes the power to kill in the name of justice. All states worldwide reserve to themselves the "sovereign" right to wage war. All 192 member states of the United Nations have agreed to a code to govern this right to wage war, the UN Charter. But the Charter is a voluntary document and infringing it does not invoke automatic punishment, especially if the infringer is a powerful state.

Domestically, the government's commitment to provide security means that government takes responsibility to preserve peace, prevent crime and disorder, and to save the populace in times of grave peril, say after military attack or natural disaster. So far, the pact is familiar, and echoes the theories of political philosophers down the ages, from Locke and Hobbes, and earlier still, Plato.

Less familiar is the second layer of the pact, one that is less often mentioned than the first, but one with more insidious effect. In addition to protecting the population, government makes a further commitment – to take care of society's problems, including education, in some states healthcare services, care for the elderly and disabled, to protect the natural environment, including now the globe's atmosphere, and above all, to provide for growth and employment – to take care of the economy. This commitment – and its consequence – are almost never explicitly stated: government will take care of these problems, so we don't have to.

Instead of admitting this pact, politicians instead declare policies and promises to manage these problems, much as Barack Obama did at Invesco Field. But by declaring government's intention to address such problems, a politician is sending a powerful if concealed message: if government is willing and able to sort out these problems, we the populace do not need to worry. In Barack Obama's case, the message was carried a step further: I the politician need your active involvement – to campaign, raise money, etc. – in order to get elected; then I will be able to address these problems.

Indeed, Obama raised the stakes a notch further: the mass involvement he was able to activate through his candidacy exploited the massive political energy and frustration of the progressive electorate: the millions who volunteered for his campaign. His implicit message was "Mobilise to elect me and I will deliver". Though still unstated, this was an implicit recognition of the pact at its most stark.

But the effects of the pact can be witnessed in what followed the election. The mass of volunteers who mobilised to campaign for Obama by and large threw away their badges and stayed at home, their job done. There was no dramatic upswing in volunteering for social causes. Even in electoral politics, hard-core party activists found that the "Obama effect" had little long-term benefit in recruiting volunteers to fight elections at the more local level. The long-run trend in volunteering for social causes remains, as Robert Putnam and others have attested, resolutely downwards[41]. In general, we are doing less and less. And here is one message that issued unintended but with subtle and powerful force from the millions watching that one charismatic man at Invesco Field. That vast crowd is *watching*, not acting. For most of us, politics is a spectator sport – we observe, they do.

The trouble with the pact is that it is breaking down. National governments are less and less able to tackle the transnational and global causes of the various problems that confront us. At the most basic level of the pact, government is unable to guarantee protection against terrorist attack; it is unable to provide an effective response to prevent climate change; it is unable to manage the global causes – and effects – of economic volatility. In society, government is unable to slow the seemingly inexorable rise in "anti-social" behaviour, a trend evidenced for example in mounting attacks on bus drivers*, but apparent in innumerable other ways including the subtle but palpable tension in our public spaces. Anti-social behaviour orders, and CCTV cameras on every corner, do little to curb this discomforting trend, though they provide ample proof of our absence of trust in one another.

As a result, trust in politicians, never high, is declining. In Britain, a well-known television presenter called the Prime Minister "a cunt" in front of a studio audience. Such disrespect is now commonplace in many established democracies. In America and virtually every democratic country, there is widespread disillusionment if not disgust with the political classes, and with politics itself. In Germany, polling before recent Bundestag (parliament) elections indicated that eighteen percent of voters would vote not for regular politicians but for a comedian playing a politician[42]. The election campaign was dominated not by discussion of education or economic policy, but by a scandal over a politician who had used her government car to be driven on holiday to Spain. Commenting on elections widely seen as "boring", one voter said, "There's just no belief that anything is going to change"[43]. In Iceland, widespread disillusionment after the catastrophic impact of the financial crisis saw another

---

* New York City bus drivers report unprecedented levels of attacks upon them, but also a rising sense of perpetual aggression. After a driver was stabbed when confronting a passenger who refused to pay his fare, drivers across the city reported that they were repeatedly threatened by unruly passengers. They said that passengers had spat on, punched and thrown bottles at them, as well as making constant verbal threats. Such reports are not news to public-transport users in London. On a bus travelling to the centre of the city, I witnessed a car driver storm onto the bus after the driver had hooted at him. The man screamed obscenities at the bus driver's protective screen and concluded his abusive tirade by emitting a voluminous mouthful of spit at the driver. When I was growing up in London, protective screens for drivers were not felt necessary. What was disturbing about this incident too was the reaction of the passengers: not sympathy for the driver but anger. "Get moving! We don't have time to wait!" some yelled.

comedian elected mayor of Reykjavík. In the US, antipathy towards politicians manifests itself mostly, as in most issues in America, in partisan terms: the other side's politicians are venal, corrupt and self-serving; the manifest failings of ours are overlooked.

The disintegration of the pact is exacerbated by a further damaging phenomenon: the deepening chasm between voters and their representatives. The evolution of democracy has been, in general, one from "direct democracy" to representative democracy, from people collectively deciding their affairs to electing others to do so on their behalf. But as representative democracy has evolved, so too and barely noticed has grown the distance between voter and the decisions that affect them.

In every national democratic system, individual participation has been reduced to mere occasional voting to choose legislators or the executive (in the British system, these are one and the same election; in the US and other systems, they are separated). Today, the executive, in cahoots with the legislature, manages society and the economy and the country's international affairs. These highly complex decisions are taken not by the population collectively, but by a small executive often comprising only a few hundred people. This pyramidal, top-down structure produces several inherent and thus inescapable features.

The competition to become one of the élite is intense and antagonistic, and in some places violent. It costs an estimated $1.5 million to win a seat in the US House of Representatives; in the Senate, $9m[44]. Once in power, there is ferocious competition to gain the executive's attention and influence their decisions. The evidence for this is clear in the growing professionalisation of this process, both of politicians and the industry established to influence them. In Britain, many politicians have spent their whole professional lives practising nothing but politics, starting as researchers to MPs, then graduating as MPs and sometimes government ministers. David Cameron, elected Britain's Prime Minister in 2010, has never had any job outside of politics, unless one counts a brief stint working in public relations; the leader of the opposition, Ed Miliband, likewise. In Washington, every politician claims to be an "outsider" as they try to ride the anti-politics wave, but in reality very few are.

The contest to secure political influence has become increasingly professionalised and has assumed the characteristics of an industry, with professional associations and its own group interests: there are now lobbyists representing the interests of lobbyists. The number of paid lobbyists has in recent years multiplied enormously. In Washington, the number of registered lobbyists has more than doubled since 2000, to nearly 35,000 in 2005[45]. While the recession may have in recent years thinned their ranks, the ratio of lobbyists to legislators remains, incredibly, hundreds of lobbyists to every member of Congress.

At the European Union in Brussels, an increasingly dominant source of legislation affecting economic interests worldwide, no one seems able to give precise numbers of professional lobbyists. It is nonetheless clear that as the power of the European Commission and Parliament has grown over recent years, so in parallel has grown a similar army of professional lobbyists: most estimates place their number at around 15,000[46]. A former commissioner for the EU's most expensive and wasteful policy, agriculture, described Brussels as a "paradise" for lobbyists; one member of the European Parliament commented that "From morning to evening, are all here"[47].

One reason for the proliferation of business lobbyists is all too clear: it pays to invest in influence. BP helped Liberal Democrat MEP Chris Davies draft climate-change legislation that secured a nine billion euro subsidy from European taxpayers, covering the entire cost of new technology to convert from 'dirty' coal-fired power stations, saving energy firms from having to pay for it themselves. The industry later gave Davies an award. Davies was at least candid about the process he conducted to prepare the new European laws, justifying his actions by using a famous quotation often mis-attributed to Otto von Bismarck: "The public should never be allowed to see two things: how sausages are made and how laws are made."[48]

Elsewhere in the European Union, a *Financial Times* investigation discovered that some of the biggest beneficiaries of the EU's regional funds, designed to foster development in Europe's poorest areas, are multinational companies, including McDonalds, GlaxoSmithKline and Coca-Cola. Tobacco companies, including British American Tobacco and Japan Tobacco International, received more than an estimated three million euros in public funds to set up factories[49].

If this is the reality of the supposedly democratic legislative process, it is unsurprising that popular enthusiasm for conventional politics is waning. Membership of political parties, one measure of popular participation in conventional politics, is in steep decline in all major western societies[50]. Global surveys confirm that while people in general prefer democracy, they are less and less happy with the practice of democratic government[51]. Voter turnout has been in long-term decline in almost all democratic systems. In the last parliamentary elections in France for instance, turnout was the lowest ever recorded. The European Parliament elections of 2009 suffered the same ignominious outcome – fewer voters turned out for them than in any election since the parliament's inception. In the US, twenty-two percent fewer people vote in elections than did in the era of Kennedy[52].

There is no clearer evidence of the separation of governers from voters than the proliferation of the lobbying industry. And despite the promises of politicians to limit this industry and its influence, it has continued to grow. Its pernicious power – an inherent function of the reductive pyramid from voters to deciders – seems greater than them. One of President Obama's first acts in government was to appoint as Deputy Defense Secretary a long-time lobbyist for Raytheon, a top weapons contractor, despite Obama's campaign commitment to prohibit any such appointments. In New York State, the successful Democratic candidate for governor in 2010 proclaimed his forthright opposition to special interests and lobbyists throughout his campaign, yet the bulk of his campaign funding came from organised labour, real-estate firms and related industries like construction, the healthcare sector and lobbying firms[53].

In 2010, the Supreme Court in its misleadingly named "Citizens United" ruling decided to allow commercial companies to pay for political advertising, absurdly defining companies as having the same rights as individuals, and over-ruling the existing feeble limits to curb their influence such as the McCain-Feingold Act, which prohibited (though did not manage to prevent) political donations by corporations. The ruling permitted corporations and other types of organisations to raise large amounts and run political campaign ads without revealing the source of funding. Sure enough, the 2010 Congressional elections saw large influxes of money from these unaccountable bodies, tilting the races for many seats. Professor Lawrence Lessig has argued that the mutual dependency of lobbyists and legislators is now so profound, and corrupt, that legislation is enacted with the sole purpose of extracting rents from corporate interests. Former senators have admitted the same thing: that all legislation is made on "K Street"[54], the infamous Washington street where lobbyists' offices are concentrated. Lobbyists for the healthcare industry spent hundreds of millions before the Obama administration legislation of 2009, and employed former advisers of Congress members and Senators from the left of the Democratic Party to the right of the Republican. One observer estimates that the lobbying industry spent $3.3 billion in just one year (2008)[55]. Private companies that run prisons now employ lobbyists to press for legislation requiring judges to impose longer sentences[56].

In Britain, the corrosive influence of lobbyists is better concealed and less acknowledged in a political class that prefers to sneer at the money politics "across the pond" than examine its own squalid deficits. But here, one way in which money rewards political action appears to be an unspoken agreement between government and lobbyists, of access in exchange for deferred rewards. In a system where vast power is concentrated in the Prime Minister's office, many of Tony Blair's advisers left office for highly paid executive positions in companies that had substantial political interests in their earlier incarnation. One senior adviser joined Morgan Stanley's investment banking division as a full-time senior managing director. Another left her job in Blair's inner team to work for the oil giant BP.

Several of Blair's press advisers formed a PR group on Blair's departure from office that now enjoys lucrative contracts with businesses, many of which had clear interests in legislation delivered by the Blair administration. After leaving office, Blair himself was awarded a position as "senior adviser" to investment bank JPMorgan for a salary of half a million pounds a year[57], a rôle to which he gave rather less publicity than his position as a peace envoy in the Middle East for the so-called "Quartet" group of countries.

It is not only politicians who seem to feel that they deserve reward from those whose interests they have been arbitrating – with supposed impartiality. Senior officials too take their turn at the trough. One of the most senior British officials involved in the planning (if that's the right word) and execution of the 2003 invasion of Iraq was recruited upon retirement by oil giant BP, which, it is no surprise to learn, has a considerable interest in Iraq's massive oil reserves; another, doubtless for the same purpose, by British Gas.

Within the political class in Britain, there appears to be a tacit understanding not to criticise such obvious conflicts of interest, perhaps because other members of that class wish to leave themselves that opportunity in future. The self-serving excuse, which can often be heard *sotto voce* in Westminster, is that such rewards are a just pay-off for the supposedly poor pay and hard labour of a career in politics.

A similar unspoken understanding is clearly at work in Washington too, where politicians "retire" from their legislative duties as elected officials to sell their contacts and networking expertise as lobbyists. When he was scrutinised by Congress to lead President Obama's healthcare effort, it was revealed that former Democratic senator Tom Daschle had earned over five million dollars as a lobbying adviser to various industries. Notably, it was not this blatant influence-peddling that provoked the criticism that met his nomination, and ultimately forced him to withdraw, but his failure accurately to declare for taxes the *gratis* use of a limousine – one client's form of payment for his services.

Republican senator Ted Stevens was acquitted of corruption charges, but his trial revealed the existence of a lobbying mini-industry, involving scores of lobbyists, that had grown up solely to secure benefits from his influence. Meanwhile, former American ambassadors after their years of public service sometimes return to Washington to act as paid lobbyists for the very countries to which they used to represent US interests, a naked breach of ethics, not to speak of the risk to national security[58]. Two senior officials from the Clinton administration, including the former President's legal counsel, later ended up as paid lobbyists for Laurent Gbagbo, the former President of Côte d'Ivoire, whose refusal to relinquish power after losing elections in 2011 led to widespread violence costing hundreds of lives. These well-connected American officials lobbied the State Department and White House on behalf of the worst of tinpot dictators[59].

As the popularity of membership of political parties declines, they are forced to depend more and more on rich donors, whose inevitable demands for political favour in return of course reinforces the disconnection between parties and voters. In the US, the proportion of income for political parties from corporate donors has dramatically risen in comparison to private-individual donations. The starkest evidence that such contributions have become wholly divorced from the real preferences of voters, is that many of America's biggest companies – Microsoft, Exxon, Boeing – now routinely give money to *both* major political parties[60]; their motive is obvious.

In Britain, data show all too clearly that the bulk of dona-tions to the major political parties came not from mass members but a much smaller number – just a few hundred – of very large donors. The major sources of finance for the top parties are unions (for the Labour party) and very wealthy individuals (for the Conservatives), as well as corporations, such as large account-ancy firms, that give to all major parties. These contributions far outweigh those from such old-fashioned political actors as party members[61]. All the major political parties run, with little fanfare, secretive donor circles where, for a certain fee, contributors are given guaranteed but discreet access to ministers and other senior politicians with sway over policy. In a particularly notorious recent case, former cabinet ministers offered their services to a fake lobbying firm, set up by television investigators, charging several thousand pounds a day for access to their political contacts. Contrast this with the access granted ordinary voters, for whom an audience with a junior minister on any subject, unless they happen to be rich or have managed to garner press attention, is all but impossible.

Given the pernicious forces at work in the current political system, it is unsurprising that the decisions produced are often grossly divorced from the needs of electors, or even of the state itself. In the US, where the lobbying industry is most developed and where politicians are highly dependent on campaign contributions, these effects are most noticeable. For instance, members of Congress in 2009 demanded that the government purchase seven extra F-22 fighter aircraft, at nearly a quarter of a billion dollars each, which the Department of Defense itself had not requested, despite the trillion-dollar size of its defence budget. At this point, the US was at war in two countries – Iraq and Afghanistan. Although by that time already in USAF service, the F-22 had not been used in either conflict. In the UK, the government has been convinced by the defence industry to purchase two enormous aircraft carriers, to "maintain Britain's ability to project force", even though the carriers offer a far greater capability than Britain has enjoyed for many decades, if not ever.

Trade sanctions are commonly instituted by the US to pressure countries that have committed some grievous breach of international peace and security, or stand accused of "state sponsorship" of terrorism, like Iraq, Libya or Iran. Some American companies however have managed to win exemptions to rules preventing trade with these countries. Unsurprisingly, most are large companies with a commensurate lobbying presence in Washington. Kraft Food, Pepsi and some of the nation's largest banks have secured thousands of exemptions for their products to be sold to countries like Iran, allowing them to do billions of dollars of business despite swingeing measures to prevent commerce with states that sponsor terrorism[62]. Wrigley's chewing gum was classed as "humanitarian aid" and thus exempt from sanctions, permitting millions of dollars of sales to Iran and other sanctioned countries. One official later admitted that while the government debated whether chewing gum counted as food, and was thus exempt, lobbyists too had played their part, "We were probably rolled on that issue by outside forces".

On another patch of the carpet, the oil giant BP revealed that it had "expressed concern" to the British government about slow progress in diplomatic negotiations between Libya and Britain on the transfer of prisoners, on the grounds that it might negatively affect BP's oil exploration contracts with the Libyan government. These contracts were worth $900 million. The company claimed that such an expression, and indeed its concern, was nothing to do with the incarceration of the Lockerbie bomber, Abdelbaset al-Megrahi, whom Libya was campaigning to have transferred to Libya from his Scottish prison, where he had been sentenced to life imprisonment for the 1988 Lockerbie bombing, which killed 270 people.

BP admitted its intervention on the prisoner-exchange issue only after al-Megrahi's transfer to Libya, and following a public outcry. The delay in the negotiation had been caused by the British government's insistence that the Lockerbie bomber be excluded from the prisoner-transfer agreement. It backed down, and no exclusion to the agreement was specified. Al-Megrahi was transferred, much to the outrage of many of the families of those killed.

Thanks to pressure from lobbyists and agricultural special interests, the US Department of Agriculture has spent millions of dollars, under both Republican and Democratic administrations, encouraging the consumption of cheese, including the promotion of extra-cheese Domino's pizzas which contain forty percent more cheese than "regular" pizzas. Pressing this foodstuff upon consumers is directly contrary to the interests of citizens themselves, whose consumption of cheese, and with it saturated fat, has tripled over the last thirty years. Other parts of the government, including the Agriculture Department's own nutrition committee, meanwhile, are busy telling Americans to reduce their consumption of highly saturated fats[63]. Perversely, the government's promotion of cheese is a direct consequence of consumers' growing preference for low and non-fat milk and dairy products. This has created vast surpluses of whole milk and milk fat which the dairy industry turned to the government to help offload – as high-fat cheese. Thus, even as consumers exercise their own choice to eat less fat, the government, pressured by cheese lobbyists (hilarious but true), exploits the consequence – unused high-fat milk and cheese – to persuade the consumer to eat more of it.

In a similar case in Britain, the government in 2011 published a list of healthy eating guidelines, including the advice that consumers should eat no more than seventy grams of red and processed meat per day. The Department of Health produced a list helpfully indicating several meaty items alongside their respective weights. Alongside a cooked breakfast and the Sunday roast and other common meals, only two branded products were mentioned by name: Big Mac and Peperami. It just so happened that both items came in under the 70g limit. The previous November the government had set up five "responsibility deal" networks with the food business to come up with health policies. At the time, this was criticised as being akin to letting Big Tobacco draft smoking policy. Two of the companies were McDonald's and Unilever, who happen to be the manufacturers of the Big Mac and Peperami, respectively[64].

In another notable instance in the US, a Democratic senator opposed the Obama administration's plans for healthcare reform, brazenly arguing that the interests of the health insurance industry, which had given him over $200,000 in campaign contributions, were not best served by the proposed legislation, saying he opposed the public plan because "it would be too attractive and hurt the private insurance plans"[65]. He did not even bother, it was reported, to claim that he was representing the interests of his voters. Though these examples are especially gross, such distortions are apparent in most other democracies too.

The political space is more and more occupied not by citizens, but by big business and the wealthy. Not content with the purchase of lobbying power in our nations' capitals, oil companies are using the political techniques of environmental activists to promote their own interests: in this case to prevent curbs on carbon emissions. In a memo leaked in 2009, the American Petroleum Institute (API), which represents the US oil industry, wrote to its member companies asking them to "move aggressively" to stage up to twenty-two "Energy Citizen" gatherings, mostly located, it turned out, in the Congressional districts of representatives with weak majorities. Without irony, the memo declared that the objective of the demonstrations, which would be organised and funded by API, would be to "put a human face" on the impacts of "unsound" energy policy i.e. efforts to limit climate change. The memo encouraged oil-industry executives to mobilise particularly aggressively in those states where there is an "industry core", where there were significant numbers of oil-industry employees, contractors and retirees, a cynical strategy suggestive of nothing so much as the manipulative political techniques of the Communist Party.

Elsewhere, wealthy philanthropists use their foundations, and financial pull, to promote their political preferences. The foundation of Wall Street billionaire and Nixon administration Commerce Secretary Peter G. Peterson, for instance, is seeking to address the issue of taxes, deficits and fiscal responsibility, using advertising and public appearances by foundation experts to educate the public and increase engagement on the issue of the fiscal deficit. The foundation's website offers sample op-ed articles and letters to public officials and editors, some of which have appeared in newspapers. All members of Congress received a copy of a report by the foundation[66]. This is an interesting twist on the traditional understanding of philanthropy; some foundations now act – with tax-free benefits – as a kind of "force multiplier" for the political preferences of the "philanthropist". These activities may be beneficent, such as Bill Gates's efforts to improve school curriculums, or malign, but either form of influence shares one common characteristic – it is accountable to no one.

It is not only big business that engages in the lobbying business. To compete in the overcrowded and cacophonous halls of modern "democratic" legislatures, anyone with an axe to grind has to follow the same tactics. Whether car-drivers or environmentalists, so-called "interest groups" have become a growing force in contemporary politics. Both Greenpeace and the Automobile Association deploy skilled full-time teams of lobbyists and advocates in legislative centres (the latter claiming to represent the interests of its fifteen million members, even though most have joined for breakdown insurance).

At international conferences, invariably there are now "NGO forums" to accommodate the scores and sometimes hundreds – as at the Copenhagen climate conference – of organisations with views to present. There is no assessment of the democratic legitimacy of these groups: some represent many millions of members; others are tiny, and represent nobody apart from themselves. The more skilful use direct tactics to get their message across to legislators: the National Rifle Association, one of the most accomplished at this practice, maintains an on-line roster of the voting patterns of members of Congress, "scoring" them according to their support for – or hostility to – pro-gun positions. Such tactics are now becoming commonplace across the political spectrum.

The number of non-profits in the US increased by over thirty percent between 1996 and 2008, to well over 1.5 million[67]. Such organisations are today more likely to be located in Washington and have a "subscriber" base of members who pay dues but do not attend or participate in local meetings. There have been similar trends in Britain. Such organisations are in effect turning political activity into a business, what some have called a "business of protest". The organisational model for many contemporary political non-profit organisations now resembles that of a commercial business, which defines its target audience, purchases relevant mailing lists and advertising to reach that audience, and asks minimal participation (usually just membership fees) from them to achieve their lobbying goals[68]. Whereas active participation in community organisations correlates with political participation, there are no such "positive externalities" of paying membership dues to a non-profit. In essence, we are contracting out politics to be done by others.

Common to these interest groups is that they are in general focused on single, narrow issues: gun rights, fuel duties, environmental protection, abortion. Their aggressive tactics and sheer numbers fill the domestic political space and have created a new culture of politics, where legislators are confronted with a panoply of groups and lobbyists, so erecting a kind of wall between them and individual voters.

Such groups also contribute to a growing and unpleasant

extremism in political debate. Adept at one-sided presentation of the evidence, these groups advocate black-and-white positions with aggressive vigour, and armfuls of one-sided research – often representing those who oppose them as foolish and sometimes evil. The compromises inherently necessary in political decision-making thus become harder; deadlock becomes likelier. Facts and reasoned analysis are invariably the victims.

One effect of these trends is the polarising rise of "partisanship". Many have commented on the growing ugliness and vituperation of public debate. For the first time in living memory, a lawmaker shouted "You lie!" at the US President when he spoke to both houses of Congress. It is a long way from the method of the Indian "talking stick", introduced by the Iroquois to Ben Franklin, and reportedly used by America's founding fathers, which requires participants to be able to articulate one another's position before having a chance to speak. During "town hall" meetings on proposed healthcare legislation in the summer of 2009, politicians were shocked by the anger and hostility of some participants.

At the conservative *National Review*, which had prided itself on its high-minded and thoughtful debate, the columnist Kathleen Parker received 11,000 email messages when she argued in an article during the 2008 Presidential campaign that Governor Sarah Palin was unfit to be vice-president. One message lamented that her mother did not abort her[69]. On the internet, which some extol for its invigorating heterogeneity and debate, it is clear that the opposite is also true: on-line, people tend to choose views that confirm their own[70]. There are even dating sites to accommodate lonely hearts distinguished by their political views.

In Britain, recent elections saw the first ever accession to a parliamentary seat – in the European Parliament – of a far-right party, with the victory of the British National Party. In the US, Republicans and Democrats are increasingly choosing to live apart from one another, and locate themselves with others of similar political views[71]. Red and blue are now more starkly drawn than ever*.

The polarisation of political views, the intercession of business, lobbyists and interest groups between voters and their representatives, the growing number and power of political actors who are neither politicians nor conventional political parties, accountable to no-one but themselves yet nonetheless wielding considerable influence; together these factors suggest a deepening divide between the public and their nominal representatives; they suggest nothing less than a crisis in democracy.

The pact between citizen and government is never explicit. You can spend an entire life paying taxes, obeying laws, without once being asked whether you wish to contract into or out of it. Government insists upon your registration at birth, and to be notified upon your death. At no point does it seek your consent. You never get the chance to contract into the pact: your parents are legally obliged to do so on your behalf whether they like it or not. And there is only one way to contract out.

The pact rests on one central pillar (and, oddly, it is the same whether a country is democratic or not) – that government more or less represents the collective interests of the populace. The democratic process provides – in theory at least – for continual feedback, as Karl Popper once theorised, from governed to governers, the only way, Popper believed, to optimise policy so that it reflects the needs and preferences of the people. But if that feedback is interrupted,

---

* Though there is not the space here to explore this phenomenon fully, this sorting – or to put it more bluntly, segregation – by political views, which also occurs according to income, religion and race, is a characteristic of complex systems. Economist Thomas Schelling won the Nobel prize for explaining how the choice made by a few, say, Democrats, to live in a particular location can, over time, transform or "tip" a hitherto-mixed neighbourhood into one that is uniformly of one political persuasion. Even if individuals are tolerant at the micro level, over time a neighbourhood will become segregated, a phenomenon called "micro level tolerance; macro level segregation".

government policy, at best approximate to the collective wishes of the people, starts to diverge. People and government become estranged. When this happens, the pact breaks down. The evidence is accumulating in the 21st century that this is indeed happening.

If government cannot provide for the stability, safety and just arbitration of our common affairs, who can? The answer is both radical and discomforting. For there is only one alternative if government cannot successfully provide: we must do so ourselves. Self-organised government is one term; another rather more loaded term is anarchism.

But this is not the anarchism of early-20th-century bomb-wielding Russians, or nihilists charging police lines at G8 summits. It is a different vision, of individuals and groups peacefully organising their affairs, arbitrating necessary business directly with one another, guided by their conviction and direct experience and not by party-political dogma. It is more evolution than revolution, for it is dawning on people across the world that in order to fix our problems, there is no one to look to but ourselves. The minimalist act of voting is looking less and less adequate as a solution.

This vision may animate people, but it does not prescribe. Instead, this new way of doing things is just that – a way of doing things, a method, and emphatically not an end in itself, nor a design to be imposed upon others. Only a fool would wish the abrupt or violent overthrow of the current system for the certain result would be violent chaos – anarchy of the worst kind. Today, we are too accustomed to distrusting one another, to perceiving the "other" at home or abroad as hostile and malign. We are too accustomed to letting government take care of matters. If the crude policing of the current order were removed, it is easy to predict that we would likely fall to fighting one another.

But if it's true that government is less and less able to manage our collective affairs, it seems we have little choice but to take that burden upon our own shoulders. We must learn anew to look to ourselves to produce the effects we desire, to take responsibility for ourselves and for others, and to cooperate and negotiate with each other, instead of leaving that arbitration to an evidently imperfect mechanism. As these habits spread, a new and more durable order may emerge, not – as now – legislated from above but built from the ground up, by people acting upon their beliefs and engaging with each other.

For curiously it is perpetuation of the existing way of doing things, not anarchism, that may pose the greater risk to our peace and security. It is the alienation of government from people, and us from each other, that more endangers our fragile stability. It is no coincidence that this is the commonest criticism of anarchism, that it engenders disorder, that Anarchy=Chaos. Let us examine this, most serious, objection to this different way of doing things. I know about anarchy, violence and chaos, because I have seen it.

3

ANARCHY = CHAOS

WHEN THE TROUBLE FIRST IGNITED, I WAS IN GENEVA, AT a conference designed – ironically, it turned out – to promote reconciliation between Kosovo's Albanians and Serbs. An adviser to Kosovo's Prime Minister, a friend, drew me aside: "Three Albanian children have been killed", she whispered conspiratorially, "by a Serb". With deliberate portent, she added, "There will be trouble." Curiously, she seemed excited by the news. It was as if she was relieved that, at last, *something* was happening.

Next day, back in Pristina, Kosovo's capital, where I then lived, it was clear that her premonition was correct[72]. Tension was palpable in that city's polluted air, straining people's faces. The rumours were widespread, amplified by irresponsible journalists: a Serb had driven three children to their deaths, the reporters claimed, by drowning*. Not only that, but they had died that horrible death in the Ibar, the very river dividing Serb and Albanian halves of Mitrovica, Kosovo's most divided city.

That afternoon, at UN headquarters where I worked, we received reports of crowds gathering in towns and villages across the province. Suddenly, the security guards announced over the

---

* The deaths were later found to have been accidental.

office loudspeakers that a large group of young men was approaching the headquarters. Soon, their chanting "UÇK! UÇK! UÇK!" – roughly, Ooh-Chay-Kah – reverberated around the building, loud and aggressive. UÇK is the acronym for the Kosovo Liberation Army, the Kosovo-Albanian guerrillas who resisted Slobodan Milosevic's repression, including during the 1999 war that led to the withdrawal of Yugoslav forces.

Without warning, the loudspeakers announced that the building was immediately to be evacuated. But there was no information on how the evacuation should proceed or where the UN staff would go. There was a sudden and anxious sense of panic. People began to run up and down corridors. Mobile phones stopped working – it was later discovered that the riots had overloaded the networks, partly because some had used their phones to organise the riots. For some reason, the lifts stopped functioning too. Some began to weep, perhaps with fear.

I was with my wife, who had come to my office for its greater security. My Albanian assistant took charge. Besnik ushered us down the fire escape and into a car. We drove out of the compound and back to our house. On the streets, groups of young people were gathering. Many were children. They looked excited and agitated. That night, the groups merged into mobs.

I had agreed that evening to take part in a television discussion with political leaders at the main television studio in Pristina. Driving to the studio, near our house, a large mass of people was blocking the streets. It was dark and I could not tell their number. The mass swelled and shifted; it had a shape and intent beyond its individual components. There was shouting and the bangs of what I thought at the time were firecrackers. I later realised it was gunfire. There was no police in sight.

The television debate was ugly. Along with an American diplomat, I argued that the riots must stop immediately. Parents should tell their children to go home. But the political leaders from Kosovo's Albanian majority did not agree. According to them, the trouble was the UN's fault. In their version, the riots had been triggered by the UN's decision to allow Serb protesters from a village near Pristina to block one of the main roads to the south.

The Kosovo-Albanian leaders argued that the anger on the streets was legitimate protest at the many injustices Kosovars had suffered, past and present. From the tenor and aggression of the debate, it was clear that some of the leaders sensed a revolutionary moment when the UN, the *de facto* power in Kosovo, might be overthrown. They grasped the tail of the tiger. By the end of the programme, my back was in painful spasm from the tension gripping me. I returned home through a city smouldering with violence.

Back at home with some Albanian friends, I sat listening to the gunfire and occasional explosions. A red glow appeared at our window. We looked out to see sparks and flames spurting into the air nearby. We realised it was the Serbian church at the top of our street, alight. There was an awful sound: a bell ringing, incessantly.

After a while, when things seemed calmer, my friend Ardi suggested we go out to see what was going on. We walked up our street to the church. It was ablaze like a summer bonfire, its steeple a column of flame. Atop, the church bell rang with a desperate rhythm. The heat and flames were somehow making it ring: thankfully, there was no one still inside the blazing building. At last the bell stopped. Scores of young men surrounded the church. Their work done, many were sitting, gazing at the fire, smoking and chatting. Someone was selling cigarettes.

We walked away. Ardi, a Kosovo-Albanian, would not look at me. He was beside himself with anger and shame. Spent cases of plastic bullets and rifle cartridges crunched under our feet. The UN riot police had confronted the mob here. But they had been overwhelmed and retreated, leaving the church to its fate. All across Kosovo, the forces of law and order – the UN and local police and NATO peacekeepers – had lost control. In one town, a contingent of German soldiers had remained in barracks while a mob of thousands roamed the town for hours, moving from district to district, picking out Serb churches, houses and UN offices, ransacking buildings and putting them to the torch. When we later visited the town, we saw at its centre a blackened hillside, studded with the shells of burned-out houses, as if a forest fire had swept through it.

The next day, the violence continued. There were reports of buses transporting rioters around the province to attack different Serb enclaves. In southern Kosovo, a large mob was prevented from besieging a Serb Orthodox monastery by the intervention of a local Albanian former KLA guerrilla leader (he was later to become Kosovo's prime minister). In the divided town of Mitrovica, where the Albanian children had drowned, NATO troops shot and killed several Albanians trying to cross the river to attack Serbs in the northern part of the city. Riots went on around the country into the night. Every UN office in the territory was attacked, over 150 UN vehicles were destroyed. At least 550 homes and 27 Orthodox churches and monasteries were burned, and over 4,000 people – mostly Serbs, but also Roma and other minority groups – were driven from their homes[73].

Eventually, the violence died down. Local political leaders claimed that their calls to end the turmoil had worked, rarely confessing that these entreaties had been made under pressure from international officials. But in truth it appeared more that the chaos and violence had simply petered out. On the streets, the rhythm and the momentum of the violence pulsed through the city. Before the violence erupted, you could feel it build up as an urge needing expression. As the violence played out, that dark energy was ventilated. As it ended, somehow you could tell that the force that had driven the chaos and rage had at last been exhausted.

It is commonly held that society requires authority in order to enjoy peace and stability. Without such institutions – law, the police, the army – society will collapse into anarchy and disorder; the many will fall victim to the criminal few. In case we need reminding of what this might be like, movies abound with depictions of anarchy, even if often an anarchic world perpetuated by zombie hordes (*28 Days Later*, *I am Legend*) or provoked by alien invasion (*War of the Worlds*): either way, the anarchy shown is entertainingly terrifying. It seems there is only a fragile veil dividing us from the jungle. Television offers ceaseless titillating depiction – both real and falsified – of the criminals who lurk to destroy us, but for the thin blue line of law and order to hold them back.

But in these illustrations lies a clue. There is scant entertainment involved in the real and actual horrors of humanity – the Holocaust, the Khmer Rouge's "Year Zero" or the butchery of Charles Manson. If anarchy were so close, and so awful, we wouldn't find its Hollywood depiction entertaining; instead, we would find it horribly frightening.

One criticism of anarchism as a political strategy is so ubiquitous that it merely requires a reshaping of the word: anarchism = anarchy. Without a superstructure of institutions to maintain order, it is claimed, disorder and chaos will surely result – Hobbes's "war of all against all".

This is indeed a frightening prospect that few dare contemplate. When disaster strikes, like an earthquake in Haiti or a hurricane in New Orleans, it is never long before commentators, safe in their television studios, issue dire warning of social disorder and breakdown, as if this is more frightening than the original natural disaster. In post-Katrina New Orleans, reports of carjackings, rapes and murders flooded the news. Thousands of law-enforcement agents were deployed from other states as Louisiana's governor warned, "They have M16s and are locked and loaded. These troops know how to shoot and kill and I expect they will". Police in one suburb neighbouring the flooded city were so alarmed at the prospect of looters and other malcontents that they blocked the bridge from the city, preventing the hungry and desperate from getting help. Others shot fleeing refugees, in the notorious case at the Danziger Bridge.

As Fareed Zakaria has noted, the federal government's fastest

and most efficient response to Hurricane Katrina was the establishment of a Guantánamo-like prison facility in which 1,200 American
citizens were summarily detained and denied any of their constitutional rights for months, a suspension of *habeas corpus* that, Zakaria
commented, reads like something out of a Kafka novel[74]. Later
accounts, such as Dave Eggers's *Zeitoun*, told stories ignored at the
time, like that of Abdulrahman Zeitoun, who after the hurricane
paddled around the flooded city in a canoe offering help, ferrying
neighbours to higher ground and caring for abandoned pets, only
to be arrested by National Guardsmen and held *incommunicado* for
several weeks without charge and without medical attention along
with other Arab-American companions. As Rebecca Solnit has
written, disasters in fact often produce the opposite of disorder in
human society: instead of violence and anarchy, community and
solidarity[75]. I saw this myself in New York City in the days after the
9/11 attacks. Rather than the jingoistic blunderings of government,
it was the community and compassion of ordinary New Yorkers
that has stayed with me from that awful experience: the huge piles
of food and water stacked outside the Salvation Army on 14th
Street, the almost tangible air of grief and sympathy on the streets.

A recent letter to the *Financial Times* makes a common claim:
that civilisation is fundamentally fragile and requires government
to protect it. The correspondent cites the example of the arrival
of the mutineers from the *Bounty* on the isolated Pacific island of
Pitcairn:

When the nine Bounty mutineers and 17 Tahitian men and
women arrived there in 1789 it was as close to the Garden of
Eden as anywhere in the real world: generously endowed with
water, sunshine and fertile soils, and uninhabited by anyone else.
The perfect test of Hobbes versus Rousseau. In the event, Hobbes
won. The British sailors fought among themselves and tried to
subjugate the Tahitians. The Tahitians resisted and fought among
themselves.

By 1800, 11 years later, only one of the mutineers, nine Tahitian women, and many children were left, most of the others having died unnatural deaths. The surviving mutineer created political order by establishing not just an autocracy but a theocracy, with himself as the link between God and man.[76]

The writer concludes, quite reasonably given the episode he offers as an example, by emphasising "the importance of continued efforts to sustain governance organisations that bring together the specific interests that count most in the definition of a common (national, regional, global) interest, in order that, through repeated interaction, convergent interests will prevail over divergent ones".

The writer's conclusion is entirely correct. Unfortunately however, it is not clear that contemporary political institutions, whether national or international, do in fact successfully give sufficient attention to the common interests of humanity. Instead, it's increasingly evident that these institutions elevate the interests of the most powerful interest groups over collective interests, and, thanks to the short-termism of the political cycle and the beggar-thy-neighbour "zero-sum" calculus of international bargaining (analysed later), neglect long-term primary needs, including the environment.

One can also argue that the worst outrages in human history occurred not in the absence of authority and government, but were instead perpetrated by governments claiming to act in the common interest: Nazi Germany, Stalinist Soviet Union, Khmer Rouge Cambodia – the list is a very long one. The criminal acts undertaken by these governments were permitted and in all these cases ordered by government in the name of the collective interest; the individual perpetrators were thus rendered immune. Democratic governments are also fully capable of terrible crimes, legitimised by government's ultimate moral immunity of *droit d'état* or "state interest" (on this too, more later). But in any case the correspondent's argument is widely shared: institutions protect us against ourselves, above all against what would otherwise prevail: chaos and disorder.

It's worth examining this specific proposition in more detail by taking the opposite case: a thought experiment – imagine a world without institutions. And let us take a difficult context: the sometimes venal and secretive world of financial investment.

The gigantic "Ponzi" scheme orchestrated by the financier Bernard Madoff was the world's largest fraud ever perpetrated by one man. It ruined thousands of investors and symbolised the most grotesque excesses of Wall Street. Despite the abject failure to catch Madoff by the government body established to police and regulate the investment industry, it was almost universally agreed that the best way to prevent such crimes in future was tighter regulation and scrutiny of the investment industry. The overwhelming reaction was that the government should have protected the innocent investors: something must be done!

But there may be a solution that overturns every assumption we have about how to deter, prevent and punish such crimes in future. It may be that the very rules and institutions established to protect us in fact do the opposite.

Madoff's fraud was simple. He encouraged investors to deposit money with his firm, paying them returns that were consistently higher than the going rate. With the appeal of above-market and above all steady returns, Madoff had little difficulty in attracting new investors. Their fresh deposits would be used to fund returns to the earlier investors. All the scheme required was a never-ending flow of new investors, with deposits sufficient to fund the above-market returns to the earlier investors, and to pay off the occasional depositor who wished to withdraw their whole investment: and for obvious reasons, those wishing to withdraw from this cash-cow of easy money were few.

Madoff and his co-conspirators manufactured a huge volume of falsified reports and data to pretend that their fraudulent scheme was in fact a legitimate and highly successful investment business. Madoff's cover was effective. On three occasions in the 1990s, he was elected chairman of the NASDAQ. By his own admission, he perpetrated this massive fraud for nearly two decades, and was uncovered only when the precipitous market collapses at the end of 2008 prevented him from raising the funds to pay off those wishing to withdraw their money. In the end, it was estimated, Madoff's fraud cost his investors perhaps twenty billion dollars.

Less simple is why a scheme of such magnitude and pervasive dishonesty succeeded for so long. Madoff lied systematically to both his investors and to the supervising federal authorities. In this criminal endeavour, he was assisted by colleagues and, perhaps, family members, some of whom have been prosecuted or face further investigation. But the scale of profits from his fund should have provoked more intrusive suspicion. Others within the industry tried to calculate how his company could consistently make such high profits, against market trends, outperforming all competitors year-after-year. They couldn't work it out.

The institutions designed to prevent such crime completely failed. The Securities and Exchange Commission (SEC), the federal body established in the 1930s to supervise the investment industry, conducted several investigations. Madoff himself has said that he had "hundreds" of contacts with SEC staff[77]. Prompted by tip-offs from others in the industry who questioned Madoff's fantastic profits, the SEC failed however to uncover the crime.

A later report on how the SEC missed Madoff found many failings: staff were over-specialised, devoted to particular subsets of fraud, and were rewarded for pursuing that particular kind of crime[78]. Different parts of the SEC investigating Madoff were unaware of one another. Each individual section cleared Madoff of other allegations against him. Together, they managed to miss the big picture. One commentator compared the SEC to twelve blind men examining an elephant.

Elsewhere, the report revealed not only that SEC staff were

often incompetent in understanding Ponzi schemes, but that Madoff intimidated SEC investigators because of his stature on Wall Street. The investigation at one point describes investigators as "enthralled" by Madoff: some of them asked Madoff's staff if they could work for him[79].

This failure appears part of a disquieting pattern. It was only *after* the BP Gulf oil spill of 2010 that the many failings of the body assigned to monitor and regulate the oil industry surfaced. In the aftermath of the disaster, it emerged that the Minerals Management Service (MMS) had allowed BP to skip environmental assessments ahead of drilling the well that spewed millions of barrels of oil into the Gulf. MMS inspectors had also permitted oil-company employees to fill out inspection forms in pencil, which they would then ink in. Others had accepted illegal gifts, consumed drugs and literally gone to bed with officials from the companies they were supposed to regulate[80]. One inspector had negotiated a job with an oil company while at the same time inspecting the company's operations.

With Madoff, the financial industry's own self-regulatory bodies did nothing to investigate or stop his suspiciously profitable activities. This was unsurprising given that Madoff was a prominent member of many of them. Madoff was at various times chairman or board member of the National Association of Securities Dealers, a self-regulatory securities-industry organisation. The Madoff family had long-standing, high-level ties to the Securities Industry and Financial Markets Association, the primary securities-industry organisation. Madoff's brother Peter served two terms as a member of this organisation's board of directors.

Madoff was regarded as a dominant figure in the investment industry, one of the largest "market makers" at the NASDAQ. He and his company were major political donors: notably he donated nearly a quarter of a million dollars to *both* Democrats and Republicans, indicative not of any political preference, but a more naked purchase of influence. Some have suggested that his political connections, and links to the SEC, helped deter a more thorough investigation of his activities.

The testimony of financial analyst and would-be Madoff whistleblower Harry Markopolos to Congress, after the fraud was uncovered, was revealing. Giving evidence to the House of Representatives capital-markets subcommittee, Markopolos said that he had investigated Madoff on behalf of a group of private investors[81]. After only a short examination of the numbers, he came to the conclusion that Madoff's spectacular returns could be explained only by one investment technique: fraud. Markopolos testified that for nine years he had repeatedly tried to get the SEC to investigate and shut down the Madoff Ponzi scheme. The SEC had not only ignored these warnings, according to Markopolos, but was fundamentally incapable of understanding the complex financial instruments being traded in the 21st century. And here lies one clue to what might be done to prevent such crime in future.

Another lies in an uncompromising look at the investors themselves. Many suffered terribly from Madoff's fraud, losing life savings, being forced to sell homes or return from a well-earned retirement to work indefinitely, their nest egg stolen. In many cases, their lives were utterly ruined. But why did these investors give their money to Madoff without the most cursory scrutiny of his company? Madoff's returns were so implausible that any sensible investor should have held back, but many committed their entire life savings. Harry Markopolos told Congress that investing in Madoff was a "no-brainer" in that "you had to have no brains whatsoever to invest into such an unbelievable performance record that bears no resemblance to any other investment manager's track record throughout recorded human history".

Some commentators have suggested that one of Madoff's techniques was to hint at a vague air of wrongdoing to help justify his otherwise inexplicable returns. The right to invest in his company was by invitation only, creating an air of desirable – and perhaps disreputable – exclusivity, that something special was going on, maybe something if not illegal then a little bit questionable: insider-trading perhaps, of some kind. For several years, potential investors who approached Madoff were told that the fund was "closed". Such false allure is the classic sign of a Ponzi scheme.

In the *New York Times*, business commentator Joe Nocera has argued that for these investors to blame the government for their decision to give every last penny to Bernie Madoff "is like a child blaming his mother for letting him start a fight while she wasn't looking". But here lies one explanation of why people may have invested in Madoff. The mere existence of the SEC, with its claim to supervise, scrutinise and protect, must inevitably lower people's own sensitivity to risk. If the teacher is present, what is going on in the playground must be, in some way, acceptable.

Research suggests that when measures are in place to protect people from risk, they tend to indulge in *more* risky behaviour. In his 2006 book *Market Failure Versus Government Failure*, Clifford Winston, an economist at the Brookings Institution, cites consider-able and divers research which shows, for instance, that people drive faster in vehicles that feel safer, cycle more dangerously when they wear helmets and take less care bathing infants when using child seats designed to reduce the risk of drowning.

This research makes sense. We tend to lower our guard when told that the coast is clear. Indeed, so evident is this fundamental human tendency that one can make a further, and perhaps provoc-ative, presumption: that criminal frauds like Madoff are actually made more feasible by the presence of institutional authorities designed to prevent them. The evidence for this seemingly outra-geous claim is in front of our noses: the fraud happened, right under the SEC's.

Moreover, as the Madoff example has clearly shown, it is naïve to expect any single authority to keep up with the massive complex-ity and dynamic changes of an industry like securities investment. There is a fundamental and insoluble imbalance in such supervi-sion. Government bodies suffer the constant depredations of budget cycles, cuts, and the intrinsic disadvantages of employers who can offer salaries equivalent to only a tiny proportion of those available in the industry they supervise. Given this fundamental and persistent power imbalance, it is surprising not that institutions like the SEC fail, as they regularly do, but that investors expect such institutions to keep up with the free-wheeling, greed-tainted and secretive world of securities investment.

On the broader scale, it is often claimed that the recent global credit crisis was caused by the absence – or more precisely, the withdrawal – of the correct controls on the financial industry. It is persuasively argued that it was the proliferation of certain financial instruments, collectively known as derivatives, and specifically so-called Credit Default Swaps (or CDSs), which helped spread the poison of the sub-prime mortgage crisis across the world. CDSs are essentially legalised gambling: they are bets on whether certain financial indices, like mortgage repayments or stock prices, will rise or fall; a financial instrument that Warren Buffett has called "financial Weapons of Mass Destruction". Some have called them the 21st-century version of the "bucket shops" of the 1920s where people could bet on whether stocks could rise or fall without actually owning those stocks. The bucket shops were blamed for the wild speculation that helped fuel the Wall Street Crash of 1929. They were subsequently outlawed. In 2000, Congress passed a little-known law that essentially permitted such betting again. As for the industry's own alleged safeguards, banks *paid* the ratings agencies to rate and thus endorse the mortgage-based investment instruments that "sliced and diced" and concealed and spread the dangerous risk of sub-prime lending.

Many commentators have therefore reasonably concluded that the obvious answer is further regulation, to ban CDSs and rely on legislation to tame the industry. The problem however with this analysis, so tempting in these turbid days, is that it rests on an assumption about the legislative process that is perilous indeed: that legislators act upon the interests of voters, and no one else. The law in question, the Commodity Futures Modernization Act, was passed in 2000 by a Democratic administration; it was proposed by the Clinton administration and passed quickly through both Houses; the bill passed by 292–60 votes in the House of Representatives, and by "unanimous consent" in the Senate. Not one member of Congress raised objections to this particular provision, which was secreted away in a bill of many hundreds of pages. Needless to say, that year the financial-services industry, which strongly supported the bill, contributed large amounts to both Democrats and Republicans.

After the crash, on both sides of the Atlantic, politicians roared their populist anger against the banks and mortgage companies that helped precipitate the crisis, then demanded massive government bailouts for their companies, while continuing to pay their executives grotesque bonuses. In all countries, political leaders queued up to decry the greed and swear their commitment to legislation "never again" to allow such abuse to recur. But out of this bellowing public rage, the legislation actually delivered resembled more a mouse's squeak.

The legislation is complex. In the US, the bill finally passed in July 2010 allegedly to "reform Wall Street", is a document of thousands of pages[82]. Many of its provisions are highly technical in nature, allowing politicians to claim to an ill-informed public that the new law amounts to more than it in reality is. The press, in its complacency as the "fourth estate" in the body politic, did little to enquire into and explain the complexities. In the American bill, for instance, much was made of the prohibitions against "proprietary trading"; most people would have no clue what this actually is.

In fact, this prohibition, in any case very limited, will do almost nothing to prevent the kind of collapse that the global economy experienced in '08/09. Within months of the "reform Wall Street" legislation, banks were finding ways to circumvent the so-called "Volcker rule" to limit trading – perhaps better known as betting – on their own accounts: precisely the activity that helped bring down Lehman Brothers in 2007[83].

Most financial commentators agreed that there was one simple and easily explicable measure that would surely have limited the ability of banks to create the chaos that they did: substantially higher requirements for capital-to-loan ratios, i.e. to require banks to hold more capital relative to their lending. In the confusion and obscurity of new measures, such rules were largely absent or, if present, in watered-down form. Instead, in a telltale signal that the necessary tough decisions had been dodged, Congress set up new bodies, and new mechanisms, to deal with these problems in the future. Likewise, amendments designed to address the problem of banks "too big to fail", by limiting their capital and thus the risk they pose to the whole economy, were rejected. Instead of passing the necessary measures in the immediate aftermath of the crash, when they might have been politically possible, the Congressional legislation empowers a new regulatory body to pass them in future, when without doubt still less political support will be available. In a sure sign that the legislation was indeed to the benefit, not detriment, of the banks, shares in all financial-service companies significantly rose immediately after the Senate vote.

Meanwhile, at the global level, neither the G20 nor the global banking regulatory mechanism, the Basel Committee, have managed to agree measures to ensure banks hold sufficient deposits against lending. The "Basel III" proposals in 2010, celebrated by the banking industry as a major step forward, were judged by a more independent and disinterested group of distinguished academic finance experts as "far from sufficient to protect the system from recurring crises"[84]. Clive Crook in the *Financial Times* commented that the new Basel rules were an improvement on the preceding arrangements, but "not by much"[85].

The reason for this failure is not hard to find. As soon as anyone suggested more effective measures, like higher capital/lending ratios, legions of banking-industry spokesmen would rise as one to complain that such requirements would render US financial companies "uncompetitive" in the global marketplace. The CEO of

JPMorgan Chase, for instance, wailed that new financial regulation including stricter capital controls would be the "nail in the coffin" of big American banks, adding for good measure that this would "greatly diminish growth"[86]. This was a powerful argument in a country deeply enmired in recession. But the argument rarely needed to be publicly advocated: there was precious little public debate on the bill, since politicians, both Democrats and Republicans, conspired to pretend that the bill had sharp teeth when in fact it was but a set of crummy plastic dentures.

This too was unsurprising since the financial industry had taken care to donate generously to both sides. In advance of the Congressional bill, financial institutions spent $1.4 million a day on lobbying; they had hired 70 former Congress members to their payroll, and 940 former federal employees. Senator Scott Brown (R) of Massachusetts raked in "off-the-charts" donations from the financial industry while working to water down the financial bill[87]. On the Democrats' side, President Obama's then budget director, Peter Orzsag, left the White House and waited a seemly four months before joining Citibank, which of course was busy marketing new credit cards to indebted Americans.

The Congressional debate was in fact not a substantive discussion of what was really required to prevent another financial meltdown in the future. It was instead a kind of theatre show, presented for the public's benefit to reassure them that "something was being done". The chairman of the House Financial Services Committee, Spencer Bachus, with refreshing candour soon afterwards remarked that "My view is that Washington is there to serve the banks".

The answer then may be to do the one thing that no one seems prepared to contemplate: take away the teacher in the playground. Let anarchy reign. It's interesting to contemplate what might follow. Some pointers are already available: in the behaviours and systems that have grown up on the worldwide web.

*   *   *

On eBay and other on-line marketplaces, there are few certain methods to prevent fraud. It's easy for a seller to take payment on-line for imperfect or non-existent products then disappear into the anonymous jungle of the internet. When eBay began, the anonymity of the web did little to produce trust. On the contrary, buyers and sellers were quick to complain about each other – often directly to Pierre Omidyar, the founder of eBay, who in the early days would answer customer-service complaints himself. He was soon overwhelmed with the volume of complaints.

Omidyar decided to introduce a system under which eBay participants could rate each other on-line – not just to say when they were dissatisfied, but when they were happy too. This feedback system is one of eBay's most well-known features: sellers advertise their positive ratings as a selling point. Sellers without positive ratings struggle to find buyers. Thus, there is a huge incentive for sellers and buyers to treat each other well, if they are to do any repeat business. And interestingly, like the accumulation of friends on Facebook, which takes months and years to build up, the accumulation of trust indicators within this system is also a huge barrier to entry for prospective competitors to eBay.

The idea – and effect – was to incentivise sellers to behave well: to deliver what they sold promptly and in good order. The system seemed to work. Introduction of the ratings system helped drive a massive increase in transactions on eBay and a reduction in the number of criminal cases of fraud arising from eBay purchases.

In China, things have worked slightly differently, but prove the same point. Here eBay lost market share to a competitor that understood better how customers wanted to build trust with one another. On its Chinese site, eBay did not offer ways for buyers and sellers to chat on-line, fearing they would close their transactions off the site to avoid paying fees. By contrast, eBay's rival Taobao.com understood that live conversations were necessary for Chinese consumers to cultivate trust, and offered an instant-message service to allow them to haggle over deals. eBay forfeited the Chinese on-line market to Taobao partly as a result.

The on-line classifieds site Craig's List did something similar to eBay, following the philosophy of its founder, Craig Newmark that "people are good and trustworthy and generally just concerned with getting through the day"[88]: all you have to do is build a minimal infrastructure and let them work things out for themselves. The primary mechanism of the site is the red flag: if other users flag an unacceptable advertisement enough times, it will disappear. The mission of Craig's List is simple: to enable local, face-to-face transactions. This formula clearly works despite the many aesthetic flaws and frustrations of Craig's List. It is by far the most popular community site in the US, and is reportedly viewed by forty-seven million unique users each month.

The very openness of the web has however brought to the surface some of mankind's worst aspects. In its transparency, it has made visible and in some cases exacerbated behaviours that were hitherto kept hidden – from "snuff" videos to child pornography. After celebrities, grisly battlefield videos shot with the cell phones of soldiers are among the most popular downloads. But with the transparency, others are learning to combat the most undesirable and sometimes criminal activities.

For instance, in 2010, campaigners demanded that Craig's List remove its "Adult services" section because it was being used by sex traffickers to pimp underage girls. Craig's List at first refused, citing its commitment to freedom of speech, but eventually succumbed to the pressure and removed the offending section, rather childishly replacing it with a notice saying "Censored". Likewise, Amazon removed a self-published book on paedophilia, advertised on the Amazon site, after mass Twitter and email protests. In both cases, the action to address the offence and the reaction of Craig's List and Amazon to comply took place with no government intervention. In Amazon's case, the protest and reaction took place in a matter of hours.

Small businesses everywhere must rapidly adapt to a world

where their services and products are discussed openly and critically on the web by customers, more or less all the time. Local
listings now offer customer ratings on all types of business, from
the local plumber to the bakery – and bank. Discomforting for
some, the enforced visibility and criticism on the web is proving for
others a liberation, and sales advantage. The evidence is mounting
that of two otherwise identical businesses, the one that responds
quickly and positively, and above all transparently, to customer
complaints on-line, will rapidly gain the better on-line ratings, with
obvious consequences for their likely sales.

A new phenomenon is emerging on the internet, which one
commentator has called the "Panopticon"[89]. The original
Panopticon was an imaginary prison, designed by Jeremy Bentham,
where all parts of the prison were visible from one central point,
without the prisoners knowing that they were under observation at
any particular moment. But the Panopticon of the internet is not
for the purposes of monitoring the incarcerated, or of observation
by one over many, but more of "all watching all". As our lives are
lived increasingly on-line, so are our traces apparent. More and
more it is possible to locate, identify and examine people from their
on-line presence.

There are obvious privacy concerns here, which we have yet
properly to contend with. It is a new and disquieting world when a
trainee teacher can be denied a college degree because she has
posted a photo of herself, drunk, on MySpace*. And we should

---

* The *New York Times* reported that Stacy Snyder, then a 25-year-old teacher
in training at Conestoga Valley High School in Lancaster, Pennsylvania., posted a photo on her MySpace page that showed her at a party wearing a pirate
hat and drinking from a plastic cup, with the caption "Drunken Pirate". After
discovering the page, her supervisor at the high school told her the photo was
"unprofessional", and the dean of Millersville University School of Education, where Snyder was enrolled, said she was promoting drinking in virtual
view of her under-age students. As a result, days before Snyder's scheduled
graduation, the university denied her a teaching degree (see *New York Times*,
19 July 2010, "The Web Means the End of Forgetting" by Jeffrey Rosen).

remain concerned that the internet itself does not fall under the control of a few and unaccountable agencies (as will be discussed). But at the same time there is also the potential for a new form of collective security. Already, it is possible easily to access the human-rights and environmental records of major companies[90]; one website allows you to research all the components, and the labour history embodied in them, of even complex products like comput-ers or TVs[91] . It is easy to see how this scrutiny will spread more widely. Already, employers google prospective employees to scruti-nise their on-line history. Prospective lovers do the same. The Panopticon is already reality.

On-line transparency and criticism may help improve the services offered by competing local plumbers. It's harder to see how it may work for the securities industry, a world that is not only secretive but also so complex that many of the most sophisticated financiers (George Soros for instance) freely admit that they do not fully understand the financial instruments now available. Here, we return to Harry Markopolos.

After conducting his own investigation of Madoff, and concluding that something very fishy was going on, Markopolos sought to inform the SEC which, as we now know, failed to follow up his suspicions. This he was permitted to do by law. Markopolos was not however permitted to publicise his concerns, for to do so would have immediately made him vulnerable to punitive lawsuits by Madoff. Indeed, Markopolos testified that the failure of the SEC to investigate his complaints made him fear for his safety. In his testimony, he repeatedly talks about the risks to him and his team of investigating Madoff. Markopolos tried to interest the *Wall Street Journal* in the story, but apparently the journalist concerned was never given the go-ahead to publish by editors, no doubt also fear-ful of lawsuits. The net effect therefore of the laws existing at the time of the Madoff fraud was not to inform and protect investors, but to protect Madoff.

Perhaps it is naïve to expect ordinary investors to enjoy the expertise to scrutinise investment funds like Madoff's, even if one might expect them to exercise more diligence than that demonstrated by Madoff's unwise and unfortunate investors. It is not unrealistic however to envisage a system whereby disinterested experts might offer advice on the wisdom of investing in certain funds. Looking at the way e-commerce is developing on the web, this might consist of several connected elements: a ratings-system for buyers anonymously to rate their investment "experience", independent sites which offer disinterested advice on various investment alternatives, and, finally, investors might form groups – like cooperatives – such as that which hired Harry Markopolos to conduct more partial research on their behalf.

Above all, the web shows that it is transparency that wins business custom. Ergo, those that eschew it – or actively reject it, as Madoff did – should pay the penalty in lost business. Madoff himself has argued that his claimed "black box" investment strategy – the series of computerised algorithms to decide equity trades – was unintelligible to most of Wall Street, let alone ordinary investors, claiming that many other hedge funds are similarly opaque to outside scrutiny: "Does anyone know how, say, Renaissance really makes its returns?" Madoff asks in an interview with the *Financial Times*, referring to the wildly successful hedge fund[92].

Perhaps he is right. However, what is beyond dispute is that from 1992 onwards Madoff, by his own admission, conducted no trades at all and faked the documents pretending that they had taken place. This fraud should have been easy to detect, with only the most cursory scrutiny, if the market were more transparent: it should be straightforward to corroborate the trades with the counter-parties, those who supposedly bought and sold Madoff's equity holdings. In other words, transparency does not need to reveal the secret investment strategies of successful funds, but it can – and simply – reveal other telltale signs of fraud like Madoff's. Unlike his faked investment strategy, Madoff's fraud was devastatingly simple.

There is perhaps a final and subtle lesson to be learned from this miserable episode. It is clear both from victims and Madoff himself that the wealth and power of big Wall Street players, including Madoff, was a deterrent against scrutiny and investigation, intimidating those who sought to question, including the SEC. From many accounts of the Madoff scam, Wall Street appears as a layered hierarchy governed not by the SEC but by an exclusive club of powerful financiers, whom Madoff sought and succeeded to join. This club was bound by a wary but mutual trust, including not to question each other's affairs too closely. Madoff claims that many major Wall Street figures and banks, including JPMorgan, knew what was going on. Once Madoff joined the club, and hobnobbed with its members, he was all but untouchable. Madoff himself is far from alone in suggesting that the SEC concentrates mostly on minor infractions, and fails to go after the big banks and institutions, arguing that recent "reform" legislation has done nothing to correct the problem[93].

This analysis suggests that a more fundamental levelling is necessary to avoid such crimes – and indeed dramatic global crises like the credit crunch – in future. Clearly, it is a mistake to believe that alone the punishment of Madoff is sufficient to address the deep and systemic danger – and risk to us all – that his crime, like the '08 financial collapse, has uncovered. We have been culturally conditioned to accept that the prosecution of the occasional Madoff somehow proves the effectiveness of law and the intrinsic justice in the system; in fact, the story unearthed by his case proves the opposite: the system is revealed as fundamentally iniquitous and persistently vulnerable to crime and violent instability. The gross inequality of contemporary society permits a culture of unaccountability and, sometimes, criminality amongst the richest and most powerful. The most extreme results of this imbalance are scandals like Madoff but also, with the credit crunch, economic volatility that destroys millions of jobs and endangers the entire global economy.

Methods to address this inequality will be discussed later. Money and power are of course hard to assail as sources of influence and secrecy. But what can be changed is the attitude of those outside the private circle. We should no longer be intimidated. One clear lesson of the Madoff scandal is the requirement for individual investors themselves to use greater care and scrutiny: to exercise, in short, their own agency rather than submitting their choices to the care of others. Everyone has the right to question. This is a right that cannot be taken for granted but must be continually asserted, by one and by all. The more that each of us demands it, the easier it will be for all of us.

The exercise of collective and individual scrutiny, disinterested analysis shared publicly, insistent questioning: none of these elements would necessarily suffice alone to deter or prevent future Madoffs. But together they would create a lattice of checks and balances whose collective effect would be to force greater transparency within and scrutiny of a notoriously closed, clubby and corrupt industry: a result that decades of government supervision and legislation have signally failed to achieve.

That lattice would not have a fixed structure, and it would likely change over time in response to changes in the industry it was monitoring. It would not have the reassuring bricks-and-mortar institutional presence, and claim to expertise and authority, of a body like the Securities and Exchange Commission – itself a comforting name, at least prior to Madoff. The lattice may not be imposed by legislation, and its origin may be in a state of affairs some might call anarchy – the absence of rules – yet its result would be not the disorder usually associated with that word, but its opposite.

For two days in 2004, there was anarchy in Kosovo. The "authorities" – in this case the local police, UN and NATO peacekeepers – lost control. This was never publicly admitted. The candid admissions of failure in reports by UN officials in Kosovo itself were altered at UN headquarters in New York before they were reported to the UN Security Council, the ultimate authority which supervised the *de facto* government of Kosovo. It wasn't the UN's fault,

the Security Council was told. The violence was deliberately instigated by extremist Kosovar leaders, an allegation for which there
was little hard evidence.

The journalists who arrived in Kosovo after the violence chose
their own convenient narratives: this was a typical, if depressing,
cycle of the familiar ethnic violence that had plagued Kosovo, like
the Balkans, for generations. Only a few chose to report the more
complicated truth, including that the violence had been in part a
kind of rebellion against the ruling authorities in Kosovo, the UN.
Only one NGO, a specialist in conflict, whose two staff were deeply
embedded in Kosovo's complicated stories, managed to capture the
many strands of what had happened here[94].

In truth, each chosen narrative carried some weight. The story
of generational ethnic hatred was, in a sense, a true one. Serbs were
attacked by Kosovo-Albanian mobs across the territory. Many
Serbian houses were burned. Some Serbs were physically assaulted;
eight were killed (the remainder killed in the violence were Kosovo-
Albanians shot by NATO and UN forces[95]).

A second narrative was better concealed than the first, conventional, account. This was that the anger was directed as much against
the UN rulers of Kosovo as it was against the Serbs. Despite having
their own democratically elected government, the people of Kosovo
were excluded from the crucial decisions about their own future. I
saw the evidence with my own eyes. The UN was attacked in all its
manifestations – offices, cars, staff. Other international organisations, such as the EU, were not attacked. There was already
considerable and vocal discontent with the unaccountability and
incompetence of international rule. But this version of events was
suppressed by the UN itself, in its reports to its political supervisors
in the UN Security Council, which misleadingly absolved the UN of
any criticism. The member states of the UN interested in Kosovo
like the US, UK, France and others, tended to accede, at least in
public, to this revisionism.

There was a deeper flux at work too. The boys and young men

in the rioting crowds were not sophisticated political critics. If you had asked them why they were rioting, they would not have said it was because Kosovo's people were excluded from political decision-making about their future. They might have said, we hate the Serbs. But many said, it is because we are angry. Angry at the potholes and the lack of jobs; angry at the endless power cuts; angry because the girls and the luxury we see on MTV are unavailable to us.

So far, so political. But it was clear, because you could feel it, that there was a collective emotion at work. An emotion that was evident in individuals, but took greater force, and found expression, only when the crowd formed. The violence felt, in some inadmissible way, like a release. This was why the girl in Geneva was excited by the prospect; this was why the men smoked and laughed after burning the church; this was why teenagers rushed to join the mob. It was exciting. This was the power of the crowd, a force that can be felt benignly in the exhilaration of a cheering crowd at a sports match, malignly in a rioting mob. It is powerful and terrible, all at once.

After the violence subsided, I returned to my work at the UN. My job had been to guide the local elected Kosovo government to adopt so-called "standards" of democracy: the rule of law, minority rights and other measures of a state's worthiness to exist and be accepted in the community of nations. The "international community" in this case was embodied in a small and secretive group of six countries known as the "Contact Group", which ran international policy on Kosovo. This group had insisted that such standards be established, and in some way fulfilled, before Kosovo could be considered for "final status" – whether it could become a state, as the large majority of its people desperately wanted.

Politically, the imposition of these standards was one reason why the violence had erupted. Because Russia, the US and others disagreed in principle on whether Kosovo should become a state, no one in the "international community" was prepared to say *what* precisely Kosovo had to do to become independent. Kosovo was caught in a state of perpetual limbo, like being told every day to sit an exam but never told if you'd passed or failed, or indeed what a pass or fail required.

The two-day orgy of violence therefore represented a total failure for my work. I sat at my desk, facing Besnik my loyal assistant, and stared at the stacks of papers elaborating the democratic, rule-abiding "standards" that Kosovo was required to meet. We discussed whether to take the papers to the street outside the UN building, make a little pile, and set light to them. In the end we decided it would be a ridiculous and futile gesture: the rioters had already done it for us.

Later, it occurred to me what had happened here. It wasn't an analysis that fitted in with the political narratives that were convincing, but somehow insufficient. And this is not to claim that my explanation is in any way the "correct" one, for all these threads in their way help explain what took place, and there may well be others.

One incident, seemingly unremarkable, had stuck in my memory, long after the violence was over. On the morning of the second day of the trouble, the head of the UN mission, a former President of Finland, had summoned Kosovo's political leaders to his office. He demanded to know what they were doing to stem the violence. Reading from a note prepared by his staffers, he looked over his spectacles at the leaders across the conference table, peering at them like a remonstrative school teacher at his unruly pupils.

And the leaders were silent. They sat, glumly, looking a little shifty, like naughty schoolboys who had been caught smoking cigarettes behind the bicycle sheds. A few muttered excuses, but those uttering them seemed as unconvinced as we were. There was a general air of embarrassment.

I pondered this incident. Why had the leaders not spoken up for their political demands? Why had they not blamed the UN and the international community for stoking the frustrated anger of the Kosovo-Albanian majority? Why had they resembled nothing so much as a bunch of adolescents being punished after school?

(Indeed, many in the "international community" regarded Kosovo's political classes as "immature": one well-known liberal commentator referred to them as "teenagers"[96].)

Slowly, it dawned on me. This was the reaction of the irresponsible. No one was prepared to take responsibility for the violence, because no one *felt* responsible for it. The behaviour of Kosovo's leaders was immature and childish, because that is what was expected of them. The international community had refused to give these political leaders the real responsibility to run the country, telling them instead that they and their country were not yet ready for the burdens of statehood. My work in elaborating and implementing the "standards" sent, and made concrete, this very message.

Kosovo was permitted to have elections, an elected government and a parliament, but the real power resided in an unelected official – the UN Special Representative, the Finn, appointed by the UN Secretary-General – who could veto any decision made by the local elected government. Kosovo's own leaders were like the class captains from schooldays – expected to keep order – but ultimate power lay with the teachers.

The dramatic events in one small Balkan province (now a state[97]) were unique, but there are nevertheless lessons of broader significance. Western democracies are not on the cusp of violent disorder, although it cannot be ruled out if the current system is not improved. The violence and unrest on the streets of Kosovo, but above all the feckless behaviour of Kosovo's elected but powerless politicians, carried one crucial lesson: if people do not have responsibility, do not expect them to behave responsibly.

This episode suggests a broader lesson about democracy, stability and anarchy. Defenders of the current order argue that to abandon the system of representative democracy is to invite anarchy, a war of all against all. But the 2004 disorder in Kosovo suggests a more subtle and unexpected lesson. It is this: the less people have agency – control – over their own affairs, and the less command they feel over their futures and their circumstances, the *more* inclined they are to take to the streets. The best way indeed to invite anarchy and violence is to *reduce* the agency and sense of control that people need to feel over their lives.

The disconnection between voters and their governments along with government's declining ability to deal with problems of global origin are combining, in the current dispensation, to produce this very effect. The frustration, disillusionment and growing extremism all too evident in today's democracies are symptoms of this phenomenon: loss of agency. Kosovo may represent an extreme case, but for it not to become a harbinger, action must be taken. Our way of doing politics, indeed our way of thinking about politics, needs to change, from passivity to action: reclaiming agency.

And in that reclamation, we must find better ways of doing business with one another. If too distant and corruptible institutions are proving inadequate, what might work? Some believe that technology alone, and the internet in particular, can deliver the necessary revolution. Some even believe that the internet *is* the necessary revolution, and that its inherently heterogeneous and transparent nature amounts, in itself, to political change. Closer analysis reveals however a more complicated and ambiguous reality. Something else is needed. And that something else turns out not to require fancy technology, web-based platforms and Twitter feeds (though they may help). That something else turns out to be simple indeed.

4

THE IMPORTANCE OF
MEETING PEOPLE

DURING THE SPANISH CIVIL WAR, MORE THAN 30,000 people from over fifty nations volunteered to fight the Nationalist armies of General Franco. Many gave up jobs and left families in order to fight the emerging global threat of fascism, and to defend a nascent socialist, even anarchist republic.

They joined Republican forces that were in many cases under-trained and equipped with antique and inadequate weapons. In *Homage to Catalonia*, George Orwell vividly describes the miserable conditions of the front-line troops, dug into faeces-strewn trenches with neither the clothing nor arms properly to fight the Francoist armies, which by contrast received substantial international support from Italy and Nazi Germany*. Yet Orwell compellingly evokes the

---

* An international embargo was in theory supposed to stop arms supplies to both sides, but its enthusiastic enforcement by Britain, France and others had the principal effect of denying arms to the Republicans. Nazi Germany and Mussolini's Italy meanwhile breached the embargo to support the Francoists with impunity. A similar situation arose during the break-up of Yugoslavia in the 1990s when a UN arms embargo, proposed and enforced by the UK, US and others, failed to diminish the military effectiveness of the genocidal armies of the Bosnian-Serbs (mainly because they already enjoyed the considerable military resources of the former Yugoslav army). The UN embargo however considerably hindered the defences of their victims, the Bosnian-Muslims and

comradeship among the Republican troops, the abolition of traditional hierarchies and the appealing idealism of both the Spanish and international volunteers. He recounts too that anarchist principles were no obstacle to effective military organisation: although there was debate within army units – and a welcome absence of the cringing deference of many military organisations – there was also discipline, not least thanks to the unity of purpose among the troops.

Much history since has given the impression that the international volunteers were mainly middle-class intellectuals. But in fact eighty percent of the volunteers from Britain were manual workers who left their jobs or were unemployed[98]. The "International Brigade" of foreign volunteers fought in several key battles of the civil war, including a notable rôle in the Battle of Madrid, where Republican forces successfully beat back a Nationalist assault in the autumn of 1936. The fighting was intense and bloody: infantry fought at close quarters, room by room, with bayonets and grenades.

Of the 30,000 or so foreign volunteers who went to fight for their beliefs, nearly 10,000 were killed in action and another 8,000 or so were wounded. Of those who survived, many returned to a less than welcoming reception in their home countries. Some were imprisoned, others were denied citizenship, while some, such as the 3,000 or so anti-fascist Germans, were unable to return home at all.

The war in the Darfur region of Sudan has been raging since 2003. Civilian casualties are enormous, with some estimating that several hundred thousand people have been killed, and perhaps three million refugees displaced. The killing has been sustained and deliberate, leading many to depict the conflict as a planned genocide of the indigenous inhabitants of Darfur, engineered and led by the Sudanese government in Khartoum and executed by militias under its control, including the notorious *Janjaweed*. In 2008, the

---

Croats. The effect of that embargo therefore, as with Spain in the 1930s, was to deliver a military advantage to the fascist aggressor. In the 1930s, this was indeed the intent.

President of Sudan, Omar Hassan al Bashir, was indicted for war crimes by the International Criminal Court in The Hague. At the time of writing, however, he has not been handed over to the court for trial*. On the contrary, all the signs indicate that the "international community", including the US, is prepared to allow the indictments to be quietly forgotten.

The international reaction to the killing in Darfur has been vociferous. Across the world, hundreds of protest groups have demanded action to stop the killing, calling for the intervention of foreign troops either under United Nations or African Union (AU) auspices. Some protest groups, such as *Not on Our Watch*, were set up by famous film stars, including George Clooney and Brad Pitt[99]. Students from a US college set up a telephone hotline which received considerable press acclaim[100]. Calling the hotline immediately connects the caller to the office of their representative in Congress, whom they can demand take action about Darfur. There have been a large number of internet petitions about Darfur, some attracting many millions of signatories.

This vast expenditure of campaigning energy has resulted in scant additional protection for Darfuri civilians. As the war raged, the response of the "international community" amounted to a small and under-equipped AU force, which several years after the conflict began comprised only a few thousand lightly armed troops to provide security in an area approximately the size of Spain. Even the force's defenders make no claim that the AU force is in any way adequate to deter or prevent attacks against civilians. And indeed the killing has continued up to the time of writing in late 2010.

Some commentators have suggested that the rhetorical heat generated by Western pressure groups, and in particular their use of the word "genocide", may have made the chances of finding a

---

* In its first ten years of operation, the Court has failed to secure any convictions

peaceful outcome locally more difficult[101]. Just as distant govern-ments must simplify the complex realities of foreign conflicts in order to pronounce policy about them, so too did the simplifying lens of distance enable campaigners to turn a complicated and fluid situation into a compelling black-and-white narrative of good and evil, leading some to argue that the simplifications of celebrity campaigning have actually helped prolong the conflict[102]. No foreign citizen has taken up arms themselves to defend the Darfuris.

The advent of the internet has released a wave of enthusiasts who believe that democracy can be improved – saved, perhaps – by tech-nology alone. There are now innumerable websites where on-line petitions can be created and propagated on any topic from freeing imprisoned Burmese democracy leader Aung San Suu Kyi to liber-ating socialite Paris Hilton from her brief incarceration for drunk driving. Politicians have been quick to cotton on to the petition trend. The website of the British Prime Minister, like that of the White House, encourages their submission though there is little mention of what becomes of any petition thus delivered. The woefully undemocratic British House of Lords, where every member is either appointed or inherits their seat, recently estab-lished an equally pitiful blog site to encourage "dialogue" between their lordships and the grateful public[103]. Even the British sover-eign, to whom all Britons are subject, now has a Facebook page where the Queen's subjects can vent their feelings.

Not one to miss out on a trend, China's Communist Party, a body not best known for accountability and transparency, has launched its own discussion forum, "Direct line to Zhongnanhai". (Zhonghnanhai is the huge and secretive compound in the heart of Beijing where China's leaders live and work.) As one commen-tator aptly put it, "The site appears to be an effort to persuade people that the leadership is listening to their very personal concerns . . . It is clearly designed to demonstrate that the leadership is attentive and sensitive."[104] But, as the *Financial Times* reported, although the new message board is trying to demonstrate responsiveness, it does not actually provide responses from the leaders addressed. In this aspect, the Communist Party site is identical to the on-line forums, petition sites and other such efforts in transparency and "citizen engagement" in more ostensibly democratic countries.

A further problem with "internet democracy" was revealed when such an attempt was mounted during the transition period after the Presidential election of 2009. When the new administration of President-elect Barack Obama created an on-line "Citizen's Briefing Book" for people to submit ideas "virtually" to the President, they received over 40,000 proposals and nearly a million and a half votes for those proposals. The most popular idea was to legalise marijuana. Legalising on-line poker topped the contributions in the technology category. Revoking the Church of Scientology's tax-exempt status garnered three times more votes than raising funds for childhood cancer. *The New York Times'* conclusion from this episode was that advocates of the internet as the incarnation of real-time participatory democracy – "Athens on the web" – still had some arguments to answer[105].

There are now websites that invite views on proposed legislation, scrutiny of campaign finances and details of your representatives' voting patterns. "See, click, fix" allows citizens to identify local problems on-line for government action[106]. But all these supposedly new forms of political action rely on a very traditional mechanism of political change – *up/down*: pressuring, scrutinising, demanding that representatives and government take action. There has been no change to the fundamental model of politics.

It is correspondingly easy for government and other embodiments of the *status quo* to adopt these new technological tools, and thus reduce any benefit. Governments are now replete with their own tech fetishists, wittering (or tweeting) on about "government 2.0" and organising podcasts, tweets and blogs saying more or less the same things that politicians have always said, albeit through a different medium.

Despite the repeated claim from government that the flow of information is from people to government, the evidence suggests that the true direction is the opposite. There is scant evidence to suggest that any significant government policy has been informed or altered by tweeting or the fancy on-line tools set up for instance by the US State Department to encourage a "global conversation". The basic power structure is unchanged – up/down – the only difference is the *form* of communication. Revealingly, the most palpable results of this "new" web activism are to be found in the most traditional manifestations of "old" politics: organising get-out-the-vote volunteers and, inevitably, raising money.

Celebrants of the new technological democracy often cite examples from "abroad" where technology has brought about political change, like the so-called "colour" revolutions in Ukraine or Georgia, or the "Twitter" protests against the government in Iran in 2009, and most recently the revolutions in Tunisia and Egypt in the so-called "Arab spring" of 2011, where indeed it is clear that social media played an important rôle. They rarely mention that there are equally many examples where technology has had a more malign effect. In Nigeria, deadly riots in the city of Jos were fuelled, according to one authority, by text messages sent between rampaging mobs[107]; the same thing happened in the violence that gripped Kosovo in 2004 (described in the previous chapter). In London, the killing of a fifteen-year-old boy was coordinated by his attackers on Facebook*. The "Twitter" protests in Iran have not led, yet, to the overthrow of government; many protesters ended up in the same prison very traditionally used by different regimes to house

---

* In American prisons, the proliferation of smartphones has allowed criminals to continue to organise drug trafficking and gang activity outside even while incarcerated; Facebook, Twitter and email listservers were used to coordinate recent protests across several prisons (source: *New York Times*, 2 January 2011, "Outlawed, cellphones are thriving in prisons").

political prisoners – Tehran's notorious Evin jail. These prisoners now include Iran's most well-known blogger, Hossein Derakhshan, known as the father of Iran's bloggers, who in 2010 was sentenced to nineteen years in jail for alleged collaboration with foreign governments, spreading "propaganda" against the Islamic regime and setting up "obscene" websites.

In early 2011, the dictatorial regime in Sudan learned quickly from the Mubarak regime's mistakes in managing internet-based protest in Egypt. Khartoum turned the internet against the protesters, setting up fake pro-democracy pages on Facebook and arresting all those who showed up for the demonstrations advertised on the site. Eventually, activists avoided using internet-based tools at all, returning to more traditional and covert forms of organisation[108]. The lesson is stark: power adapts to new technology, and swiftly.

After an initial spasm of excitement at the liberating possibilities of the worldwide web, it is now emerging that China's adoption of the internet does not necessarily herald a new dawn of transparency and incipient democracy. Every major internet company in China employs scores and sometimes hundreds of internet "administrators" to search for subversive content. The city of Beijing recently advertised for 10,000 volunteers to act as monitors[109]. Twitter, Facebook and YouTube remain blocked at the time of writing. China is adapting search technology similar to Google's to hunt down and prosecute dissent. The search company that pioneered the anti-dissident algorithms is now a successful commercial company, listed on the Chinese stock exchange – a neat rebuttal of the naïve equation that free markets *ipso facto* produce freedom of speech. Indeed, Western companies too have profited from the widespread adoption of web censorship tools like Netsweeper, Websense and Smartfilter by undemocratic regimes across the world: these programs can block access to thousands of sites at a stroke[110].

In general, the protection of basic freedoms on the web relies on the good will and good intentions of the very small number of people who control its most powerful institutions: the very opposite of the ideal condition required for the maintenance of freedom and democracy.

Large companies – Yahoo, AOL, Google - dominate decisions about what content may appear on the web; one can only hope they are beneficent. Google alone controls sixty-three percent of internet searches. In deciding what can or cannot be published on the web, and listed in its searches, and whether to comply with censoring governments, Google is taking decisions of immense consequence for freedom of speech, in China, Turkey and across the globe. Its decision to confront censorship in China in early 2010 was a decision of political, and not merely commercial, consequence. As Google stood up to China, Microsoft without apology continued to offer a censored search service.

As one commentator has argued, Google's legal team "arguably have more influence over the contours of on-line expression than anyone else on the planet"[111]. The remark of Google's legal counsel on how she saw her rôle in deciding on-line content is hardly reassuring, "I definitely am not trying to pass judgment on anything. I'm taking my best guess at what will allow our products to move forward in a country, and that's not a judge rôle, more an enabling rôle." [112] YouTube, which is owned by Google, offers no explanation for its decisions to remove videos it determines, sometimes after flagging from viewers, as "offensive". Eli Pariser of MoveOn has warned of a more subtle danger: that Google and Facebook's filtering mechanisms are creating a "filter bubble" around us; the algorithms applied by these sites to "personalise" our browsing experience are effectively rendering much of the web invisible[113]. We think we are surfing the entire worldwide web, but in fact we are seeing only the sites Google's and Facebook's filters deem appropriate to our interests. The web surfer in China experiences the same phenomenon. There is no outward sign that the sites they are visiting have been vetted – or filtered – for their consumption by the sophisticated filtering technology used by the Chinese government.

Unwitting, they think that they are surfing the whole web. In this regard, they are just like web users in the West.

Yahoo and Microsoft have been accused by Amnesty International of abetting censorship and repression in China by supplying equipment and adapting their search engines to block certain sites and, in Yahoo's case, assisting the Chinese authorities in identifying on-line anti-government critics. In response, they have argued that no company alone can change Chinese law, by which they must abide.

As Stanford University's Professor Lawrence Lessig has argued, it is hard always to square the interests of a commercial company seeking to expand market share with the protection of freedom of speech: "[Google has] enormous control over a platform of all the world's data, and everything they do is designed to improve their control of the underlying data. If your whole game is to increase market share, it's hard to do good, and to gather data in ways that don't raise privacy concerns or that might help repressive govern-ments to block controversial content."[114] Companies like Google and Microsoft are making intrinsically political decisions of considerable consequence for the rest of us.

At least the internet, it is argued, will encourage debate and interaction, albeit virtually rather than in person. But here, it appears that instead of encouraging debate among those of differ-ing views and thus convergence, the opposite may be happening. The web offers multiple locations to find those one agrees with, and to avoid those one doesn't. As columnist Nicholas Kristof has commented, we select the kind of news and opinions that reflect our own prejudices back to us, an emerging news product Nicholas Negroponte of M.I.T. has called "The Daily Me"[115].

One result is that any clash of opinions, especially in the anything-goes anonymity of the web, is increasingly violent, hostile and insulting. Name-calling is frequent; reasoned debate, rare. Particularly when opinions differ from the party line – whether of left or right – criticism tends to escalate, and coarsen. It's not only domestic debates that witness such growing vituperation. In China, when a Chinese fighter plane crashed, killing its pilot, after colliding with a US reconnaissance aircraft over the South China Sea, the Chinese blogosphere erupted with violently anti-American and nationalist sentiment: views that the Chinese government was happy, at least at first, to allow, perhaps as a means to vent more general political frustrations. Demonstrations followed, and the American embassy in Beijing was attacked by stone-throwing hordes. Some demanded that China declare war on the US. The traditional state-controlled press, while critical of the US, had taken a more measured tone. The Chinese authorities struggled to contain the situation and began to downplay the issue in public. Some of the more rabid blogs were closed down. Eventually, the riots died down. Back in the US, the government's Director of National Intelligence has observed that the internet is a fertile breeding ground for terrorism, warning that, "When it comes to susceptibility to radicalisation, virtual communities have become as important as physical communities."[116]

The antagonism and hostility of political debate on the internet reveals an essential truth of the modern condition, which is in fact a perpetual condition of humanity, but one which modernity places in starker relief: the more detached people are from one another, the more they can cloak themselves in anonymity and be shielded from the consequences of their views, the more violent, hostile and irresponsible they are likely to be. It is a peculiar but retrograde feature of modernity that its facets – the nature of modern work, communications, political interaction and the modern state itself – have heightened that detachment.

A parallel from the military world is perhaps instructive. In the century's new wars of Iraq, Afghanistan, but also Yemen and Somalia, Unmanned Combat Aerial Vehicles (UCAVs) are being increasingly used to attack and destroy remote targets – cars containing suspected "terrorists" or houses in Waziristan where intelligence suggests "AQT" – Al Qaeda/Taliban – may be present.

Remotely piloted aircraft such as the Predator or Reaper have launched missile strikes in Pakistan, Somalia and Yemen*, controlled by pilots sitting in booths at airbases in Nevada (Britain's Royal Air Force also deploys both aircraft). This form of remote killing, which has dramatically increased during the Obama administration[117], gives rise to obvious moral questions. Military psychologist Dave Grossman for instance has written that the more detached the soldier is from his target, the more likely is he to commit abuses or ignore prohibitions against killing civilians[118].

P.W. Singer's fascinating recent book on robot warfare suggests disquieting evidence that may affirm Grossman's findings[119]. As the military turns more and more to robots to fight war, so humans are increasingly dislocated from the battlefield. Singer reports one US Air Force Predator commander who suggests that the virtual "pilots" who steer the distant aircraft and instruct it to fire its weapons sometimes seem to forget that there are real humans on their video screens: "You have guys running the UAV saying, 'Kill that one, don't kill that one.'" At Langley Air Force Base, soldiers monitoring banks of screens carrying the feeds from drones over Afghanistan, Pakistan or elsewhere, have nicknamed the video-streams "Death TV"[120]. Singer quotes the ethics instructor for the Soldier Support Institute at Fort Jackson in South Carolina, that,

---

* The US is not legally at war with any of these countries, illustrating the confusing status and realities of these new borderless wars. Command and control of Unmanned Combat Aerial Vehicles (UCAVs) lies with the Central Intelligence Agency (CIA), whose programme is covert and receives its direction from 'Presidential Findings' – executive directives from the White House. It is in these operations that UCAVs have been deployed above western Pakistan and, on occasion, in Somalia and Yemen. In March 2010 US State Department Legal Adviser Harold Hongju Koh argued that the US was in armed conflict with Al Qaeda, the Taliban and its affiliates, and was allowed to use force consistent with its inherent right to self-defence under international law. The US practice, therefore, complied with the laws of war (source: *International Institute for Strategic Studies*).

as war becomes safer and easier, as soldiers are removed from the horrors of war and see the enemy not as humans but as blips on a screen, there is a very real danger of losing the deterrent that such horrors provide.

There are obvious parallels here with the disembodied anonymity of the worldwide web, or disembodied decision-making by any institution, or by anyone . . .

The answer then suggests itself, and it is not an internet petition: there is a form of politics which produces more consensus, a better understanding and respect for alternative points of view and a deeper acknowledgement of facts over opinion. It does not require an expensive computer or any technical equipment at all, for the internet often excludes the poor and otherwise marginalised*. It is as old-fashioned as the earliest parliaments, where people gathered on a hillside to arbitrate their common business. The academic who has pioneered the technique calls it "deliberative democracy", but really it can be called something simpler: meeting people.

After Hurricane Katrina, much of the infrastructure of New Orleans was devastated: more than seventy percent of housing was damaged and entire neighbourhoods were almost completely destroyed; schools, hospitals and police stations were shut down. Nearly a hundred thousand jobs were lost and eighteen months after the hurricane more than half of the city's population had not returned.

In the aftermath, plans to rebuild New Orleans confronted a ravaged infrastructure, enormous financial losses, a local government in disarray, and a citizenry whose trust in government had been sorely undermined. The early planning efforts by city officials were met with anger and protest as the community struggled with the challenges of distributing resources and reviving an entire city.

Faced with this crisis of confidence, city officials decided to

---

* The so-called "digital divide".

involve the citizens in a full discussion, face-to-face and in-depth, on the priorities for the city. Most of the city's inhabitants were still spread across the US, not yet able to return. Four thousand New Orleanais met in "Community Congresses" staged across the country to discuss recovery priorities for their city. As decision-makers listened, citizens discussed how to ensure safety from future flooding, empower residents to rebuild safe and stable neighbourhoods, provide incentives and housing so people could return, and establish sustainable and equitable public services[121].

At the end of the deliberations, fully ninety-two percent of participants agreed the "Unified Plan" for the city. Critically, this approval rating represented the collective view of the citizenry: participants reflected pre-Katrina New Orleans – in proportion to both race and income. At earlier similar events, blacks and the poor were often severely under-represented. This time citizens had participated not only at home but in cities across the country where hurricane refugees were then living. Thus, the city's new plan was discussed and endorsed not only by its officials, but also by its citizens, who overwhelmingly committed to support the plan.

There has been a more sustained experiment in such "participative" or "deliberative" democracy in Porto Alegre, one of Brazil's largest cities. "The Porto Alegre Experiment" again shows that better outcomes result when citizens are directly involved in decisions over their own lives. In 1989, when the experiment began, the city suffered some of the worst inequality in the continent. The poor – one-third of the city's population – lived in deprived slums around the periphery; the rich controlled the city's government and budget. Over the last ten years, the city has gradually developed a multi-layered approach to participatory budgeting. Starting at the most local level, citizens are encouraged to participate in debates about local spending priorities – water, schools, hospitals, housing, roads. Of the city's 1.5 million inhabitants, every citizen is informed about the budget process; around 50,000 now take part in it; notably, their participation is unpaid.

According to a World Bank study, the participatory process has fostered direct improvements in facilities in Porto Alegre. For example, sewer and water connections increased from 75 percent of households in 1988 to 98 percent in 1997. The number of schools has increased fourfold since 1986. The high number of participants, after more than a decade, suggests that participatory budgeting encourages increased citizen involvement, according to the paper[122]. The city is at the cutting edge in developing progressive recycling and renewable energy projects. The participatory process is overwhelmingly supported by the city's population. It has also, reportedly, encouraged a change in the tenor of local politics. Less and less a partisan contest, the common enemy is the occasional crisis. Everything is transparent, from decision-making to the awarding of contracts.

Participatory budgeting is slowly spreading to cities and municipalities across the continent and more widely, including in Britain[123], where there are now some 120 participatory budget or "PB" processes, delivering better services, better partnerships between citizens and government and greater social cohesion[124]. In Keighley, Bradford, local elections of the traditional kind saw unprecedented success for the racist British National Party. By contrast, in the locally organised "PB" process, where over 250 people turned out to vote on how to spend funds in their area, the majority of the participants were from the Asian community, largely women who traditionally weren't involved in the wider community: one benefit of such processes is that they tend to encourage groups – the young, the elderly, minorities – often marginalised in representative processes. But the two most popular projects selected in the process, with the highest votes, were submitted by groups from 'white' areas of the town. There was also evidence of increased cooperation within the Asian communities as a result of attending the event.

These deliberative processes are locally driven and designed for local circumstances; there is no "one size fits all". The general benefits – of greater citizen empowerment, of greater consensus over local spending – are clear: they flow directly and crucially from the *agency* of those involved. People participate not to be consulted by government and service-providers but to make real decisions themselves about their circumstances. And when people are trusted and informed to make decisions, they tend to make good ones. Such deliberative processes, with real decisions as their result, are not to be confused with the heated "townhall" meetings of recent memory in the US, or the vulgar arguments on internet "forums". The town-hall meetings are not designed to take decisions. Politicians claim that they are intended as a place to hear the views of the public. Typically, however, the local angry brigade line up to denounce politicians and their plans, providing an unpleasant experience for everyone except those who enjoy public confrontation. Rational discussion and respect for the facts are, unsurprisingly, rarely the result.

In a recent book, Cass Sunstein has noted that very often when groups of people are placed together to debate an issue, they often end up more polarised than at the beginning[125]. But Sunstein's book also suggests how to create greater unity. The more detached groups are from society, the more extreme their decisions are likely to become. The less that a decision debated within a group actually *matters*, the greater the likelihood of dispute and conflict. A lesson becomes clear: when nothing is at stake, and when no one has agency, it is predictable that heated disagreement will be the outcome.

The case for participatory systems was well put by a minister in Western Australia, which held one of the largest such consulta-tions, on the future of the city of Perth:

"My concern is that we are increasingly functioning in a climate where making good decisions becomes very difficult ... The media wants clear black and whites – big headlines, little words – it wants dramatic divergence – it wants outrage – not considered partial disagreement . . . This mitigates [*sic*] against good governance."

It is not only hurricane-struck New Orleans that suffers a crisis in democracy. With turnouts falling and disaffection with "politics" growing in all democratic countries, its model, like that of Porto Alegre, offers lessons applicable beyond the occasional management of disasters.

One particular example of that crisis is found at the European Parliament, an institution designed with the best of intentions to remedy the so-called "democratic deficit" of the European Union, but in its way exacerbating that very snazzily named problem. Originally conceived and empowered to give European peoples a voice in EU decisions largely dominated by governments, its problems highlight weaknesses increasingly apparent in other democratic legislatures.

At the most recent elections to the parliament, extremist parties jumped at the opportunity offered by the dismal turnout of Europe's voters – the lowest in the parliament's history. Realising that many mainstream voters would stay away, extreme and far-right parties made special efforts to mobilise their supporters. The result was that such parties were represented in greater number here than in their own national parliaments. The British National Party joined Italian and Lithuanian proto-fascists, Dutch anti-immigrant parties, and other assorted representatives of the fringe in the home of European "democracy".

Neither phenomenon – low turnout, extreme political parties – bodes well for the legitimacy, popularity or effectiveness of the decisions arising from the parliament. It is more than ironic that after this result Europe's governments pushed ever harder for the adoption of the Lisbon treaty that would give the Union's institutions, including the parliament, even greater power. Both phenomena however point to a future of democratic politics, of both disenchantment and extremism, that may become more and more evident, in more established parliaments and congresses too. What is to be done?

The *Financial Times* reported a recent exercise which sought to address this problem, asking the question: how much longer can the EU continue as a project controlled by élites and disregarded by the masses?[126] What is the solution to this "democratic deficit"? One answer was attempted by Professor James Fishkin, a social scientist at Stanford University. He conducted an experiment in which a balanced sample of 348 Europeans from the EU's twenty-seven countries were brought to Brussels for a three-day dialogue on the elections and the policy issues surrounding them. This is a procedure known as "deliberative polling", a concept Professor Fishkin invented in 1988.

One outcome of the exercise was that many participants changed their voting intentions as a result of the dialogue. Beforehand, 40 percent said they would vote for mainstream centre-right parties, 22 percent for socialists, 9 percent for centrist liberals and 8 percent for Greens. After the exercise, support for the centre-right dropped to 30 percent, the socialists were almost unchanged at 21 percent and 8 percent respectively, and the Greens shot up to 18 percent. The rise in support for the Greens came about as a result of detailed discussions among the participants on climate change. Participants were asked to choose between the view that "we should do everything possible to combat climate change even if that hurts the economy" and the alternative view that "we should do everything possible to maximise economic growth, even if that hurts efforts to combat climate change". Before the discussions, 49 percent wanted to emphasise the fight against climate change. Afterwards, this figure rose to 61 percent.

As the newspaper reported, Professor Fishkin thinks that "deliberative polling" of this kind helps to connect policy-makers to the general public in a constructive way, because it gives the former an insight into what the latter would support if they knew, thought and talked more about the issues. It is a tool with more potential than a standard opinion poll because an ordinary poll is merely a snapshot of people's views, no matter what their level of knowledge.

Exercises like that performed by Professor Fishkin, and the New Orleans reconstruction plan too, have shown repeatedly that when a group of people gathers together to consider their affairs and collective response to them – and, crucially, make decisions – a number of valuable benefits follow:

(i)   Participants pay greater heed to each other's positions, and are more likely to acknowledge the concerns that underlie other people's political views;

(ii) There is a deeper consideration of facts – including scientific data – than normal political debate, composed largely of opinions, allows;

(iii) Partly as result of (i) and (ii), such exercises usually produce a greater degree of consensus within the group;

(iv) The group feels a much greater commitment to decisions reached collectively in this manner, than decisions imposed by any other authority.

Fishkin calls this "deliberative democracy". It is a process of a different order from the current system, prevalent in all democratic states, of *representative* democracy, whereby citizens elect representatives to take decisions on their behalf. Indeed, deliberative democracy in its fullest form, where people take genuine decisions of consequence as a group, or a grassroots, community-based democracy, is in fact ultimately incompatible with representative democracy. It is not possible to have two sources of decisions: what if their choices are contradictory? One must be supreme.

Professor Fishkin attempts to bridge this problem, and render deliberative techniques compatible, by proposing that deliberative *polling*, of the kind described above, should help inform the regular structures of representative democracy – the legislators and members of the executive who make up the decision-makers. But despite his efforts to construct such groups as representative of the general populace – by selecting their members in proportion to the political support for different parties in the broader population – such "deliberative polling" groups fail in one fundamental regard: they lack legitimacy. They are not elected, so why should their voice, however proportionately it might represent the rest, be heard above others? The representatives who run the EU – the President, the Council and the parliament – are, after all, at least *legally* legitimate in that they are chosen by member states (and the parliament by the people, at least a few of them), even if their selection is for most voters pitiably distant and dissociated from their everyday concerns.

Polling – like frequent referendums – fails in another regard too. While polls may provide an indication of what people think on a particular question at a particular moment, they leave out one crucial component of Fishkin's experiments – the deliberation: the talking, the to and fro, the listening, the compromise. Any citizen of California, where referendums are frequent, will recognise that they have done little to contribute to responsible and effective government of the state – rather the opposite. This is also why internet surveys of opinion, or petitions, tend to the extreme, and are so pathetically inadequate as a new form of democracy.

In his essay, *The Pursuit of the Ideal*, Isaiah Berlin concludes that in deciding what to do, the only option, in private life as in public policy, is to engage in trade-offs – rules, values, principles must yield to each other in varying degrees in specific situations, adding that "a certain humility in these matters is very necessary" since we have no guarantee that any particular course we choose will be right. This is the essence of democracy: discussion of differing views and options on how we together must live, with a view – ultimately – to collective decision. The mere venting of opinions, whether in person or on-line, does not qualify.

At the most microcosmic level, it is self-evident that encounters and negotiation offer a greater possibility for respect and agreement than either the virtual chatroom or a distant authority. Difficult discussions with friends or family can quickly degenerate on-line as misunderstandings and WILFUL misinterpretations multiply. No one pretends that meetings in person are necessarily easier, or less painful, but somehow we are able to see and feel more and thus achieve a greater comprehension than we can in a more detached method of negotiation. Perhaps, above all, we simply spend more time.

Professor Fishkin's excellent books are filled with examples of deliberative democracy, and his comprehensive analysis of why and how it works and the impressive results it clearly delivers. But by and large deliberative democracy has remained a matter for academic discussion, and occasional illustrative, yet tantalising, exercises of the kind that took place in New Orleans or Porto Alegre, or the experiments practised by Professor Fishkin.

The trouble with deliberative democracy is of course that it poses a direct challenge to the existing constitutional order of representative democracy, where the few are elected to arbitrate the affairs of the many. Deliberative polling, while imaginative and revealing in its insights, fails to bridge the gap. For in the existing system, it is not tolerable to the existing authority for citizens to gather to sort out their affairs and make decisions with real effects: that is what governments are for!

For deliberative decision-making to function properly, and for the citizens to enjoy its full and evident benefits, a condition must apply which, oddly, even the most ardent academic proponents of deliberative techniques seem loath to confess: there must be no other authority, *at all*. This condition is sometimes known as anarchism.

Though it is rarely mentioned, even in the histories of that period, the Spanish civil war saw a moment, tragically brief, of real existing anarchism. In the area of Spain under Republican control, anarchists for a short while held sway, as far as that term means anything when no one was completely in charge. This was not anarchy, an absence of order, it was a society that for a period decided to govern itself not by centralised authority, but by the wishes of local communities, workers, men and women, led by values of equality and mutual respect.

It came about thanks to a coincidence of forces – the collapse of the old order, widely shared and elaborated anarchist thinking in the trades unions – and was snuffed out by forces at that time greater than it, above all communism: a refutation, and there are many, to those who equate anarchism with communism. This happened between 1936 and 1938 and was confined mostly to parts of Catalonia in northern Spain, including Catalonia's capital, Barcelona. It was estimated that perhaps ten million people participated in this "Spanish Revolution" where farms and factories, and even shops and barbers, were collectivised and run along communal lines – neither owned by the state nor private capital, but run by the peasants and workers themselves. Decisions were made on libertarian principles – by those affected, without bureaucracy. In many areas, agricultural production significantly increased.

By 1938, it was over. The Communist Party in Moscow decided that Spain was not ready for proletarian revolution – at least not this kind – and ordered its cohorts in Spain, the local Communists, to suppress the anarchists. There were mass arrests, street fighting, and executions. Anarchist leaders and parties were denounced. This repression was one of the reasons for the ultimate defeat of the Republicans, and the ensuing four decades of fascist dictatorship under Franco.

George Orwell's memoir of his experience in Catalonia contains vivid depictions of what anarchism, in practice, was really like. When published, *Homage to Catalonia* was attacked in Britain and elsewhere above all by Communists and the Left in general, who rejected its account of Communist suppression of the anarchists, preferring Moscow's propaganda that the anarchists were somehow in Franco's pay or otherwise to blame for the in-fighting within the anti-fascist ranks.

Still to this day overshadowed by Orwell's anti-totalitarian fiction like the cartoonish *Animal Farm* and *1984*, *Homage* sold very few copies on initial publication. Even now the book is rarely seen for what it truly is, and is instead interpreted as a tragic and picturesque account of failed resistance against fascism[127]. Orwell had joined a small Marxist-oriented party POUM* in order to fight fascism, but later in the book confesses that, if he had the choice again, he would have been an anarchist. He describes life in Barcelona during anarchism:

> Many of the normal motives of civilised life – snobbishness, money-grubbing, fear of the boss, etc. – had simply ceased to exist. The ordinary class division of society had disappeared to an extent that is almost unthinkable in the money-tainted air of England; there was no one there except the peasants and ourselves, and no one owned anyone else as his master. Of course such a state of affairs could not last. It was simply a temporary and local phase in an enormous game that is being played out over the whole surface of the earth. But it lasted long enough to have its effect upon anyone who experienced it. However much one cursed at the time, one realised afterwards that one had been in contact with something strange and valuable. One had been in a community where hope was more normal than apathy or cynicism, where the word "comrade" stood for comradeship and not, as in most countries, for humbug. One had breathed the air of equality.[128]

This description tantalises with its suggestion of what might be possible if self-organised government were to become reality. *Homage to Catalonia* also tells a vivid story about how one generation chose very directly to tackle the problems of the world, in this case fascism. And it is to this global stage that we must now turn. For here particularly, perhaps even more than in the domestic realm, governments

---

* Partido Obrero de Unificación Marxista.

and their organisations claim to have matters in hand. And in general, it seems, we are happy to believe them. On the world stage, in general, the management of "international affairs" is left to practitioners like statesmen and diplomats, which I once was.

It seems at first sight a reasonable bargain. The world is complicated; it requires professionals to sort it out. But, as we shall see in later chapters, the bargain, like the pact between government and voter at home, seems to be breaking down. Established systems of inter-state cooperation do not seem to be producing the solutions the world needs. But there is a worse and more pernicious effect too.

Somewhere along the way, it has become accepted that, in representing a state, normal moral rules are suspended. Under the catch-all moral permission of *droit d'état*, officials acting in the name of the state, even a law-abiding democracy like Britain or the US, are entitled to forsake normal moral inhibitions, like those against killing or causing harm to others. If such actions are justified by the needs of the state, they are not only excused, they are explicitly available. Indeed, the good diplomat is told to reject the soft-headed morality of ordinary people if he is to practise his trade as it must be practised – *realpolitik*. If death and the suffering of others are the result, this is a necessary price of protecting our own.

I have not come by this criticism by way of academic study, or historical research. I know this, because once I did it. I helped do harm to innocent others, with the explicit moral cover of the state, safe in the knowledge that I would never be held to account. With the comfort of impunity, I once committed violence in the name of the state.

5

THE MAN IN THE
WHITE COAT

THE EXPERIMENTS CONDUCTED IN THE EARLY 1960S BY
the psychologist Stanley Milgram are a well-known demonstration
of how authority can incite people to undertake heinous acts.
Conducted soon after the 1961 trial of the Nazi Adolf Eichmann,
Milgram's experiment showed how otherwise normal individuals
could be instructed to commit horrific acts including torture and
murder, if commanded to do so by a person of sufficient, even if
feigned, authority.

But the experiment also illustrates a problem that pervades the
current international system and the current practice of diplomacy.
That problem has a name, amorality: the profoundly negative moral
consequences of officials, in this case diplomats, not taking responsibility for what they do. And as we shall see, it is not only a problem
of diplomacy, it is a problem of any system that suppresses people's
sense of agency over their actions.

Milgram arranged a fake experiment whereby unknowing
volunteers were instructed to give ever-greater electric shocks to
another participant in the experiment, unknown to the volunteer, an
actor. As the subject failed to give correct answers to the instructor's
questions, the volunteer was told to give higher and higher electric
shocks. As the shocks increased, the actor pretending to be the subject

would bang on the wall in feigned agony, complain about his heart condition and, eventually, as the shocks increased to the normally fatal level of 450 volts, fall silent. If the volunteer hesitated in administering the electric shocks, a white-coated "instructor" (in reality, another actor) told the volunteer that they must continue. If at any time the unwitting volunteer asked to halt the experiment, he was told, successively, by the "instructor":

1. *Please continue.*
2. *The experiment requires that you continue.*
3. *It is absolutely essential that you continue.*
4. *You have no other choice, you must go on.*

If the volunteer still wished to stop after all four successive verbal injunctions, the experiment was halted. Otherwise, it was halted after the volunteer had given the maximum 450-volt shock three times in succession. Of Milgram's subjects, sixty-five percent (26 of 40) administered the experiment's final – and theoretically fatal – 450-volt shock. Only one participant refused to administer shocks *before* the 300-volt level. Notably, all were told during the experiment that they would not be held responsible for what happened.

Traditionally, and by Milgram himself, this experiment has been cited to demonstrate the pernicious effects of authority upon moral conduct. If people are told to do something awful by someone who is clearly in authority – in this case, a professorial type in a white coat – all too often they do it. But another lesson is also evident in the fact that the volunteers who administered the electric shocks, crucially, were told that they had no responsibility for the results.

The nasty human truth of Milgram's experiment has been demonstrated many times in recent history. Mass warfare offers many examples. During the Second World War, German reservists were called up by the government to join regular military units but also police units, like Reserve Police Battalion 101. The members of this unit were "ordinary" men: teachers, bankers and plumbers drawn from a wide variety of backgrounds, from across Germany. As is the way with groups put into difficult circumstances together, the battalion quickly bonded into a close-knit team. The battalion was deployed to the Eastern Front, where it followed closely behind the *Wehrmacht* advance across Eastern Europe and into the Soviet Union.

The battalion was not recruited on any particular ideological basis, though some were also members of the Nazi party (a good percentage of Germans were at the time). But these were not *Waffen SS* ideologues; they were largely middle-aged men with wives and families, gardens and pet dogs.

The battalion, in other words, was unexceptional, banal (as Hannah Arendt might have put it[129]). In a little over a year, this battalion of approximately 500 "ordinary men" killed 38,000 Jews and dispatched approximately 45,000 more to extermination camps[130]. The battalion did most of its killing by shooting civilians at close range after rounding them up from villages and towns over-run by German forces. In the course of this murderous year, not one member of the battalion questioned their orders, or sought to leave the unit. When given the option by commanders to opt out of specific opportunities for mass murder, fewer than 15 men of 500 did so.

In case tempted to the conclusion that it was something about the Germans that permitted this appalling conduct, there is evidence of similar (if less horrifying) group behaviour in World War Two by Americans, Russians, Britons and many others. They may not have murdered *en masse* innocent civilians face-to-face but, as chronicled by several authorities[131], Allied troops raped innocent women in their thousands during the invasion of Germany towards the end of the war[132], actions that were of course utterly impermissible in peacetime but during war were somehow condoned by the group, at least by omission of condemnation[133].

The Milgram experiments were recently repeated, to test how people today might submit to authority when ordered to inflict pain upon innocent others[134]. As reported in the journal *American*

Psychologist, Professor Jerry Burger replicated part of the Milgram studies – but stopping at 150 volts, the moment at which the subject cries out to stop – to see whether people today would still obey[135]. There were some changes to account for modern ethical rules and social sensibilities. University ethics committees barred researchers from pushing the unwitting subjects through to an imaginary and "lethal" 450 volts, as Milgram did.

But despite these restrictions the results were very much the same. As in the 1960s, once again more than half the participants agreed to proceed with the experiment past the 150-volt mark. Burger interviewed the participants afterwards and found that those who stopped generally believed themselves to be responsible for the shocks, whereas those who kept going tended to hold the experimenter accountable. This reveals a crucial distinction: it was the participants' assumption or relinquishing of agency that determined their actions.

Milgram's experiment is today so well known that it has entered the collective consciousness – but for the wrong reason. Although the experiment is ostensibly about the pernicious effects of authority, in fact it reveals a more important truth: that when people feel no agency and no responsibility for their actions, they can commit horrific crimes. The Milgram experiment nevertheless seems remote from our normal lives. One problem with such an experiment is that it is hard to imagine ourselves in a situation where we would have to give electric shocks to an innocent person. But the uncomfortable truth is that such situations do not come announced; the chance to perform cruelty upon others comes disguised. I know this now because I was once in a position of one of Milgram's test subjects, asked to inflict suffering upon others. Except in my case, unlike his experiment, the suffering was real.

For almost as long as I remember, I have wanted to be a diplomat. As a schoolboy, I read *The Times* (of London) every day, pretty much all the way through, gripped by its accounts of détente, the proxy wars between East and West and the terrifying, yet intriguing, calculus of nuclear war: first strikes, the "missile gap" and the strange but compelling logic of Mutually-Assured Destruction. Thanks to inherited colour-blindness, I couldn't fulfil my original ambition to become a fighter pilot. The next best thing would be to become a diplomat and enter this weighty but arcane and closed world, to learn its terminologies and codes.

I was moreover fired by more emotional urges. My family exuded a certain awe of "the Foreign Office" where British diplomats worked: several relations had tried and failed to enter the élite ranks of the diplomatic corps. One childhood memory stands out. At perhaps age twelve, I announced to my family that I wanted to become a diplomat. My father, who later denied having said this, turned to me and said, "you have to be very clever to become a diplomat". Thus was my ambition sealed.

University came and went. Eventually I managed to enter the fast-stream of the Foreign Office, a tiny group: some twenty-odd of the many thousands who applied. We were a chosen élite, given to expect that in due course we would become ambassadors and under-secretaries, the most senior exponents of our country's wishes. I was elated to join this exclusive club and happy to undergo the many compromises membership of this group entailed.

Among them was the process that all new entrants must undertake in order to join the foreign service, and therein become party to the state's secrets. "Positive vetting" is a deeply intrusive examination of friendships, family relations, habits and personal history designed to discover whether the proposed new diplomat poses any kind of security risk.

To check its prospective sharers of secrets, the Security Department of the Foreign Office assigned an investigator to examine my personal background, quiz acquaintances and friends, in order to find out whether my behaviour, past or present, might render me vulnerable to approaches from foreign intelligence services. Without this clearance, the would-be diplomat cannot begin work since a great deal of work in the "office", as it soon became known to me, involves access to Top Secret material, the compromise of which, in theory at least, poses a grave risk to the security of the state.

Others who had gone before told me that the process was straightforward "as long as you don't tell them anything". Unfortunately for me, my personal referees had already told my investigator various things, including the fact that I occasionally drank too much at university, played poker and that I was sharing a flat with a gay man. I took the naïve view that since I had nothing in my life to be ashamed of, I would tell them the truth. This approach proved to be a serious mistake.

My vetting took place almost exactly as the Cold War was ending, in 1989. But the Foreign Office still feared the corrupting attentions of the KGB and others and it was felt that being homosexual, which I am not, risked exposing the officer to blackmail. It did not seem to have occurred to the mandarins in charge of Security Department that a blanket prohibition on homosexuality was more likely to force serving or potential foreign-service officers to lie about their true sexual natures and thus increase their vulnerability to blackmail. So my vetting officer subjected me to a long series of absurd and insulting questions about my sexuality, culminating in the conclusive "So you've never been tempted off the straight and narrow then?"

Meanwhile, my investigator had found out from application forms that my grandmother was Polish. Poland was at that time undergoing its transformation to democracy. But Security Department suspected, following policy, that the mere fact that I had Polish relations posed a security risk, since the KGB might "get at" them and use them to "get at" me (it had happened in the past when Poland was a vassal of the Soviet Union). My family was thus forced to dig up long-buried records and tell the awful investigator exactly when, where and how all my Polish ancestors had died, in order that the KGB couldn't discover their names and impersonate them to "get at" me. This led to the discovery that some of my Polish forebears, captured as members of the Polish resistance, had died in Auschwitz.

I was obliged to attend several interviews with the investigator in a sparse office in an anonymous building near Parliament Square, furnished with sinister-looking steel filing cabinets. His desk, like that of an interrogator, was bare but for one government-issue swivel lamp, the only light in the otherwise gloomy room. Sometimes the interviews would last for hours. My family and friends, who were subjected to separate questionings, were at first amused by his questions, but soon became irritated and in some cases upset.

The planned start date of my work at the Foreign Office came and went and I had not passed my "PV" as Positive Vetting is known. The personnel officer assigned to my case took some pleasure in telling me that it was extremely unlikely that I would eventually be allowed in. I considered withdrawing from the process and abandoning my application to join, but I decided instead to swallow these humiliations. Too badly, I wanted to become that rarefied species, a diplomat.

In retrospect, I realise that this process was only in part about guarding against security risks. The investigator was far too amateurish and superficial in his approach to be plausibly effective. If I had simply chosen to lie to him, and coached my referees to do the same (as presumably any determined spy would), my vetting would have proceeded without hitch. Many of my colleagues later admitted to me that they had lied systematically to their vetting officers to avoid unwanted intrusion into their personal affairs.

Instead, this process was akin to a kind of "hazing" ritual, of the kind practised in certain American colleges, the military or similar institutions. It was a form of ritual humiliation, where my sexual habits, personal finances and most intimate relations were probed and exposed. Once complete, not only was I permitted to join the élite club of those permitted to see state secrets; I felt that I had shared with them – through my investigator – something of me, something private and personal. This was more, much more, than a regular induction into a job.

The inculcation went further when the new entrant to the diplomatic service entered training. Immediately, we were encouraged to undergo a subtle but crucial transformation; the "I" became "we". In describing to us the arcane and fetishised practices of the foreign service (the use for instance of special paper for ministers and senior officials: green coloured paper called, perversely, "blue"), our instructors did not talk of how they saw things with the personal and individual "I". Instead, they talked about how "we" saw the world. Telegrams, then the principal form of communication between the Foreign Office and British embassies worldwide (there are now "E-grams"), were written in the first person plural. The author did not describe his or her own view of politics in Iran; instead they described how "we" saw the prospects for engagement with the Islamic regime.

A young diplomat from the British High Commission[*] in Pretoria lectured the new entrants about how "we" thought sanctions on apartheid South Africa were a bad idea (these were the days of Margaret Thatcher's policy of "constructive engagement" with the white minority regime). A diplomatic despatch was presented to us as an example of how to write such pieces. In it, the Ambassador wrote about how "we" had got Iran "wrong" and "we" needed a new approach. In a number of different ways, the new recruits were taught how "we" saw the world. What we were never taught, however, was *why* it was that "we" saw the world that way. This method was assumed, implied, never confessed but nonetheless supreme.

One training exercise involved a game revolving around a crisis in a fictional country, "Boremeya", and what "we", meaning Britain, should do about it. It was a good game, and fun. It lasted about   a   day   and   consisted   of   crisis   meetings,

---

[*] In former colonies that are now members of the British Commonwealth, British representations are not known as embassies but as High Commissions.

submissions to ministers ("make sure to use 'blue' paper!") and difficult encounters with the Boremeyan Foreign Minister, played by one of our instructors. Throughout the game, the new entrants were told to consider what "we" wanted or needed in the situation. Within such exercises, and infused in all our training, was a clear, if only rarely explicit, assumption. As diplomats, "we" were the embodiment of the state, Britain. What we thought was right was thus implicitly right for Britain.

This assumption suffused everything we were taught and everything we subsequently did in our careers in the Foreign Office. It began at the beginning and very quickly became a habit of speech and writing. Above all, it became a habit of thought. Writing telegrams or policy submissions, never did I write what I, Carne Ross, thought was right, instead I wrote about "our" interests and what "we" – Britain – should do. I became We. It was quite literally an instructed shift from thinking as an individual into groupthink. Even after I left the foreign service, I found myself saying "we think that the Zimbabwean government needs to . . .". "We" was wired pretty deep.

It is obvious to the reader that such a transformation from the individual to the group must imply a loss both of individual agency and of moral autonomy. Processes such as that I underwent to join the Foreign Office have parallels in military induction, including in more striking form, Police Battalion 101. But it was not obvious to me at the time. I still felt the same person. I still believed that I was autonomous and free to make my own choices, within certain limits that I freely accepted. I convinced myself that if faced with a morally unacceptable instruction, such as murdering Jews, I would have the courage to refuse. Little did I know that today's moral choices rarely come so clearly signalled as the choice of whether to pull a trigger.

I had been in the foreign service some nine years by the time I was posted to the British mission to the United Nations in New York. By then I was deeply steeped in the culture and mind-habits of my institution. Many of my friends were in the Foreign Office. The "office", as we called it, was a kind of brother- and sisterhood: all over the world there were co-members with whom I shared a common language and experience. I had experienced with them excitement and boredom, from the corridors of the United Nations to the mountains of the Hindu Kush. I was with them as they wept at the frustrations of negotiations, and as gunfire crackled on the streets of Pristina. They have been at my side in Hebron and Dresden, Oslo and Islamabad. With them, I watched wars begin and end, wrote and argued international law, and shared the many joys and miseries of a life lived in the glamour of overseas embassies, of high-level meetings and the dinginess of Whitehall offices. It was not an ordinary job.

And my job in New York was not ordinary either. I was to be the head of the Middle East section at the British Mission to the UN. It was an exciting and challenging task. My responsibilities covered the Arab-Israel dispute, the 1988 Lockerbie bombing by Libyan agents, and the long-standing and unresolved injustice of Morocco's occupation of the Western Sahara. But my primary responsibility was Iraq – ensuring its disarmament and containment after the 1990 war, and the sanctions agreed at the UN Security Council to effect these goals. For Britain at the UN in those days, there was no more important task, and it was my responsibility. In the early days of my posting, I was so excited by the prospect of my work that I would whoop with joy as water poured over me in my morning shower.

One central part of my job was to maintain the UN Security Council's support of restrictive economic sanctions against Iraq. When first told of this task, I relished it. I had no question that the sanctions were justified. Their purpose was after all to punish and contain that most evil and lawless of dictators, Saddam Hussein. When briefed in London before my posting however, the first doubts began to assert themselves. Sanctions on Iraq had been imposed, I naïvely thought, because Iraq had not disarmed itself of its famed Weapons of Mass Destruction (WMD), in this case defined as nuclear, chemical and biological weapons, and ballistic missiles with a range of over 150 km. This failure presented a clear case for the maintenance of sanctions. However, when I asked one of my briefing officers in London whether the UK believed Iraq maintained significant stocks of WMD, he looked a little sheepish. "Not really" he replied. How then do we justify sanctions, I asked, trying to contain my astonishment. He replied, on the basis that Iraq had failed to answer multiple questions about the destruction of its earlier stocks. In summary, sanctions were in place because Iraq had not correctly answered questions.

And indeed it was on this flimsy premise that the UK and US argued at the UN that sanctions should be maintained. Despite the weakness of this justification politically, it was fully borne out in the legal texts, the resolutions, adopted by the Security Council after the 1991 Gulf War. As a diplomat, I was happy to bear the challenge of defending sanctions against those who would undo them. They made this easier by their barely concealed sympathies for the odious Saddam regime, and their commercial interests in easing pressure upon it (I speak of course of Russia and France, who were during this period closely allied with Iraq in its efforts to lift sanctions).

None of my colleagues questioned our policies; our allies in Washington and in the US delegation did not either. Never was such debate encouraged in my ministry, either formally or informally. Thus was it indicated that such questions were discouraged, if not to say impermissible. Thus, moral doubt and questioning of my country's position was suppressed – above all by me, myself.

By the end of 1997, when I joined the mission, British and American policy at the UN Security Council was under severe pressure. Iraq's allies on the Council, particularly France and Russia, were arguing for an easing of sanctions on the grounds that Iraq had complied fully with its obligations, following the Gulf War ceasefire, to disarm completely of its nuclear programme, chemical and biological weapons and long-range missiles. The UN weapons inspectors were however clearly saying that this was not the case, and that there remained many unresolved issues about Iraq's WMD. We, the US and UK, deployed these unresolved issues to argue support for sanctions – what had happened to all the missiles Iraq had imported? Why the discrepancy between chemical bombs produced and those verifiably destroyed? etc. etc. Sanctions, we argued with great vigour, were necessary to force Iraq to disarm, fully and verifiably, as it had demonstrably not yet done. It was a tough diplomatic fight, not helped by the absence of hard evidence that Iraq was maintaining any significant WMD stocks, however hard the inspectors looked.

Opponents of sanctions argued that they were unjustified and caused immense human suffering in Iraq. Iraq *had* demonstrably disarmed; the weapons inspectors' endless probings and questions were pointless. Our counter-arguments were plausible: Iraq had failed on many occasions to cooperate fully with the weapons inspectors, leaving important questions unanswered; Saddam Hussein obstructed the operation of the UN's oil-for-food programme, which was designed to lessen the humanitarian suffering. In northern Iraq, where the UN, and not the Iraqi government, fully controlled the programme, all indicators showed the positive benefits of the programme in health, sanitation, education and the like.

It was my job to cull and collate the innumerable statistics, reports and testimonies in support of this latter version of the story and to deploy them in speeches and debates in the Security Council. On the other side of the table, the diplomats opposing sanctions – led by Russia and France – could cite myriad reports detailing the suffering under the sanctions regime and the inequities of the oil-for-food programme. They could provide convincing arguments that the north received an unfair share of oil-for-food funds. Like me, they could deploy an arsenal of facts and details to validate their version of "the truth". But, oddly, they often cited the very same reports that I did, for the UN reports provided ammunition for both sets of arguments.

It was, of course, a complex story that we managed to divide into two distinct and opposing narratives. The atmosphere between the delegations on the Security Council was aggressive and adversarial, as it remained until – and after – the 2003 invasion. Political divisions were allowed to degenerate into personal animosities. The Council, its chambers and corridors became a diplomatic battle zone where the more we fought, the more we entrenched our positions into competing blacks and whites. Thus were we able to obscure the more complex, deeper and more important truth, perhaps even *the* truth.

This reality was only slowly revealed to me by the many humanitarian workers, UN officials and ordinary Iraqis, including those bravely opposing the Saddam regime, who actually lived and worked in Iraq rather than those who wrote or read reports about it from far away. Their human testimony was in the end infinitely more eloquent and convincing, in the main because all of them, without exception, said the same thing. And this was that there was undoubted human suffering in Iraq, of a quite appalling scale, and that not enough was being done – by anyone – to address it. Put this question to a British official today and he or she will tell you – as I would have done when it was my job – that we tried to ease the impact of sanctions, but it is clear now, and frankly it was clear then, that it was much, much too little, too late. We – the US and UK – could have done a great deal more. Meanwhile, the Russians, French and others in the Security Council could have done a lot more to support the weapons inspectors and to help control illegal smuggling by Iraq, which was the main sustenance of the Saddam Hussein regime and itself something that reduced the funds for humanitarian supplies.

This example illustrates how governments and their officials can compose convincing versions of the truth, filled with more or less verifiable facts, and yet be entirely wrong. I did not make up lies about Saddam Hussein's smuggling or obstruction of the UN's humanitarian programme. The speeches I drafted for my ambassador to deliver to the Security Council and my telegrams back to London were composed of facts filtered from the stacks of reports and intelligence that daily hit my desk. As I read these reports, facts and judgements that contradicted "our" version of events would fade into nothingness. Facts that reinforced our narrative would stand out to me as if highlighted, to be later deployed by me, my ambassador and my ministers, like hand grenades in the diplomatic trench warfare. Simple details in otherwise complicated reports would be extracted to be telegraphed back to London, where they would be inserted into ministerial briefings or press articles. A complicated picture was reduced to a selection of facts that became *factoids*, such as the suggestion that Saddam Hussein imported huge quantities of whisky or built a dozen palaces, validated by constant repetition: true, but not the whole truth.

In the end, it became clear even to us that comprehensive sanctions were counter-productive. They targeted the wrong group of people, and their effects undermined the necessary international support for the containment of the Saddam regime. This reality slowly percolated into our small policy-making group, and eventually led to a change in policy. As the century turned, the US and UK initiated a shift in Security Council policy towards what became known as "smart sanctions" – whereby Iraq could import all civilian goods except those with potential military application: so-called "dual-use goods". But by then, the damage both political – to the consensus supporting containment at the UN and in the international community – and humanitarian – to the Iraqi population – had been done.

That damage has been more fully revealed since the 2003 US-led invasion of Iraq. One assumption of those planning that war was that Iraq's middle class would quickly recover from Saddam's removal, and Iraq's economy would rapidly thrive. That assumption quickly met the brute force of the reality that there was no Iraqi middle class and no economy to speak of. Iraq's non-oil economy had been more or less completely destroyed by the dozen years of sanctions that I, and others, had helped enforce. Anyone with the chance – mostly the educated and professional classes – had left as soon as they could. Within a year of the imposition of sanctions, Iraq's GDP had dropped by about three-quarters of its 1990 value to approximately that of the 1940s. By 1996, one million children under five were malnourished. In a country that had been cholera-free, by 1994 there were 1,344 cases per 100,000 people. Even after the oil-for-food programme came into operation, water-treatment plants lacked the proper spare parts and maintenance; there were extended power cuts. The population had no choice but to obtain water directly from contaminated rivers, resulting in turn in massive increases in water-borne diseases such as typhoid and cholera. Though the statistics are debated still, and data from Iraq during this period are unreliable, a recent and thorough academic history of the sanctions era concludes from a review of epidemio-logical studies that for the period from 1990 to 2003, there was an "excess mortality rate" of more than 500,000 for children under five. In other words, half a million children may have died[136]. Though Saddam Hussein doubtless had a hand too, I cannot avoid my own responsibility. This was my work; this is what I did.

I have no way to assuage the shame I feel when contemplating this episode. I was aware of the reports of humanitarian suffering, but I did little about them. In discussion within my ministry, I may have occasionally argued for easing the effects of comprehensive sanc-tions. But if I did I suspect that I argued the political grounds for such a shift – the loss of support for our policies – rather than presenting the urgent moral and humanitarian arguments. In our ministry's culture, it was often deemed "emotional" or "immature" to burden arguments with moral sentiment. Real diplomats were cold-eyed and hard-headed, immune to the arguments of liberal protesters, journalists, and other soft-heads who did not under-stand how the "real world" worked.

For years afterwards, I wondered how this might have happened. Why did we permit this? Or, rather, the actual, direct but more uncomfortable truth: why did I do this? My colleagues and I were decent people, or so I preferred to think. Likewise, my ministers and officials who endorsed the policy and defended it in parliament and before an increasingly critical press. It was this very decency that helped still my doubts, that persuaded me that we could not have been doing wrong. Later, in recounting this story, my former colleagues or friends would say, "you were doing what you were told", implying thereby that I bore no guilt and, needless to say, that they bore none either. Thus the state shows its similarity with the Church, and God himself. The state says: I will take your sin, your shame, and make it mine – which is in fact no one's. You are thus cleansed and free to go on your way. We are absolved of what we do in the name of the state.

And as in all institutions unscrutinised from outside, the hold of "groupthink" was a firm one upon our little group of policy-makers – no more than half a dozen or so people in the British government, more in the US. We reassured one another that we were doing the right thing. Our arguments sounded all the better the more we rehearsed them to one another.

The comfortable succour of my institution, in this case the British Foreign Office, allowed me to ignore the dictates of my own conscience. My bosses and colleagues were to me as the white-coated instructor in the Milgram experiment. The man who knew better. The man who held authority. Paid and committed to my profession and its enveloping persona, I was more than happy to press the button.

But here the parallel with Milgram ends. Milgram was an experiment. No one was hurt. Nothing really happened except a point was proven. Sanctions on Iraq were, unfortunately, no experiment. Though the arguments we played out in stuffy rooms in the UN in New York often seemed abstract, the effects of sanctions on ordinary men, women and children were to them all too painful. In the end, the difference between what I did and the Milgram experiment was this: in Milgram, the victim being electrocuted was an actor. In my case, the screams of pain and anguish coming from the other side of the wall were real.

The "man in the white coat" problem, as the insight from Milgram's experiment might be called, is not just a problem of diplomacy. It takes little imagination to see how, to varying degrees, it is a problem intrinsic to any system where people feel dissociated from the consequences of their actions – where they feel that someone else, not them, is really in control. Thus, the ultimate paradox of government, however well-meaning in intent, is revealed. The more that government seeks to act to tackle particular problems, the less that individuals are likely to feel responsible for them. Whatever is legal is thus rendered morally permissible. Evidence for this is all around us in the decaying standards of public behaviour, in many realms, from the shameless greed of Wall Street bankers, to the brutality and exploitation perpetuated in the anonymity of the worldwide web, to the thuggish antics to be witnessed on public buses, or subway trains.

The answer is obvious. Confront the individual with the consequences of their actions. Restore the moral understanding that each of us is responsible for the world as it is, and for each other. Take away the man in the white coat.

6

WHY CHESS IS AN INAPPROPRIATE METAPHOR FOR INTERNATIONAL RELATIONS, WHY JACKSON POLLOCK PAINTINGS ARE A BETTER, BUT STILL INADEQUATE, METAPHOR, AND WHY THIS HAS PROFOUND POLITICAL CONSEQUENCES

THE CHESS GAME IS A FREQUENT METAPHOR FOR THE business of international relations. Artfully shot photographs of kings and knights adorn many a book or scholarly article (particularly those about the theory of "IR"). The chess game appeals as parallel because it is complicated, it involves two clearly defined opponents and, above all because, although a very difficult game, it is ultimately comprehensible: there may be a very large number of permutations (according to Garry Kasparov, there are 10^{120} possible games), but there are a limited number of outcomes. Computers can be programmed to play chess, as well as if not better than the best human players.

Such metaphors therefore have a reassuring quality, that if the game is played well (by a state, a government), they will win, or at least prevent a loss – as long as our players, or computers and software, are good enough. The shape and possibilities of the pieces and board are known and finite. It's comforting to think that foreign policy is a bit like pulling a lever and, after some whirring and clicking, a result pops out at the other end. Historians and commentators reinforce this suggestion: their articles and books abound with the linear narrative: decision A leads to policy B leads to outcome C; if *only* Washington adopts policy *x*, result *y* will surely follow.

Maps and atlases evoke a similar effect. None of them portrays a world as it is: no globe is big enough. Jorge Luis Borges suggested such a map in his wonderful story *Of Exactitude in Science*: a map to the scale of the Earth, with every manhole cover, every goat path depicted as it actually *is*. Such a map would be perfectly accurate but of course wholly useless. All depictions must therefore reduce and thereby distort. All maps are nonetheless imbued with a certain implied confidence that their delineations are meaningful and significant. The neatly drawn lines, dots and shadings convey a message that the world is ultimately known and demarcated: complicated but clearly defined.

There are several problems with the chess metaphor, and indeed with the conventional way of thinking about international relations. In the discomforting reality of the world today, the number of relevant actors who may affect the outcome is invariably far greater than two, the potential moves of these multiple players are not limited (instead they are infinitely varied), and therefore the number of possible interactions in a globalised world is certainly greater than 10^{120} even though this is already an unimaginably big number.

Multiply the billions of connected humans in today's world by the actions available to them, then throw in the reactions and counter-reactions to these initial actions, run the calculation for even a short while, and you will end up with an impossibly large number of possible outcomes. That number is massive and possibly infinite: there are doubtless insufficient atoms in the universe to equal it. Given this reality, the hope of a foreign policy of deliberate action to produce predictable results looks increasingly vain. Instead of pulling a lever on a machine to produce a predictable result, foreign policy-making starts to look more like a roll of the dice – a dice with an infinite number of sides.

Few dare acknowledge what increasingly appears to be the truth, that the world has no defined shape, aside from its continents, rivers and oceans – and even these shift form and location, now at an alarming speed . . . That instead of a chessboard, or a web, it is in fact a swirling miasma of billions upon billions of interactions, not on a fixed pattern, or a net, but an ever-changing mesh of connections, some significant but temporary, some long-lasting but inconsequential, a reality more evocative of the swirls and spatters of a Jackson Pollock painting than a chessboard, though even a wall-sized Pollock can barely suggest this vastness, this complexity.

Some illustrations drawn from this maelstrom, themselves abstracted and polished and thus, to a degree, falsified for contemplation:

In 2009, a spate of high-profile kidnappings in Phoenix left Arizona the kidnapping capital of the USA. That same year, 18 people were killed in Mexico City after a gang of hooded gunmen attacked a local drug-treatment facility, apparently a refuge for rival gang members. The connection between these two phenomena was a seemingly harmless US policy aimed at improving border enforcement with Mexico. The policy was designed in part to placate a domestic constituency alarmed at high rates of illegal migration. But it had the adverse and unexpected consequence of aggravating a series of drug wars in Mexico. By slowing migration from Mexico, so too it slowed the transfer of drugs to the north. But as drug supply in the US fell, supplies increased dramatically in Mexico, lowering domestic prices and fuelling a spike in local drug consumption. Over the next months, gang-related violence and kidnappings surged as new and old gangs alike sought to mark out their turf in the newly developing marketplace. With thousands dead and the violence spreading back to American territory, US policy-makers are now forced to contend with the unintended consequences of actions once thought to bring greater stability to America's southern border.

It is now well known that Osama bin Laden's involvement in the battle of the Afghan *mujahideen* against the Soviet army served as the springboard for Al Qaeda's campaign of global *jihad*. The defeat of that army's occupation of Afghanistan, among other factors, helped contribute to the fall of the Berlin Wall and the collapse of the Soviet empire. Though Bin Laden and Saddam Hussein were wholly unconnected, the 9/11 attacks created the political momentum for the invasion of Iraq*. That invasion indirectly led to the *de facto* separation of Iraq's Kurdish north, the rise of Iran as the dominant regional power and, likely and tragically, the demise of the Christian community in Iraq, driven out by sectarian violence. None of these outcomes was predicted, even by the invasion's most imaginative planners.

The weapons and influence of Al Qaeda were a function of Bin Laden's personal wealth, which was itself a consequence of his father's large fortune, made from building for the royal family and

---

* As the UK's Middle East and Iraq "expert" at the UN from 1998 to 2002, I was required to read a thick folder of intelligence every day on Iraq, its WMD and efforts to rearm. There was not a single report suggesting a connection between the Saddam regime and Al Qaeda nor would such a connection be plausible given the radically different natures of these entities – one secular and Ba'athist, the other fundamentalist and Islamist. The head of Britain's Secret Intelligence Service (often known as MI6) also confirmed the absence of connection.

others well-connected in oil-rich Saudi Arabia, his home country, a long-standing US ally. The "original" Al Qaeda, as some analysts now call it, has meanwhile spawned several deadly affiliates or "franchises", a term reminiscent of the spread of McDonalds burger restaurants – Al Qaeda in the Islamic Maghreb (AQIM), Al Qaeda in the Arabian Peninsula (AQAP), AQ in Somalia, AQ in Afghanistan, the "Nigerian Taliban" Boko Haram and terrorist groups without names in London and Miami – and has helped inspire murderous attacks in Fort Hood, Bali and Mumbai. One of the planners of the Mumbai rampage, which cost nearly two hundred lives, was an American who also, it turns out, was for a while an agent for America's Drug Enforcement Agency, which wanted his help in locating heroin suppliers in Pakistan. The DEA, it appears, failed to inform other parts of the massive US intelligence machinery.

Elsewhere, Al Qaeda is also loosely associated with, and serves as inspiration for, the Al Shabaab Islamist militia which currently controls much of southern and central Somalia. Here, the insatiable global appetite for fish has driven international fishing fleets – from Japan, Russia and Europe – to plunder Somalia's unprotected waters, denying a livelihood to Somalia's many coastal fishermen. Partly as a result (there are other reasons too), some have turned to piracy, hijacking vessels in a lucrative trade which a substantial flotilla of heavily armed ultra-modern warships deployed in the area has failed so far to prevent. This naval fleet, sometimes numbering as many as twenty or more vessels, embodies unprecedented international cooperation, including warships from former antagonists like Russia, NATO, India and China. "Combined Task Force 150" also includes the European Union's first ever joint naval deployment. Yet so far this unique and expensive military collaboration has failed to stop or deter the pirates. More people were taken hostage at sea in 2010 than in any previous year on record[137].

(Meanwhile, in the northern province of Puntland, one donor nation is secretly creating a thousand-strong force of armed militia to take on the pirates. A leading London insurer is reportedly pushing ahead with radical proposals to create a private fleet of about twenty patrol boats crewed by armed guards to bolster the international military presence off the Somali coast[138]. Just as the US admits it is now dependent on the services of private military contractors to secure its forces in Iraq and Afghanistan, in the Horn of Africa too conflict and war, hitherto monopolised by nation states, are being contracted out.)

Some of the proceeds of that piracy, where ship owners often pay several million dollars to liberate their captured vessels and crews, have found their way to Al Shabaab, which has used the money to purchase weapons with which to fight its insurgency against the internationally backed Somali Transitional Federal Government in Mogadishu. Young men are now travelling from the US, Britain and elsewhere to train with Al Shabaab and their piracy-funded weapons. National security agencies – MI5, the FBI – have warned of the danger that these radicalised young men return to their "home" countries, trained and ready to commit further acts of violence. In late 2010, a young Somali-American sought to detonate a bomb at a Christmas-tree-lighting ceremony in Portland, Oregon.

Such effects are inherently unpredictable and can appear random, even though some causes and some effects are, at least in retrospect, discernible. They do not follow the neat patterns of a flow chart or a mathematical equation. Though multiple and complex, the model of a chess game is no more appropriate either. What we witness in the world is not ordered, at least in a sequential, logical fashion, but neither is it chaos. It is entirely wrong to say that the pattern of cause and effect in the world today is chaotic or anarchic, even if sometimes it seems that way. It may *resemble* chaos, but in fact it is a hugely complex and dynamic mesh of multiple cause and effect and back again (even Jackson Pollock paintings comprise an underlying order). Given this reality, any model or any metaphor may oversimplify and thus distort this nature – an artificial simplicity imposed upon complexity. Instead, it would be best to see the world as it is in all its massive complexity and microcosmic wonder.

Only later will historians, masters of the reductive art of the narrative, be able to put shape to what seems today formless and even then they will be capturing but a tiny part of what comprises existence now. Instead, a better depiction suggests itself, a fantastic mélange with ends and connections that shift, merge and disappear. To shape this mesh, to put form to it, to give it names, is to change it, to reduce it and ultimately to fail to understand it completely. Unfortunately this is precisely what governments are required to do.

It is conventional wisdom that with myriad international problems that cross frontiers, the world needs ever more international diplomacy and engagement. But it may be in fact that we need less, at least of the kind that currently predominates – the lattice of state-to-state relations and multilateral institutions.

There are now a great many international negotiation processes addressing a bewildering array of problems, from the familiar – climate change, nuclear proliferation – to the obscure – postal standards and the standardisation of measurements. But on the most acute and urgent problems, the evidence is mounting that these processes are not delivering the necessary results – effective solutions to the world's international problems. The measure of the effectiveness of this form of politics must be as for any form of politics – what are the outputs? What are the real effects on real problems and people?

The climate change "process", with its summits at Copenhagen (2009) and Cancún (2010), has comprised hundreds of meetings involving thousands of delegates and, on more than one occasion, "world leaders". But the process has yet to produce any substantive agreement, let alone concrete and plausibly effective measures, to reduce atmospheric carbon, despite the vast expenditure of negotiating energy and voluminous reams of treaty text and media commentary. Meanwhile the concentration of carbon in the atmosphere continues to rise.

The G8 Gleneagles summit in 2005 was notable for the extraordinary length and height of the fences erected, and the 10,000 police required, to keep protesters away from the tiny group of decisionmakers meeting in the remote Scottish location. The summiteers themselves sought to make history by their commitment to $50 billion in new aid money. This announcement was claimed to "make poverty history", echoing the rhetoric of the huge "Make Poverty History" campaign, which culminated in several massive "Live8" concerts that summer, where those enjoying the music in person or on television were encouraged to lobby their leaders by sending them text messages asking them to relieve Third World debt. At the UN World Summit later that year, all member states of the UN re-committed themselves to the goal of reducing absolute poverty by half by 2015 – the headline target of the so-called Millennium Development Goals.

It is depressing to relate the utter failure of those making these commitments to keep to them[139]. Of those making the Gleneagles declaration, all major countries and seven of them more or less democracies, not one fulfilled the promise they had made. Five years after Gleneagles, it was estimated that G8 pledges would fall short by $20 billion[140]. The US and European Union had done virtually nothing to remove the import barriers and agricultural subsidies that do much to stymie economic growth in developing countries. By 2010, the G8 itself, perhaps out of embarrassment, had ceased mentioning its aid goals in its communiqués. It did however make play of yet another new "initiative", this time to target maternal health. The most recent assessment of the "MDGs", as they are known in the diplomacy and development "business", is that they will certainly not be attained, an unsurprising assessment given the paltry efforts made by the signatories of the UN declaration to substantiate their rhetoric. Of one thing however we can be sure: there will be more such declarations, freshened up with new slogans and impassioned speeches or tweets, or Facebook pages, or whatever, in future.

The recent financial crisis has occasioned massed bouts of international hand-wringing over global regulation of banking and investment. The G20 group of countries has emerged as the leading forum to discuss such measures, clearly necessary to manage the out-of-control flows of unintelligible financial instruments, like the infamous Collateralized Debt Obligations (CDOs) that spread debt and risk with no oversight. But despite repeated meetings, communiqués and speeches, here too no effective policy response has emerged. It has instead become clear that the financial industry's lobbyists in each country have conspired to ensure that every government is unwilling to trade their supposed competitive advantage for collective measures, like substantially higher and globally agreed capital requirements for lenders. To allay public concern, instead these meetings offer *commitments* to effective controls, and *processes* to discuss them – no doubt without cease until the next crisis erupts. Thus, the impression of activity is created, the absence of concrete action obscured.

Given the gravity of the problems that these international processes are supposed to address, and yet their feeble outputs, it is urgent to consider what is going on. The cynical might argue that these processes are simply rackets run by the powerful who have no intrinsic interest in success. In its own way, this is a comforting and self-serving excuse that requires little response, save cynicism, on our part. But my own experience of diplomacy, and international negotiation, suggests something more subtle is the problem.

Invariably, when these negotiations and conferences fail, commentators are quick to point fingers at one participant or other for derailing the process: the Chinese for eviscerating Copenhagen, France for blocking Security Council authority for the invasion of Iraq in 2003. But these accusations may be missing the point: the problem of international diplomacy is not the actors within it, though their actions may hint at the more submerged problem. The real problem may be concealed within the very system itself. Indeed the problem may *be* the system.

Diplomacy is a system. Any system – like a club – requires certain characteristics of its members. And it reinforces these characteristics merely by existing and by requiring its members to exhibit these characteristics. The conventional institutions of diplomacy comprise the current international system. From these institutions, we can see clearly what characteristics are required of its participants.

Diplomacy and international relations are, by their nature, about *nation states*. The United Nations, the European Union, ASEAN, the World Trade Organization, the G20 are all associations of states. This may seem a very obvious and trite point to emphasise, but it is essential. For my experience suggests that states, and their exponents, do not accurately reflect what humans are about, nor what they want. Thus, it is naïve to expect that their machinations, in the form of inter-state diplomacy, will produce results consistent with humanity's needs in general.

This problem takes several different forms, and the evidence for it, if you choose to look, is manifold. The first is that the connection between what states do and say in international negotiations and what their populations think is now extremely tenuous, to say the least. In democracies, the international representative of the state is accountable to their home ministry, which is led by a politician who is accountable to the legislature, which is ultimately accountable to the population which elects its members. This is already a very long chain of explanation and accountability.

A good example of an acutely important but complicated issue is Iraq policy. My experience dealing with Iraq policy was that only the very small group at the coal face of the policy had any hope of a comprehensive grasp of the many and diverse issues at stake: WMD, sanctions, international law, the dynamics of the UN Security Council, to mention just a few, all of which themselves were extraordinarily complicated. My ministers, whose job it was to explain and "sell" the policy in public and to parliament, usually had only a very general and hazy grasp of the subject. In parliament, there were no MPs who could equal the officials' knowledge and expertise, and thus properly hold them to account. In any case, during the 4½ years that I worked on Iraq policy inside the British government, I was never questioned by any MP directly about my work nor did any journalist ever closely question me with any serious expertise. The picture in the US is similar. Questioning by foreign-affairs committees – and I have been questioned by them (and only after I left government service) – is at best general, at worst ill-informed to the point of incompetence.

One consequence of this extraordinarily dissociated chain between diplomat and citizen is that the diplomat can have no accurate idea of what the citizen wants. This requires the diplomat to assume, or rather *invent* what they think the citizen – his nation – wants. I know this because I did this myself many times. It is a function of the inculcation process the diplomat must go through to join and then embody their profession – the assumption that "we" know best. The diplomat, by the nature of their job, is encouraged to believe that they can determine what is in their nation's interests, without consulting those in whose name they claim to be operating.

This process of assuming or inventing the desires and requirements of a state, often called *interests*, is usually conducted in secret by exchange of telegrams, or classified emails, or in policy submissions to senior officials and political masters. I have participated many times in such exercises. With exquisite concision, the official will describe the issue at hand then he or she will articulate what is at stake for "us" – our "interests", in short. In recent years, it has become fashionable for the exponents of foreign policy to talk about "values" as important in diplomacy – things like democracy and human rights. But in truth the underlying calculus remains little changed, as does the diplomatic mindset, and this is no surprise, for it is only natural for the exponent of the state to think in terms of what his state needs and wants; it is to the diplomat as to a cow eating grass or mooing; it is what they *do*.

It would be absurd for a diplomat to adopt a different set of criteria to guide their work and policies, and would certainly guarantee a short career. Such interests typically, and by inherited tradition, take the form of a hierarchy of priorities where security – the requirement to secure the state and its population – ranks at the top, followed by economic interests. There is little rigour in these delineations and orderings, and indeed only rarely do officials distinguish between types of interest, instead talking in more general terms about what "we" may want in any given situation. The identification between diplomat and state cannot be overemphasised. While both security and economic interests would fit onto most people's lists of what is important, only a very few people would, I suspect, declare them as paramount in all situations or as their sole requirements in any situation.

The premise of the international system, and the state exponents who populate it, is a fundamentally incredible one – that the needs and wants of the Earth's billions of people can be boiled down into separated and discrete subsets of interests which can then be meaningfully arbitrated. This is difficult to grasp because we have become so accustomed to the state-based system: the international diplomatic forums with their neatly lettered name cards adorning serried rows at the UN General Assembly or European Council. But reflect for a moment and the absurdity becomes clear: how is it a tiny group of people can possibly know what is best for their country of millions? By extension, it is equally implausible to expect that a collection of such tiny groups, meeting at say the UN or G20, can produce meaningful and effective agreements for the whole globe. The disconnection is simply too great. They are required to assume, to guess. They know it, as I knew it. But it is the rest who believe it.

The problem is more insidious and damaging in its effects

than merely this. The system requires that the needs and wants of the world's peoples are reduced into such subsets – a reductive requirement. That need to reduce the complexity of reality into simplicity imposes upon the diplomats and other denizens of the system an unnatural and distorting burden – to turn their understanding of the world, and our needs upon it, into something else: the calculus of states. Most of the time this process is invisible, assumed and unremarked upon. Only occasionally are its aberrations so gross that they break the surface of our indifference – for me, it was the experience of Iraq sanctions in which I realised, and only in retrospect, the gross divide between my own beliefs and understanding of what was right, and the way I was required to think – and act – at the time.

There is an additional negative consequence of this state-dominated mode of thinking. The chess game requires two sides to be played: white and black. The process of simplifying and overstating our own needs, known as calculating our interests, requires a reciprocal technique to be applied to those on the other side of the table. If there is to be an "Us", there must also be a "Them". Thus the diplomat will not only tend to essentialise the requirements and desiderata of the millions of his countrymen, he must also essentialise everyone else. The game needs two discrete sides in order to be played.

This happened on the Iraq sanctions issue at the UN Security Council, where the diplomats gaily perpetuated the national divisions between opposing delegations even when there were no facts to disagree over. I was a willing participant in this farce: the UK/US would veto proposals made by the "other" side, in this case France and Russia, even if we ourselves had made the very same proposal a few weeks earlier and they had blocked them. The effect of such essentialising – the segregation of ourselves into two competing sides – was not to reduce conflict, but to perpetuate it.

A paradoxical example of the boiling down of what "We" and "They" want in perverse ways is to be found in trade negotiations.

International trade talks at the World Trade Organization – the most recent being the so-called "Doha round" – often revolve around the trading of concessions between national delegations or regional groups of delegations. One of the most common "concessions" is the granting of trade access to the domestic market of the state offering the concession. Such concessions are offered in exchange for access to others' markets in the same or different products, in a highly complex bargaining process. The offering of such "concessions" is however nonsensical, because the benefits of free trade flow more to the importer than the exporter: imports of cheaper or better goods give consumers more for their money and, through competition, raise domestic productivity[141]. In other words, what is being offered is not a concession at all – the party offering the concession is proposing something that will benefit them more, rather than a sacrifice. But so familiar has become the discourse of trade talks, and the calculus of concession-based bargaining, that everyone pretends that what is not a concession is such, and that what really *is* a concession, is not.

It is no coincidence that it is governments that perform this essentialising. They must. It is necessary for government, and the diplomats who represent it, and the politicians who lead it, to claim that only they can speak for the whole country. Equally, therefore, they must affirm the nature of the international system by accepting that other governments speak for their whole countries. A modern diplomat would deny that they are so crass as to generalise about other cultures and countries in the way that I have described. Of course, they aver, when they talk about Iran's policy, they mean the policy of the Iranian government, and indeed that is often how they will describe it.

But despite this designative care, the habit of referring to whole countries in the singular and referring to their government as the embodiment of that state is one as deep-rooted as the state-based international system itself. To change the naming of the actors, to remove the assumption that governments represent the whole of their countries, would be to change the nature of the international system, from one based around states as the primary unit of agency, to one based on some other unit. But as long as governments wish to hold sway in international policy and decision-making, they must continually reaffirm not only their own but each other's legitimacy to speak for their countries, even when the government is as grotesquely undemocratic as, say, Muammar Gadhaffi's in Libya or Kim Jong Il's in North Korea.

Perhaps one reason this habit persists is because of the way that diplomacy evolved. From its origins in classical times, through the Middle Ages and the development of the state-based system of the Peace of Westphalia, diplomats represented, and negotiated between, entities – cities, provinces and later states – that were discrete and separate. In contrast to today, the business between them comprised relatively limited transactions of trade and occasional conflict. These were important but they did not have the character of the massive and diverse contacts and interactions of today's world, and these terms barely convey the multiform, complex and dynamic nature of these flows.

One of the seminal texts that helped define the nature of diplomacy is by François de Callières in Paris, published in 1716[142]. De Callières saw the principal function of diplomacy as moderating and managing the clash of conflicting interests between states as efficiently as possible. The diplomat was required to assess how the interests of his state, and the other state, could be met in terms acceptable to both.

One can see how remarkably similar this conception of diplomacy is to the way it is conceived today. Yet the world is remarkably different. The post-war establishment of new multilateral diplomatic machineries – the United Nations, NATO and the European Union – has created new forums for state-to-state interactions, but has not altered the fundamental idea that diplomacy is about states identifying their interests and arbitrating them with one another: that these interests and identities are susceptible to calculation.

Indeed, these institutions are premised on the very notion that states can meet there and decide upon their common problems. It is therefore no surprise that diplomats tend to render the world and its myriad problems into these shapes. That this process is becoming more and more artificial, and disconnected from the reality of the forces at work in the world, is only now becoming evident enough to compel change.

The negative consequences of this kind of thinking can be clearly seen in negotiations over issues of common global concern, like climate change. Here, where a shared solution is clearly necessary and urgent, the habit of state-based thinking still dominates. While "world leaders" and UN officials pontificated about the lofty goals of the process, the negotiators in national delegations in the trenches of the conference resorted to type. Zero-sum bargaining over concessions and commitments dominated the discussions, with the usual rancour and finger-pointing when a deal – predictably – proved impossible to find. Some delegates suggested that the earth's atmosphere was divisible and that the industrialised nations had already taken their "share", as if the atmosphere were a cake to be sliced up.

As the head of Greenpeace dejectedly stated at the dismal end of the Copenhagen summit: "It seems there are too few politicians in this world capable of looking beyond the horizon of their own narrow self-interest, let alone caring much for the millions of people who are facing down the threat of climate change," he said. "It is now evident that beating global warming will require a radically different model of politics than the one on display here in Copenhagen." He didn't say what that model was, however.

Some would argue that the solution to this problem is more *supra*-national institutions like the European Union or the United Nations, where unelected officials chosen by the member states can somehow transcend the differences that bedevil the nation states and find solutions to mankind's common problems.

However, here too the outputs are disappointing. Again, we are confronted with a vast, confusing and obscure tableau of processes and committees and sub-groups which pretend to solve common problems, from terrorist financing to avian flu and the Middle East Peace Process. Now working on the side of those subjected to these processes, rather than those designing or running them, it is clear that the existence of such processes can have in itself a debilitative effect: the mere existence of a "process" creates the erroneous impression that something is being done, when it is not.

The Copenhagen climate process – which will now endure long beyond the Copenhagen meeting – is one example. Another, lesser known, is the "peace process" to resolve the illegal occupation of the Western Sahara. This "process" has lasted since the ceasefire in 1990 between the occupiers, Morocco, and the representatives of the indigenous people, the Saharawis – twenty years and counting – when Morocco agreed to a referendum for the territory's people to decide their status, an agreement and legal requirement endorsed many times by the "international community" at the UN. Every country in the world pretends to support this process, run by the UN, but none does anything in reality to advance it. The referendum has never taken place. In fact, the "process" is a way of shelving the issue indefinitely, to permit the existing *status quo* – of occupation – which privately suits the narrowly defined "interests" of these states, the US and EU above all. The process is thus a sham; the opposite of what it pretends to be. The Middle East Peace Process, nominally supposed to end Israel's illegal occupation of Palestinian territories, bears similar but not identical characteristics: the "Process" is a word that implies movement, even progress, but conceals a reality that there is none.

Both the United Nations and the European Union have contributed enormously to limiting the 20th-century scourge of international conflict. The EU has bound European countries together so tightly that war, once habitual, has now become unthinkable. The UN's sixty-year existence has witnessed a steep decline in the inter-state conflict prohibited by the UN's core document, its

Charter. But in these successes, new weaknesses have emerged, not least in dealing with the more fluid and boundary-less problems of the 21st century. The UN Security Council was established to prevent wars between states. Today, not less than eighty percent of its agenda concerns issues involving non-state actors, and conflicts both within and sometimes transcending states, like terrorism[143].

Fatally, all such multilateral or supranational institutions suffer an irredeemable deficit of democratic legitimacy. The greater the distance between representative and elector, the less legitimate that representative. In the EU, as in the UN, that distance is considerable. The grotesque and shameless public bargaining by national leaders over the senior appointments to these institutions proves the point. The UN Secretary-General or the President of the European Union is, at least in theory, supposed to represent us, but no one except the public is expected to believe that they do. The UN Secretary-General is well aware that it is the *realpolitikers* of the five permanent members of the Security Council who decide his appointment and, he hopes, reappointment, and he behaves accordingly, just as the President of the EU takes care to keep in close step with the major powers of the EU: France, the UK and Germany. I have often attended meetings between my ambassador at the UN and the Secretary-General in which he would be told in unmistakeable terms what party line he and his staff were required to toe. It didn't have to be spelled out in threats, merely implied and hinted at. He invariably got the message.

At the EU, touted by some as a "post-modern" institution for the 21st century to which countries have ceded sovereignty for the collective good[144], the ordinary voters seem to have been left aside, their views too awkward to accommodate in the Union's beautiful designs. The European Parliament has been given ever greater powers in an attempt to address the Union's "democratic deficit". But the treaty to give the parliament more powers was put to a public referendum in only one of the EU's twenty-seven members. It barely squeaked through. The Irish were made to vote twice when their first poll rejected the treaty. Other member states deliberately avoided a referendum for fear that their voters would emphatically reject it, as opinion polls clearly indicated they would. Dutch and French voters had both rejected the new European constitution in referendums in 2005; their opposition was quietly ignored.

Meanwhile, despite the claims of democratic representative-ness embodied in the European Parliament, the most powerful bodies in the Union remain the secretive Council of member states, whose meetings are not public, the Committee of Permanent (national) Representatives (COREPER), a body which hardly anyone outside diplomacy has heard of, and the wholly unelected but enormously influential bureaucracy of the European Commission, whose head is appointed by the leaders of the most powerful member states, currently Germany, France and the UK. The "democratic deficit" has thus hardly been remedied but merely obscured. As one now very senior European official once told me, legitimacy cannot be ordained or designed "top down", it must be earned and granted from the ground up. The architects of the EU have matters the other way around – allot the central institutions more and more power, and eventually people will begin to realise that they are important and give them legitimacy. This logic does not appear persuasive to the actual population of Europe.

For the ordinary citizen, these institutions are even more impenetrable and opaque than their already-distant national governments. I run a non-profit diplomatic consultancy. Its staff works full-time to understand the world's diplomatic and multina-tional institutions, and *we* find it difficult to work out who does what, and where real decisions are made. Pity the ordinary European citizen seeking a hearing in the shiny but dismal corridors of the EU's institutions in Brussels. Even for the acute, it is all but impos-sible to find out who is truly responsible for anything. It is reminiscent of nothing so much as the pathetic queues of provin-cial Chinese who make desperate but hopeless pilgrimage to Beijing to seek settlement of grievances against corrupt or incompetent Communist Party officials.

Moreover, but more subtly, the officials themselves are dangerously detached from the problem – and the people – they are seeking to arbitrate. I saw this in the UN Security Council – it was a curiously dry and boring place to work, despite its dramatic agenda of genocide and civil war. The blood and emotion of these conflicts was absent in its discussions and it was not a good absence: it was not conducive to better negotiation, but to worse. For one thing, the parties to the disputes on the Council's agenda were almost invariably absent from these deliberations – it is hardly a recipe for good decision-making to ignore the views of those most concerned. Moreover, the emotional and moral content of events, so crucial to the motivation to solve such problems, was missing. Between the reality of the problems and our deliberations was a huge and unbridgeable divide, not only of actual distance, for we were usually many thousands of miles from the disputes we discussed, but of import.

These deficits are intrinsic to supranational institutions just as the limits of state-centric thinking are inherent to the nation-state system, a system that has, since the Peace of Westphalia of 1648, dominated world affairs. Given these deficits, the answer to our global problems may not in fact be more diplomacy and international negotiation, at least not of the current kind. Thus conventional wisdom is turned on its head: we do not need more state-to-state diplomacy to solve these problems; we may, in fact, need less. And instead of relying on state-to-state diplomacy to manage the world, we must do so ourselves. As writer Parag Khanna has commented, "As was the case a millennium ago, diplomacy now takes place among anyone who is someone; its prerequisite is not sovereignty but authority."

The deficits of the state-based system are familiar, and commonly known, yet these systems endure, even when the operators of the system – my many and cynical diplomatic colleagues

– have themselves ceased to believe in them. As they take the stand at public inquiries, or address the press, they can hardly believe that anyone still believes them. It is a hollow, hollow feeling and I know it. These systems will continue to endure until those in whose name they claim to function withdraw their consent. The pact is broken; it doesn't work. To name a problem as "international" is to absolve oneself of responsibility and to place solution in the hands of those proven manifestly incapable. The international is not international any more; it is simply us.

And here is the most insidious and yet hidden effect of the international system – of inter-state diplomacy – as it currently exists. It is not that this system may exacerbate differences, force its players to define themselves more starkly than they otherwise might, nor that its exponents must naturally reflect a calculus not of the messy and diverse human family but of these strange and artificial units, states, or that these exponents are, as I once was, wholly separated from their sense of moral responsibility for their actions. These deficits are not the worst aspect of this system. (The "Live8" text messages to the G8 Summit provide a clue.) The most dangerous effect of the system is not that it doesn't work; it is that we, in whose name it is supposed to function, condone it, pretend to believe it, contrary to all evidence, and permit it to continue*.

It is one thing to accept this critique, but it is another to embody this philosophical shift. In a world of global terrorism, a rising India and China, and intense national competition for scarce resources, what meaningful action is available to the individual? How can the world be made to reflect its human reality rather than its inherited and inappropriate delineations of segregated states and peoples?

One obvious answer is for individuals to organise across nations and states around common causes. This is already beginning to

---

* These arguments are more fully discussed in my earlier book, *Independent Diplomat: Dispatches from an Unaccountable Elite.*

happen: witness the global movements around climate change or the protection of human rights. (Ideas to guide such action will be more fully elaborated later.) Less encouragingly, such borderless cooperation is also visible in the transnational organisation of drugs trafficking or jihadist terrorism, where extremists of many different nationalities have gathered around the flag of the new *Umma*. But this last example also illustrates the paradoxical challenges of engaging in the modern world. It is not sufficient to invade foreign countries to deal with security threats. Indeed, the evidence is mounting that these adventures are wholly counter-productive. Witnessing the violence perpetrated by "home-grown" terrorists from suburban Philadelphia or Burnley, it is clear that we must also engage with ourselves.

It is too easy to succumb to defeatism in regarding the world today: its weapons, its states, its self-serving and bumptious leaders. How on earth are we supposed to deal with that? It might be revealing to look at an issue that inspires the most pessimism and also the most horror. For nuclear weapons embody in their very existence the possibility of appalling destruction and indeed the annihilation of humanity as a species. In some ways, they manifest the gross inhumanity of the state system – that in order to defend the state, governments are prepared to use weapons that threaten the destruction not only of their own population, but the entire world's.

The conventional answer to this problem has been to look to governments to get rid of nuclear weapons. Even the demonstrators massing on the streets waving banners ultimately urge their governments to respond. Is this a realistic ambition?

The 2010 review conference of the Non-Proliferation Treaty (NPT), the cornerstone of the world's efforts to reduce nuclear weapons, lasted a month and involved highly skilled delegations from some 190 countries. The agreement they reached was lauded as a success, primarily because, unlike previous review conferences for the last decade, this gathering had actually achieved agreement.

But the content of the agreement – the *output* – was feeble, despite the international atmosphere being its most propitious for decades.

As usual, the "outcome document" was long – twenty-eight jargon-laden and barely comprehensible pages – with a misleading sixty-four "action points", most of which amount to no substantive action whatsoever. The vast majority are declarative: "reaffirming", "welcoming" or "noting". The press, focusing on one small part of the forest, made great play of the agreement to hold a conference – at an unspecified point in the future – on a nuclear-free Middle East, but even that agreement left out the only country in the Middle East currently possessing nuclear weapons, Israel. Otherwise, the conference agreed merely to *encourage* the Nuclear Weapons States to make more concrete progress towards nuclear disarmament and reduce the use of nuclear weapons in their military doctrines, but attempts to make such disarmament concrete and obligatory through a nuclear-weapons convention were fiercely resisted by the Nuclear Weapons States. As even the most favourable commentators put it, all that was agreed was a further *process*, not an output[145].

In its closing statement, Cuba noted pointedly what the review conference had *not* agreed: no timetable on nuclear disarmament, no commitment to begin negotiations on a nuclear-weapons convention, no clear commitment to stop the development of nuclear weapons, no call for withdrawal of nuclear weapons to home territories (i.e. out of Europe), and no legally binding negative security assurances – we shall come to these strange creatures later.

President Obama has declared his intention of ultimately ridding the world of nuclear weapons. The Global Zero campaign, supported by many prominent former statesmen and women and highlighted in a popular documentary film*, is advocating the same. But it is a fair bet that in the current state-based dispensation these noble efforts will fail. For it is implausible to expect that China, or

---

* *Countdown to Zero.*

Russia, or even France or Britain, let alone Israel or Pakistan, will give up this ultimate guarantor of their security, even if some reductions may nevertheless be possible. As total arsenals go down, louder and louder will become the argument that nuclear weapons have successfully prevented mass conventional war between their possessors. It's a plausible argument, as long as the proxy conventional wars that these powers fought on the territories of others are ignored. But nonetheless, the argument has force. Total disarmament relies on something that evidently does not exist – complete confidence and trust in the commitments of others that they too have disarmed irreversibly, and that they will not launch conventional attack.

The NPT's answer to this problem is fundamentally ridiculous. To the non-nuclear states who demand assurance that they will not be the victim of nuclear attack, the Nuclear Weapons States (NWS) have offered so-called "reverse security guarantees" – promises that they will not use nuclear weapons against non-nuclear states in certain circumstances. The "progress" of the 2010 review conference was that the conference agreed to *consider* making these "guarantees" legally binding. In other words, if a Nuclear Weapons State dropped the bomb or bombs on a non-nuclear state, the victim state would be able to seek redress in an international court, presuming that there would remain – post-apocalypse – a government, lawyers or courts with which to press such a claim. And such legal obligations would arise only if the Nuclear Weapons States agree them, which they have yet to do: at the review conference, they agreed only to "consider" them. Such reverse guarantees, even if legally enforceable, are unlikely to provide much reassurance if, for instance, Ukraine finds itself dealing with a fascist-led nuclear-armed Russia, which unfortunately is a more plausible prospect than the legally binding reverse-security assurances.

Under the NPT, the UK, like all other declared nuclear-armed states, is in theory committed to disarm itself of all of its nuclear weapons. The NPT was founded on a conceptual bargain – that the rest of the world would not develop their own nuclear-weapons capability, as long as the Nuclear Weapons States agreed to get rid of theirs, eventually. One indicator of the "progress" made at the 2010 conference was that the UK for the first time declared the full number of its nuclear weapons. No other declared NWS has done so. Revealingly but perhaps also most honestly, France insisted that the goal of the NPT "process" not be stated as a "world free of nuclear weapons" but the creation of "conditions which will lead to a world free of nuclear weapons".

The UK's recent "reduction" in its nuclear posture is indicative of current trends, some forty years after the NPT was signed, and twenty years after the end of the Cold War. Its 2009 announcement that it would reduce the number of Trident nuclear-missile submarines from four to three has no operational effect on the number of weapons deployed. Britain will continue to maintain one armed submarine, with up to 160 separately targeted warheads on sixteen missiles, on patrol at any one time. Unlike the US, the UK has yet to revise its nuclear doctrine to indicate that it would use nuclear weapons only if subjected to nuclear or chemical or biological-weapon attack. It still reserves to itself the right to be the first to launch nuclear weapons under certain circumstances, such as overwhelming conventional assault. We are however reassured that now we know exactly how many nuclear bombs it possesses. Neither India, Pakistan, North Korea nor Israel has any publicly articulated nuclear doctrine, and thus no one can tell under what circumstances they might use nuclear weapons.

Earlier that year, the US and Russia agreed under the START agreement a reduction in their arsenals of nuclear weapons. Heralded as offering substantial new reductions, some analysts judge that in reality the agreement barely affects the number of actual deployed weapons, and involves no reduction in the number of Russian launch vehicles[146]. Both powers continue to maintain hundreds of nuclear delivery systems at Cold War levels of alert: ready to be launched within a few minutes. One respected think-tank noted that, "While the operational readiness of some weapon systems has been reduced, there has been no major change in the readiness levels of most of the nuclear weapon systems in the post–Cold War era"[147].

This analysis is not an exercise in cynicism, but merely the necessary measurement of rhetoric against actual *outputs* – how many missiles and bombs are still deployed? These measurements suggest that it would be unwise to rely on rhetorical promises and diplomatic process to deliver the desired result.

Instead, it is more plausible to refer to, reinforce and promote a reality that the diplomats, politicians and analysts refuse to contemplate. The calculus of nuclear weapons depends upon the existence of the chessboard – a "Them" and an "Us". If you attack me, I will attack you: black and white pieces, segregated and discrete. If those distinctions no longer exist, the game cannot be played; if instead of two distinct sets of pawns and pieces, clearly separated across the board, all pieces are but varying shades of grey, intermingled and spread all over the board. This depiction is much closer to the contemporary reality, and the more time passes, the more accurate it will become. A Pakistani attack on New Delhi would kill hundreds of thousands of Muslims. An attack on Israel would kill thousands of Arabs. Any use of nuclear weapons, more or less anywhere, would have devastating effects on a highly interlinked global economy. Destroying New York would kill people from every country on earth: people of more than ninety different nationalities were killed in the destruction of the twin towers; one borough of the city contains 174 different nationalities. Killing Them would mean killing Us.

Nuclear weapons make this doubly true as even a limited strike on one country would, according to recent research, imply appalling consequences for the whole planet. Studies have shown that even a "small-scale" nuclear exchange, say, India and Pakistan launching fifty weapons each against each other, would have devastating consequences not only for the countries directly targeted but for the global environment and potentially for the survival of mankind[148]. Thus, nuclear weapons are revealed in their true nature: not as weapons of deterrence or plausible utility, but as mankind's suicide pill.

This truth is already slowly spreading among some members of the military, who are realising that the use of nuclear weapons by states is basically implausible – and self-destructive – in almost any circumstance. The most likely people to use nuclear weapons are not states but suicidal millenarian terrorists. Osama bin Laden's deputy Ayman Al Zawahiri has already written a book dismissing moral objections to the use of weapons of mass destruction, including nuclear weapons[149]. Our possession of nuclear weapons is no deterrent to such threats, but the very existence of nuclear weapons provides a possible method for these extremists. Thus, the best thing would be to do away with them altogether.

Establish this as a cultural truth, and eventually that understanding will filter through. Wherever possible, travel, interact, make love, argue, live with people elsewhere. Engage; co-mingle. Resist the efforts of governments and others to paint the other in stark colours, whether black or white. Throw away the chessboard; cut the ground from under those who would pretend humanity is but chessmen. Cease using the outdated nomenclature of a world that is already receding into history; stop naming; stop dividing.

One surprising conclusion from this analysis might come as a shock to the anti-globalisation protesters storming the next G8 summit: what might be the most effective tactic ultimately to get rid of nuclear weapons is not less globalisation, but *more*. The deeper the inter-mingling, the more dense the mesh connecting humanity, the less the chessboard may be clearly defined, the more absurd becomes the calculus of nuclear weapons, and indeed of states, as discrete entities, themselves.

Interestingly, this reasoning also applies to other harmful, if less apocalyptic, forms of warfare. Many have expressed concern that China or Russia are able to launch devastating "cyber attacks" against Western institutions, and economic and financial infra-structure. But one Chinese official has reportedly dismissed this option, primarily on the grounds of China's dependence on US financial stability – China owns nearly a trillion dollars' worth of securitised American government debt – a cyber attack on Wall Street would harm China as much as it harmed the US[150].

These examples suggest that the anti-globalisers storming the G8-protecting riot police are precisely wrong.

Instead of conventional theories of government and international relations, we need a new set of tools, and perhaps a dose of humility too, for a complex world may defy all but a general understanding of its inherent and pervasive unpredictability and contingency. In fact, we need the tools that interpret complex systems.

Malcolm Gladwell has popularised the concept of the "tipping point", the idea from complexity theory that even small events may trigger complex systems to "tip" over from one condition into another. Historian Niall Ferguson and others have begun to describe how empires, such as the American "empire", are complex systems and thus may be highly vulnerable to outside events, perhaps seem-ingly minor, over which they have little or no control, causing their downfall[151]. In finance, Nassim Nicholas Taleb has suggested that highly aberrational "black swan" events, hitherto regarded as extremely rare, are in reality much more frequent than predicted, and moreover have vastly more dramatic consequences. The May 2010 "flash crash" on the Dow Jones seemed to prove his point.

There is, then, a growing realisation that human affairs make up in their totality a complex system. Complex systems share char-acteristics which have important but barely noted consequences for politics.

Complex systems are *not* chaotic. They are not simple and ordered, but neither are they an uncontrolled mess. Complex systems are instead something "in between", as Professor Scott Page, an expert on complexity, has observed[152].

Another characteristic is perhaps the most telling, and recollects the Mexican wave or the suicide bomber. The actions of one individual may ramify in very powerful and consequential ways. This insight is a conclusion completely at odds with contemporary notions of the ranking and power of government, state and individual. The individual is not powerless, not subordinate; in fact they are a potent agent of lasting change in the whole system.

If individuals begin to behave in the way suggested in this book – to act themselves to produce desired political results, cooperating and negotiating directly with others affected – then a new dispensation will emerge, something that we may not yet be able to describe. This is the phenomenon of *emergence*, a key characteristic of complexity: that from the combined actions of many agents, acting according to their own microcosmic preferences and values, a new condition may emerge from the bottom up, almost unconsciously, and certainly without imposition by government, god or anyone else.

Individual ants behave according to very narrow and singular behavioural patterns. Each ant has a single function: one gathers leaves, another marks the way back to the colony, a third tends to the queen, a fourth takes care of the eggs and so on. But together these singular actions form something extraordinary: a huge self-sustaining colony, a *super organism*, that may cover scores of square miles. A collection of billions of relatively simple mechanisms called neurons interacting together in the human brain produces the emergent phenomenon called consciousness.

Most intriguingly, complex systems are robust – they can absorb outside disruptions without necessarily causing dramatic or catastrophic change. The tipping point only occurs when the system reaches criticality, a particular state where each element and thus the whole system becomes sensitive to even minor change. More usually, complex systems, unlike those composed of fixed and inflexible structures, are resilient and able to withstand even major external disruption. Complex systems are *adaptable*: a characteristic much to be desired in our unpredictable world.

Intellectually, we understand that turning a vast heterogeneous mesh into a chessboard of discrete players is to do something inherently reductive, oversimplifying and thus, in its way, deceptive if not downright dishonest. It is simply not possible credibly to claim that any authority, like any historian, can understand this huge pattern of interaction and connection. They cannot know, yet they must claim to.

Yet, there is something still more insidious going on. In claiming authority to organise our affairs, to order the Pollock-like mélange into something that it isn't, governments take away something more crucial from us – our own agency. Or rather, they take away our own *sense* of agency, for in truth our control over events never left us, only our belief in its existence.

Contrary to common assumptions, individuals, acting collectively, have a far greater power to control their circumstances, and indeed those of the whole world, than governments pretend. The immediate overthrow of governments now would bring only chaos. But as individuals and groups begin to assert their own agency over decisions and events within their own reach, there will eventually emerge a much wider and more fundamental effect, one that would ultimately amount to a revolution in how we organise our affairs.

How this might look is inherently unpredictable. No one can know how the sum of such deliberate actions might appear. This is, above all, a cultural change not an architectural redesign of political structures. Gustav Landauer, a 19th-century theorist, once said,

> The state is not something which can be destroyed by a revolution, but is a condition, a certain relationship between human beings, a mode of human behaviour; we destroy it by contracting other relationships, by behaving differently.

It will start with individuals acting upon their convictions. It will continue and gather force as they join together – perhaps in person, perhaps on the web – to organise, not to campaign, but to *act* and embody the changes they seek. These networks of cooperation may be temporary; they may be long-lasting. They may encompass a street, or the inhabitants of a building, cooperating to manage their affairs. They may span the globe as millions act together to address a shared concern. The embryonic forms of such cooperation are already evident: there are consumers' cooperatives that bargain for lower prices; "common security clubs" where unemployed people share job-seeking skills, barter services and organise shared childcare[153]; local groups where unemployed handymen and babysitters offer their services to the community[154]; and internet campaigns that enrol millions across the globe.

As the realisation of governments' dwindling power spreads, this new form of politics will become less about protest or petition and more about action. The sum of these collectives will not have a fixed structure; they will ebb and flow, responsive to the changing needs and passions of the population. They may be local, but they will also transcend borders, inevitably weakening the mental hold of boundaries and inherited national identities upon peoples with common interests. One day, so strong may be this new culture of collective collaboration, this mesh of myriad forms of cooperation, that our existing institutions, based on the singularising, centralising unit of national government, and indeed the notion of the nation state, may wither away, un-needed, outdated, irrelevant.

This mesh of networks, of collaborating groups both local and transnational comprises in its indefinite shapes, its dynamic changing nature and its responsiveness to the needs of its participants – us, ordinary people – a form much closer to the actual nature of the world today, its diverse and massive flows, the multiplying and shifting identities of its peoples, and above all its manifold challenges. And in its consonance with the nature of the world, that mesh, that shape – indeterminate, unstructured, changing though it may be – offers paradoxically much greater stability and coherence than the fixed and hierarchical forms of organisation we have inherited from the past. The world should be ordered according to our needs, not the projections and requirements of static institutions.

The future nature of this world cannot be foreseen; it will *emerge*. But one thing is sure. No longer would we be fooled into seeing the world as a chessboard, demarcated, separated, neat, but instead it would seem to us as it really is.

7

THE MEANS ARE
THE ENDS

IN COLONIAL INDIA, THE BRITISH FORBADE INDIANS from making their own salt, and charged steeply for it as a form of indirect taxation on the subject people, a tax that hit the poorest especially hard. In 1930, Mahatma Gandhi decided to attack this injustice directly, and organised a march to India's coast, where salt could be made from seawater – for free – directly challenging the British monopoly of salt production. Gandhi's "salt march" or "Salt Satyagraha" is rightly renowned as one of the most important acts of political protest in recent history, for its lessons are manifold and powerful.

Gandhi chose to attack the salt tax, against the advice of some of his political colleagues, because it was both a tool and a symbol of Britain's oppression of India's native population. Thus, the action to undermine the tax assumed both a practical and symbolic value. Gandhi carefully planned the march, choosing only his most disciplined cohorts from his own ashram, and sending scouts to reconnoitre villages ahead. He built up public expectations and attention with press conferences before and during the march. The salt march above all manifested a core principle of Gandhi's political philosophy – that of *satyagraha* – a synthesis of the Sanskrit words *satya* (truth) and a*graha* (holding firmly to). In the common shorthand of today's times, Gandhi's philosophy is often summarised as "non-violence" or "passive resistance", and indeed it encompasses these elements. But for Gandhi, *satyagraha* had a deeper and more positive significance, not merely an absence of violence but more a strength. In his words:

> Truth (satya) implies love, and firmness (agraha) engenders and therefore serves as a synonym for force. I thus began to call the Indian movement Satyagraha, that is to say, the Force which is born of Truth and Love or nonviolence, and gave up the use of the phrase "passive resistance", in connection with it, so much so that even in English writing we often avoided it and used instead the word "satyagraha" . . .

The terms "non-violent" or "passive" resistance may emphasise passivity, but for Gandhi the philosophy was one of strength. Above all, Gandhi believed that means were intimately connected with ends. Indeed they were to him the same thing, as connected as a tree to its seed. If you used violence, you could expect nothing but further violence in return. *Satyagraha* by contrast engaged a force – love – to which there was no resistance. The salt march demonstrated clearly how these concepts, combined with an acute political intelligence, played out in practice.

The British, at first dismissive, were confused as to how to respond to the march, which gained huge publicity in India and worldwide. The *New York Times* ran daily reports on the march. It was reported that 60,000 Indians came to hear Gandhi speak on the eve of the march. Not one to eschew any melodrama he could extract from the situation, Gandhi warned that his speech might comprise the last words of his life; he invoked a compelling spirit of self-sacrifice: "My task shall be done if I perish and so do my comrades". As the march progressed, crowds of tens and sometimes hundreds of thousands gathered along the way. Gandhi's marchers slept in the open in the villages they passed through, asking only food and water, the better, Gandhi judged, to recruit India's poor, whose support would be vital to imperialism's defeat.

After a march lasting nearly three weeks and almost 250 miles, building up expectations and political tension all the way, Gandhi arrived at the coastal village of Dandi in Gujarat, where raising a handful of mud which he then boiled to make salt, Gandhi declared, "With this, I am shaking the foundations of the British Empire." Gandhi implored his followers and all Indians to follow his example and make illegal salt, breaking the British monopoly and depriving the empire of an important source of revenue. In the weeks that followed, 60,000 were arrested for making salt. At Peshawar, British troops killed over 200 peaceful demonstrators. Gandhi was arrested while planning his next Satyagraha at the Dharasana salt works. The march went ahead, eventually under the leadership of Sarojini Naidu, a female poet and freedom fighter. She warned her fellow Satyagrahis to expect to be beaten, but that "you must not even raise a hand to fend off blows". Sure enough, soldiers beat the marchers with steel-tipped clubs. The United Press reported:

> Not one of the marchers even raised an arm to fend off the blows. They went down like ten-pins. From where I stood I heard the sickening whacks of the clubs on unprotected skulls. The waiting crowd of watchers groaned and sucked in their breaths in sympathetic pain at every blow. Those struck down fell sprawling, unconscious or writhing in pain with fractured skulls or broken shoulders. In two or three minutes the ground was quilted with bodies. Great patches of blood widened on their white clothes. The survivors without breaking ranks silently and doggedly marched on until struck down.

Although such reports, which the British tried to censor, drew the attention of millions across the world (*Time* magazine declared Gandhi its 1930 Man of the Year), this sacrifice failed to win any immediate concessions from the British, and it would be another seventeen years before India would at last be independent of British rule. Though India's first Prime Minister Jawaharlal Nehru acknowledged the enormous importance of the salt march in mobilising India's masses around the goal of independence, his Congress party, to which Gandhi then belonged, eventually abandoned *satyagraha* as a political technique. Historians today tend to view the Second World War as the more significant factor in ending imperial rule in India[155]. But the Salt Satyagraha is remembered still for its signal achievement in one crucial aspect. As one British colonial administrator noted at the time, "England can hold India only by consent; we can't rule it by the sword." And thanks to the salt march they had lost that consent.

Though technically the more powerful of the two antagonists – with the power of the state, of arrest, and ultimately of force – Britain lost the contest against Gandhi's force of will, *satyagraha*. Those who were clubbed to the ground ended up victorious, for by their reaction to the march, the British lost the consent of the Indian population, upon which they relied to maintain their colonial rule. The Salt Satyagraha thus qualifies as one of the most effective political actions of recent times. It is worth summarising why:

- It confronted its political target – Britain's colonial rule – directly: the goal of the salt march was to make salt, directly confronting the British salt tax and denying the colonialists revenue, thus the action itself contributed to the political result intended;
- It confounded and confused the British by using non-violent methods; one British administrator later confessed in an internal memo that they would have preferred violence;
- By combining means and ends non-violently, the march attracted and created enormous moral force, which not only helped recruit followers but was also crucial in garnering massive international attention and sympathy.

In an age of terrorism and violent counter-reaction, such examples can seem quaint and irrelevant, but surveys suggest that, even in the Muslim world, Al Qaeda's use of violence, and in particular its targeting of civilians, alienates more followers than it attracts. The persuasive power of self-sacrifice and non-violence remains undiminished even if violence seems once again the more fashionable.

In his short manual, *Guerilla Warfare*, Che Guevara dismisses terrorist violence as ineffective:

> We sincerely believe that terrorism is of negative value, that it by no means produces the desired effects, that it can turn a people against a revolutionary movement, and that it can bring a loss of lives to its agents out of proportion to what it produces.[156]

Guevara preferred direct military confrontation with the repressive forces of Batista, Cuba's then dictator. In modern Mexico, recognising that conditions, though unjust, were less repressive than in pre-revolutionary Cuba, the leader of the Zapatista rebels in Mexico's Chiapas region, Subcomandante Marcos, whom some have called Guevara's "post-modern" successor, prefers irony and non-violence to bring home the Zapatistas' message of the exploitation of Mexico's indigenous peoples. From early on in its campaign against exploitative landowners protected by the Mexican government, the Zapatistas, though an armed military group, have forsworn violence. As Marcos put it,

> We don't want to impose our solutions by force, we want to create a democratic space. We don't see armed struggle in the classic sense of previous guerrilla wars, that is as the only way and the only all-powerful truth around which everything is organised. In a war, the decisive thing is not the military confrontation but the politics at stake in the confrontation. We didn't go to war to kill or be killed. We went to war in order to be heard.

Gandhi himself sometimes despaired of the Indian people's propensity for violence. Exploiting his immense public standing and moral authority, on several occasions he used hunger strikes as a tool of political persuasion, including to seek an end to fighting between Muslims and Hindus. This technique too has modern relevance. The hunger strikes by Republican prisoners in the Maze prison in Northern Ireland in 1981 resulted in the deaths of several strikers, most famously Bobby Sands, who was elected as a member of the British parliament during his hunger strike. As convicted IRA members and in some cases killers, the moral standing of these hunger strikers was certainly less than Gandhi's[157]. But their determination to see the strikes through to death wrought concessions from the British government which, after ten prisoners had died, granted the prisoners certain privileges, though not the renewal of the "Special Category" status, akin to that of political prisoner, that the strikers had sought. The more lasting impact however was, like the Salt Satyagraha, deeper in its effects on that intangible: will. According to one commentator, Sands "probably did more to turn the tide of the republican struggle than any other individual"[158]. Though intangible, there were measures of a more palpable political shift. By 1985, the British government, which had hitherto forsworn all concessions to the strikers, had negotiated the Anglo-Irish agreement that gave the Irish Republic for the first time a consultative rôle in the government of Northern Ireland, and heralded the peace process which resulted in the Good Friday agreement of 1998, which largely brought an end, though sadly not yet final, to the violence and sectarian strife that had benighted the province for over thirty years.

In 2009, a 42-year-old woman named Aminatou Haidar used the hunger strike for similar effect. A native of the Western Sahara, which has been occupied by Morocco since 1975, Haidar has ceaselessly campaigned for the right of her people, the Saharawi, to self-determination[159]. For these efforts, she has been repeatedly imprisoned and abused. Returning from the United States, where she had been awarded various human-rights prizes, Haidar was prevented by Morocco from re-entering the territory where she and her children live. The Moroccans seized her passport and demanded she sign an oath of allegiance to Morocco's king in order to get it back. Haidar refused and went on hunger strike to demand its return. As Haidar approached death, international efforts on her behalf stepped up and even Morocco's allies, France and the United States, were forced to intervene. After thirty-two days without food, Haidar was taken to hospital, her respiration and blood pressure dangerously low. She remained however committed to the end, determined, she said, to return unimpeded and without conditions or to die in dignity. Morocco at last capitulated and permitted her return; a public humiliation for a monarchy that had sworn it would not back down. Thanks to her willingness to starve herself to the end, Haidar not only secured her own return to her homeland, she also succeeded in attracting unprecedented international attention to Morocco's occupation of Africa's "last colony".

Sometimes, protest can take the simplest form. In East Timor, then occupied by Indonesia, the indigenous East Timorese would approach every Indonesian soldier or settler they came across and ask, "When are you leaving my country?"[160]. The most basic declaration of discontent, repeated, sends a signal that the *status quo* cannot endure.

In the summer of 1964, about a thousand American students from Northern universities – most of them white – travelled to Mississippi as part of a campaign by the Student Non-Violent Coordinating Committee (SNCC) to fight against racial segregation in the Southern states. The students lived in communes – or 'Freedom Houses' – or with local black families. They registered voters and taught in 'Freedom Schools'. Ten days after they arrived, three students were beaten to death by segregationists assisted by the local police, killings made famous in the movie *Mississippi Burning*; many more were persecuted in other ways[161]. Like Claudette Colvin, who refused to move seats on her bus, the students' actions directly contributed to the repeal of the notorious racist Jim Crow laws, and the end of legalised segregation in the South: a reminder that laws follow action, not *vice versa*.

These dramatic actions were often taken to address grave injustices, like occupation and systematic repression. The hunger strike is an extreme action taken in response to extreme circumstances. Moreover, as Gandhi and Haidar both illustrate, it helps that the striker already enjoys some standing in public, and ideally, as in both cases, moral authority. Mia Farrow's hunger strike to protest at international inaction over Darfur was diminished in its impact by the decision to end it after twelve days, although Richard Branson reportedly "took over" her strike for a further three days. Aminatou Haidar's frightening and clear determination to see her strike through to the end was a crucial component of its effectiveness.

Such actions remain hard to transpose to our own politics. What can be transposed however are the principles embodied, and in particular the consonance of means and ends. Political actions which produce, even in small part, the political end they seek carry a persuasive force far greater than any mere campaign, both for their demonstrative and symbolic force, and for the simple reason that such actions, even if only on a small scale, contribute to the desired solution.

After a spate of robberies in the New York City neighbourhood of Bedford-Stuyvesant, a group of local men decided to escort pedestrians home from the subway. One of the founders of "We make us better" said, "I decided we can't have these people terrorising our young women and children, and we're not speaking up and making our presence felt." The members of the group don't regard themselves as political or as activists; they are just trying to make their community better by their example[162]. They plan soon to set up a mentoring programme.

This illustrates an important message – that it is changing attitudes and demonstrating new forms of behaviour, as much as laws,

that matters. This lesson is also evident in Naples, the heartland of
the Camorra organised crime ring. Here, local people have taken
the initiative to resist extortion and corruption, some pasting "anti-
pizzo" stickers on their shops to indicate that they do not pay
"protection" money, and as a signal of solidarity with those who do
the same. Others are establishing cooperatives to run the farms and
businesses seized from the mafia. As one campaigning priest argues,
the environment where organised crime may flourish is one established by general culture, as much as by the ineffectiveness of law
enforcement:

> My personal experience is not that poverty determines the
> triumph of criminality but it is the poverty of intellectual culture.
> You become a criminal not just because you are hungry but
> because you want more things and quickly . . . It is the model of
> diseducation that comes out of national and private life. The
> Camorra and television project the same cultural proposal.

In a country where several legislators and the Prime Minister
are accused of links to the mob, a judge makes the same point, "The
battle is not just won by force and sequestrations, but by a social
struggle. It is a cultural battle."[163]

In crime and its punishment, innovators in California are
showing that by bringing perpetrators face to face with the consequences of their crimes – above all their victims – they may not only
lower recidivism rates, but also give victims of crime a greater sense
of satisfaction than a system in which many feel deprived of real
and meaningful justice[164]. In the current adversarial court system,
criminals are encouraged by their lawyers to minimise and excuse
their crimes; prosecutors drive for the harshest punishment. In
America today, an astonishing 2.3 million are behind bars. The
consequences of such a system are obvious, and can be witnessed in
both the inhumane conditions of America's jails, and the high rates
of re-offending. Victims meanwhile often feel that their needs are

ignored in an arcane and impersonal legal system; the pre-sentencing statement permitted to victims of certain crimes is barely sufficient. The goal with the California initiative, lamentably distant in the current system, is to bring justice – for both victims and criminals – closer to home.

In Britain, Prime Minister David Cameron has made great play of a concept he calls the "Big Society", offering a rather sketchy blend of a vague localism with more familiar Conservative moral philosophy about individual responsibility. At the same time that the government has made severe cuts in public spending, Cameron has argued that people should play a greater rôle in local activities, hitherto the preserve of government, including schools, parks and other public services. The conjunction of cuts with the moral sermonising is not the only aspect of the "Big Society" that jars. This book argues that people will benefit by taking charge of their shared affairs locally, but crucially this means that they must also have *agency* over these decisions: control. The benefits outlined here – of better and more equitable outcomes, and social consensus – from local and participatory decision-making are not available in the "Big Society" because, in Cameron's vision, central government retains overall control. If taxes and revenues are collected and distributed centrally, it is impossible for people at the local level to have real control over budgets and thus policy.

The Porto Alegre experiment described earlier is an example of what greater local agency looks like, and its benefits are clear – above all in the more equitable distribution of government services, but also in greater social consensus underpinning policy choices. The "Big Society" by contrast has yet to amount to real autonomy at the local level. Instead, the "Big Society" seems merely to amount to the provision part of "local responsibility": local people may provide, but not decide. It is this contradiction that perhaps explains Cameron's inability to explain his concept with any clarity, and suggests that it will amount to little more than encouraging volunteers at the local library. For this half-baked philosophy entirely misses the point of real devolution of power. Indeed, it represents little such devolution in substantive terms at all. All that it offers is responsibility without power. Little wonder that Cameron's big idea has been greeted with some scepticism.

And while those at the bottom of the pile are expected to suffer cuts as they are patronisingly inveighed into taking on more local services, with their morality the alleged beneficiary, the craven morality of those who benefit from the current *status quo* is barely questioned.

CEOs of the largest American companies earned an average of 42 times as much as the average worker in 1980, in 2001, they earned 531 times as much. Britain has witnessed a similar divergence. It is hard to imagine that these bosses have in twenty years increased their contribution to company performance by such a remarkable degree. Instead, there appears to be an emerging culture amongst the top executives that because they *can* pay themselves so much, they *should*. This self-interested belief piggybacks upon and exploits a vague cultural notion that competitive economies somehow *require* exceptional rewards for the successful. Thus capitalism takes on the qualities not only of an economic system, but also a moral code.

These grossly overpaid corporate barons exhibit a brazen new morality – take what you can get away with, a norm sadly prevalent across much of corporate America and the world, and whose worst examplars are the likes of Dick Fuld, the CEO of Lehman Brothers who took home over $22 million the year before he led his bank to bankruptcy. In the fifteen years prior to the bank's collapse, he had been paid nearly $500 million. To protect his assets against legal action from the many employees and stockholders who lost out hugely from the consequences of his actions, Fuld "sold" his Florida mansion to his wife for $100. Four years earlier, it had been bought for over $13 million. The greed and excess have become so grotesque that even captains of industry feel that they can no longer defend it:

the chief executive of General Electric in 2009 attacked his generation of business leaders for their "meanness and greed".

There is nothing inevitable about such excesses, or inequality.
Such irresponsible greed is not necessary for a competitive company,
nor intrinsic to a competitive economy. Indeed, the opposite seems
to be the case. Some economists, including a former IMF chief
economist, now believe that America's gross wealth inequality lay
at the root of the financial meltdown: middle-class families, whose
incomes have been stagnant for a decade, were forced to borrow
more and more to buy houses, and maintain acceptable living standards[165]; meanwhile, the rich, who enjoyed a far greater share of the
rewards of America's economic growth over the last decade, spend
far less as a proportion of their overall income, depressing the
consumption necessary to fuel sustained growth*. In Britain, as the
small minority of the very wealthy have got richer; statistics show
that the poorest have in real terms actually become poorer.

But what might be done?

John Lewis set up his first draper's shop in 1864. His son
Spedan joined the business towards the end of the century. While
convalescing from a riding accident, he realised that his father, his
brother and he together earned more than all the hundreds of other
employees in the family's two stores put together. Spedan Lewis
instigated new systems and practices as soon as he returned to work:
he offered shortened working days, set up a staff committee, and a
third week's paid holiday, an innovation for the retail trade at the
time. He founded a house magazine, *The Gazette*, which is still
published today.

In 1920, Spedan introduced a profit-sharing scheme. Twenty

---

* According to economist Raghuram Rajan's calculations, every dollar of
growth in income between 1976 and 2007, 58 cents went to the top 1 percent
of households. The other 99 percent of American families had to scrap over the
42 cents of loose change. The result was a country as unequal as it had been just
before the Wall Street crash of 1929 – and with much the same results (source:
The Guardian, "What the £35,000 cocktail taught us" 3 August 2010).

years later it was expanded into a partnership: in effect, Lewis handed over the business to its workers. Today, nearly 70,000 partner employees own the scores of major stores and supermarkets operated by John Lewis across Britain. Every branch holds forums to discuss local issues. These aggregate to form divisional councils; partners elect the large majority of members of the Partnership Council. The councils have the power to discuss "any issue whatsoever"; the partnership puts "the happiness of Partners at the centre of everything it does".

The partnership's constitution sets out to be both commercial and democratic. The annual bonus for partners was in 2008 equivalent to ten weeks' wages. The partners own two country estates, sailing clubs, golf courses, hotels and other extensive recreational and social facilities. Pension schemes are generous; after twenty-five years' service partners are rewarded with six months' paid leave. With its well-known slogan of "Never knowingly undersold" and a guarantee that it will repay customers the difference if they can find a lower price elsewhere (though not on-line), John Lewis has been consistently profitable, despite the cut-throat competition of the retail sector. Its revenues in 2008 were nearly £7 billion.

Speaking near to his death in 1963, Spedan Lewis explained why he set up the partnership, and handed over what had been the family business to its employees[166].

It was soon clear to me that my father's success had been due to his trying constantly to give very good value to people who wished to exchange their money for his merchandise but it also became clear to me that the business would have grown further and that my father's life would have been much happier if he had done the same for those who wished to exchange their work for his money.

The profit . . . was equal to the whole of the pay of the staff, of whom there were about three hundred. To his two children my father seemed to have all that anyone could want. Yet for years he had been spending no more than a small fraction of his income.

On the other hand, for very nearly all of his staff any saving worth mentioning was impossible. They were getting hardly more than a bare living. The pay-sheet was small even for those days.

Note that Lewis suggests that his father would have been happier himself if he had paid his workers more fairly, an observation borne out in the recent book *The Spirit Level* which found that everyone in society is better off – in terms of mental health, crime and other indicators – in economies with greater wealth equality. Spedan Lewis continued that the state of affairs in the country was a "perversion of capitalism":

It is all wrong to have millionaires before you have ceased to have slums. Capitalism has done enormous good and suits human nature far too well to be given up as long as human nature remains the same. But the perversion has given us too unstable a society. Differences of reward must be large enough to induce people to do their best but the present differences are far too great. If we do not find some way of correcting that perversion of capitalism, our society will break down. We shall find ourselves back in some form of government without the consent of the governed, some form of police state.

Since this interview took place, inequality in Britain has risen more or less without interruption, despite the proclaimed efforts of recent governments to address it. In 1979, the Gini coefficient, a widely accepted standard of inequality*, stood at 0.25; by 2009 it

---

* The Gini coefficient can range from 0 to 1 and provides an objective measure of income inequality, which allows every country to be ranked against others and against its own past performance. A coefficient of 0 would mean income is shared equally between all individuals, whilst a coefficient of 1 would mean one person within the population has all the income and everyone else none. So a higher Gini coefficient figure indicates a higher level of inequality.

had reached 0.36. Inequality in the US is yet greater, at 0.408, on a par with Mexico.

Lewis believed that partnerships were a better way to run a business: "It is already dear to many hearts besides my own, for it makes work something to live for as well as something to live by."

Cooperative businesses, such as John Lewis and Spain's Mondragon, which pays its executives no more than eight times its lowest-paid employees, have shown that businesses owned by their employees can be as successful as the most hierarchical, profit-driven enterprise. At such companies, wage differentials are lower, benefits are more widely shared, and – above all – employees who are also owners feel not only more agency over the future of their business, and thus their own, but also more satisfaction. These companies are not compelled to a more egalitarian approach by legislation; they were set up that way by the free choice of their founders.

The Swiss army knife company Victorinox suffered a severe crisis when penknives were banned from airports, hitherto important sales channels, under post-9/11 airport security measures. The company responded by referring to its values of inclusiveness and loyalty to its workers. Despite a steep decline in sales, no one was laid off. The company instead stopped hiring, encouraged workers to take early vacations and reduced shifts while meanwhile expanding its product ranges, particularly in watches. The company had suffered similar crises before, such as a sharp decrease in orders from the Swiss army after the first world war. Victorinox, in contrast to the prevailing hire-and-fire model, treats its workers the same in good times as in bad; it acts according to its pronounced values (means and ends again) by establishing employee-oriented management schemes and an integration policy that better incorporates younger and older workers, immigrants and people with disabilities. It pays the highest-paid workers no more than five times the wages of the average. Founded in 1884 by Karl Eisener, who wanted to provide long-term jobs to discourage the Swiss from emigrating because of poor economic conditions, the company is going strong, with a respected global brand, nearly 120 years later[167].

In the financial sector, mutual banks and insurance companies endured the depredations of the financial crisis much better than publicly owned banks and companies. "Mutuals" by their very nature discourage excessive risk-taking and indeed excessive pay. They return banks to the old-fashioned notion that lending should not grossly outpace deposits. The trouble is that stock-market listing encourages the emphasis on short-term profits – and thus risk-taking – that contributed to such problems in the credit crunch. The ensuing government bailout of the banks reaffirmed the implicit guarantee that no major bank would be allowed to fail and risk wider economic meltdown. Thus, the current system, even after the much-heralded "bill to control Wall Street" in 2009, and thanks to government action, rewards the most destructive Wall Street behaviour.

Boston University professor Laurence Kotlikoff has proposed that all financial products be mutualised as "Limited Purpose Banking" (LPB) with benefits in reduced risk, greater transparency and less excessive executive compensation. Under LPB, mortgage lending, for example, would take place through "mortgage mutual funds" whose managers would pick loans to invest in. Mortgage applicants would provide the information they do today, and different funds could bid for their custom. The lenders would be investors owning shares in the mutual funds. At no point would any bank actually hold the mortgage on its books. Indeed, banks would not hold anything on their books at all except the modest assets needed to manage a fund – computers and offices – and the matching equity. They would neither borrow nor trade with borrowed funds. Kotlikoff extends this principle to all of finance. Insurance and derivatives for example would be replaced by funds issuing different shares, whose claims on the funds' holdings depend on how specified events turn out. Crucially, this means that all contingent liabilities would be fully backed by capital[168].

In defending the inequities and excesses of the current system, it is remarkable how often the beneficiaries of these injustices tout half-baked economic arguments – such as the economic necessity of enormous executive "compensation". In public debate, the merits of private enterprise are invariably presented as superior to government provision. These arguments come to a head over "public goods" such as the nation's health or the world's oceans, where the choice is usually presented as between private ownership or public provision and regulation: market vs. the state. Evident in these debates is an assumption that there are only two options – public or private – to resolve the so-called "tragedy of the commons" whereby common resources such as water, land or oceans will be abused by some, and neglected by all, without some form of order.

In fact, pioneering economists have shown that other spontaneous forms of voluntary management and sharing of such resources have sprung up, and are if anything more successful at husbanding these common goods than either government or the market. One such economist was awarded the Nobel prize in 2009. Professor Elinor Olstrom's work has shown that societies and groups regularly devise rules and enforcement mechanisms that stop the degradation of nature. The traditional theory holds that pollution and depletion of resources would occur because individuals fail to recognise – or do not care about – their effect on others. However, her research has shown that people can manage resources tolerably well without rules imposed by the authorities if rules evolved over time, entitlements were clear, conflict-resolution measures were available and an individual's duty to maintain the common resource was in proportion to the benefits from exploiting it. Notably, she found that the most important criterion for the success of such schemes was this (and this characteristic should be no surprise given the earlier arguments in this book): the active participation in setting and enforcing the collective rules to manage the common good[169].

The tortured debate over healthcare illustrates this problem.

In the US, a system dominated by massive private-insurance companies has created enormous and escalating costs for American business and many other distortions and inequities, particularly for the poor who have been excluded from private-insurance provision. Vast sums may be spent to prolong the lives of the well-insured for merely a few days, while many millions of the poor endure chronic or even fatal illness without treatment. Ideologues from the Right, but also the heavily lobbied representatives of both Democrats and Republicans, successfully destroyed the "public option" – that government should provide insurance – in the 2009 healthcare bill. Needless to say, the enormous health-insurance industry spent over $600 million on lobbying in the two years before the bill.

Meanwhile, in the UK, where public provision – and universal coverage – of healthcare is entrenched in the form of the National Health Service, there is very appropriate concern, amongst both doctors and patients, at the overweening and barely accountable bureaucracy seemingly necessary to run the system, and the sometimes arbitrary choices it must make, for instance, that certain drugs be denied to the sick because they are too expensive.

In both countries the fundamental truth of any healthcare system, whether public or private, is barely acknowledged – that there must be some system of rationing of care. Otherwise, demand for healthcare is insatiable; its costs would eventually consume the entire economy, as the costs of America's insurance-based system indeed threaten to do if unchecked. And in neither country does anyone moot what seems the obvious, equitable and democratic solution – that the necessary rationing decisions of who should receive care at what cost be made not by government bureaucracies or by insurance companies, but by the people most affected and most capable – doctors *and* their patients.

In Britain, proposals by the Conservative/Liberal Democrat government will devolve choices of care to GPs, allowing them to "purchase" care on behalf of their patients. But this covert attempt to introduce the market into the National Health Service is both disingenuous and inadequate: it fails to include the many other doctors and nurses in hospitals and other "service providers"; it fails to provide for any negotiation or debate among those most concerned over the necessary choices of healthcare; but above all it fails to include the patients, who, one might think, have the most at stake after all. They are instead treated as but mute and powerless objects of care and policy, as usual.

Arrangements to include both doctors and patients equally in the provision of healthcare have worked in the past, and work today. In earlier eras, cooperative or "friendly" societies pooled the contributions of working families to provide care when illness or death struck. Today, healthcare cooperatives are able successfully to manage and deploy their available resources according to what their members (i.e. patients) – and not the insurance companies or bureaucrats – regard as important. This possibility is barely mentioned in the US debate, presumably because cooperatives have no lobbyists. If it does arise, the idea of cooperatives is often hysterically attacked both by the insurance industry, which claims cooperatives are public provision in disguise, or by advocates for the "public option", who argue that non-profits cannot possibly compete with the massive cartels of the insurance giants. Neither argument stands up to scrutiny, for cooperatives would operate without taxpayer support, and by their non-profit nature would be less expensive than profit-maximising private-insurance companies: the CEO of one of the largest US healthcare companies earns over $33 million[170]. This nakedly self-interested scepticism is belied by the success of such cooperatives as Group Health, which has successfully provided reasonably costed healthcare to its members since 1947; it is governed by a board composed of its members[171].

The company, the primary unit of economic activity, is not a fixed entity and can be, and is being, transformed. The distinction between for-profit companies and not-for-profit charities is blurring as companies incorporate social and environmental responsibilities into their business model, not as add-ons but as intrinsic to the way that they work. Chris Meyer of the Harvard Business Review has called this "internalising the externalities" of the traditional economic model of the firm. While it is easy to be cynical about this development, and it is right to criticise the "greenwashing" of otherwise unchanged corporate practice, there is also here unarguably an opportunity. Encouraged by an NGO[172], scores of companies are choosing to eschew high-carbon fuel sources, like oil sands. In another initiative, thousands of the world's largest companies are voluntarily publishing data on their electricity consumption and carbon emissions in a collective effort to reduce emissions, organised by another small NGO, the Carbon Disclosure Project[173]. Utilising the power of peer and investor pressure rather than government regulation, the project organises letters to companies representing investors holding $55 trillion, pressing them to participate and thus be scrutinised on their environmental records. Other banks are ceasing to lend to the mining companies that blast the tops off Appalachian mountains in Virginia, not because this activity is illegal – it is not – but because of the growing damage to their reputations[174].

Consumers through their own choices can reinforce these trends: "when you're buying, you're voting", as the founder of Stonybridge Farms, the organic dairy producer, once exhorted. Every choice carries economic, political and environmental effects. It will soon be easy to monitor the labour and environmental records of manufacturers on the web and perhaps at the point of purchase; at projectlabel.org and other sites the embryonic form of such indices is already visible[175]. The space is available to rethink what companies do, to realise at last that their impacts are inherently political, but also to embrace and exploit that reality. Whether this transformation is positive or negative will be determined by simple, small everyday choices: the actions of those who comprise these new commercial, social and in fact highly political entities.

A French philosopher was once asked about the significance of "May 1968", the demonstrations and eruption of spontaneous

public anger in France and elsewhere[176] . He replied that the importance of May '68 was that it was the opposite of what the Communists
declared as the correct manner of the revolution. The Communists
had said that the revolution should be:

> Not here but somewhere else, like Cuba, Vietnam or elsewhere.
> Not now but tomorrow, in the future.
>
> And not you but the Communists instead, the appointed
> cadres.

> Rejecting this injunction, the May '68ers had declared instead
> "Here, Now, Us!".

The next chapter suggests some core principles that might guide any
individual or group wanting to take up the flag on any issue. This is a
politics that offers the possibility of yet-unimagined outcomes, not
those defined by our current structures and ways of doing business.

This manifesto is rather short and simple. It does not proclaim
a particular end-state or utopia, but instead a series of methods for
how the individual might engage upon the issues that most concern
them. The methods themselves are the message: a way of doing
things that promises greater mutual concern, meaning and community of purpose.

The ends are indeed the means.

8

Kill the King: Nine Principles for Action

SO MUCH FOR ALL THE THEORY, STORIES AND IDEAS, WHAT is to be done? Here is a short list of principles that may guide action, along with a few examples. The principles are by no means exclusive, nor comprehensive: mere pointers, not instructions.

1. Excavate your convictions

This is perhaps the hardest step, and I have the least useful to say about it (apart from Gandhi's and Claudette Colvin's examples, cited earlier). This must be an individual discovery of what you care most about. And this is the most fundamental point: do not let others tell you what to care about. This can only be a *leaderless* revolution, if it is to succeed. Make up your own mind. Examine your own reactions. This is difficult in the banality yet ubiquity of contemporary culture, with its cacophony of voices and opinion. Space for contemplation is all too rare. But here's one suggestion which is doubtless revealing of my own dyspeptic disposition: what makes you angry? What never fails to irritate you for its stupidity and injustice? That may be the thing you should take up arms against. It was for me, and anger puts fuel in the tank.

2. Who's got the money, who's got the gun?

Before taking action, assess the landscape. This simple axiom will point to the main sources of influence, and obstacles. Thanks to the internet, it is now possible to discover pretty rapidly who has a stake in any given situation, and thus who might alter it. When revolt against the dictatorial rule of Colonel Gadhaffi broke out in Libya in February 2011, information on which companies were doing business with his regime was available in detail, triggering immediate pressure for these companies and individuals to disengage. The same week that the revolt broke out several major oil companies announced their refusal to do business with the regime, under pressure from their own investors organised by a campaign group, the Genocide Intervention Network. The Sunlight Foundation published a chart of the lobbyists, including former Congressmen, who were paid by Gadhaffi to promote his interests. The Director of the London School of Economics was forced to resign just days after the revolt began when it was revealed that his university had received substantial funds from the regime to train its élites. One welcome consequence of the vast mesh of connections that now comprises the globalised world is that even distant situations may be affected by actors close to home, who may be susceptible to pressure. Find them, use it.

3. Act as if the means are the end

In the summer of 1968, Soviet tanks entered Czechoslovakia, crushing the "Prague spring" of emerging political freedom. Massively outgunned by the Soviet tank columns, the Czechoslovak army gave way. Demonstrators attacked the tanks on city streets with stones and petrol bombs. The Soviet troops responded with machine-gun fire. One protesting student set himself on fire in Prague's Wenceslas Square. Thousands were arrested, many to be imprisoned for long sentences. The leader who had encouraged the liberalisation, Alexander Dubček, was forced to capitulate, under duress signing an agreement with Moscow to reverse the reforms. Czechoslovakia endured more than another twenty years of communism before democracy at last dawned.

That summer of '68, thousands of Czechoslovak students had travelled abroad to work. The invasion left them stranded. Among them was P, who spent the summer picking fruit in Kent. The Soviet invasion gave him a terrible choice: should he stay in Britain, or return to Communist dictatorship? Compounding his dilemma, he had nowhere to stay. A story appeared in *The Times*, reporting on the predicament of the stranded students: an organisation was quickly set up to find them shelter.

My parents read the story and decided to offer refuge to a Czechoslovak student. P. arrived shortly afterwards. Though my parents that summer were caring for three children under four (my brother and I are twins, my sister only twenty-three months older), and had more than enough on their plate, they gave P. a bed. He stayed for several weeks while considering what to do. After much agonising, he eventually decided to stay in England. By chance, he had hitched a lift from a professor at Warwick University. That professor liked P. and offered him a place on his course. P.'s studies were duly arranged and he completed his degree, frequently spending his holidays at our house in South London. He went on to become an expert in fish storage, the father of two children and now lives in Scotland.

Thirty years later my parents gave refuge once more, this time to a Zimbabwean escaping the repressive rule of Robert Mugabe. Now they were living in a smaller flat, their children long having flown the nest. My father recalled that it wasn't as simple as giving P. a room back in 1968. Asylum laws in Britain are now strictly enforced: my father was required regularly to report to the local police station that Ngoni was indeed staying with them and had not absconded. Finding study opportunities and work was also harder, though not impossible. (Universities and other educational institutions are today themselves required to check the legal status of their foreign students, and report any non-compliance; thus, in effect, making them arms of the state.)

I asked my parents why they had taken P. in. Neither could really remember, answering my question with vague responses like "We could" or "It felt like a good thing to do". Now with my own small children, and exhausted by the tasks of their care, I marvel at my parents' hospitality. Suddenly, my mother remembered something, "This might be relevant" she said, and recalled a piece of family history of which I had had no inkling. My mother then told me that my grandparents – her parents – took in a Jewish girl from Germany during the war. My mother had been small at the time, and couldn't now remember anything about the girl except a vague memory of her name.

Life is about means not ends. There is no utopia to be gained, there is no end-state that is static and eternal, once accomplished. This was one of the great lies of communism. Likewise, capitalism offers the great deception that thanks to its machinations everyone will be richer in the future, thus justifying gross inequality and humiliation today.

Instead it's all here, and it's all now. Nirvana tomorrow does not justify avoidable suffering now. We and our world are in constant motion, responding to each other without cease. This is one reason why Francis Fukuyama was wrong to declare the End of History with the triumph of liberal democracies after the collapse of communism. No state of affairs lasts for ever.

4. Refer to the cosmopolitan criterion

This is a pretentious way of saying: give consideration to the needs of others, but based upon what *they* say are their needs, not what *we* think their needs are. The so-called "Golden Rule" states that you should do to others as you would be done to. This rule is often lazily touted as a universal rule applicable in all circumstances, thus satisfying the famous categorical imperative of Immanuel Kant*. This

---

* The categorical imperative was created by Kant as a measure of whether moral rules are good ones or not. The test of any moral rule is whether it can be universally applied, i.e. is it valid in all conceivable circumstances?

rule is in fact dramatically wrong – and indeed fails the Kantian test – for it assumes that *we* know what *they* want or need. This logic, taken to its extreme, leads to the arrogant violence of the neo-conservatives who believe that they have the right to use force in the interests of those they are attacking: to kill people for their own good. The invasion of Iraq was clearly motivated by this logic: that the Iraqi people needed democracy, even at the cost of their own lives (we know of course that the reason was not to combat an imminent threat[177]). One hundred thousand people and perhaps more died as a result. Instability was triggered that endures, with accompanying violence, to this day. Needless to say, those advocating the war never consulted those who would do the dying for their lofty goals, whether Allied soldiers or Iraq's civilians.

There is instead a much simpler way to decide what to do and how to calibrate your own action. Ask people what they want. They are usually more than willing to tell you.

With the internet, ubiquitous mobile phones and Facebook, it is no longer credible to claim that we cannot find out what people "over there" are thinking. During the Arab revolutions of early 2011, pro-democracy protesters broadcast their tweets direct from Cairo's Tahrir Square, their compelling 140-character messages shattering generations-old Western stereotypes of the Middle East and the "Arab street". Websites like Global Voices now aggregate citizen reports from all over the world, but from close to the ground. And those voices are clear and fresh and urgent.

There are in fact almost no moral rules, including very obvious ones such as "do not kill", which pass this test without controversy (for instance, would it not have been right to kill Hitler if given the chance?). This demonstrates the ultimate contingency of all moral rules, and thus the need for discussion and negotiation when rules conflict. Perhaps it also demonstrates the futility of asserting universal moral rules about anything, or perhaps the futility of declaring universal tests of moral rules.

5. Address those suffering the most

A few years ago, my wife and I travelled to northern Mali, to the southern reaches of the Sahara desert north of Timbuktu. We were on our honeymoon. We decided to take a camel tour with some Tuareg tribesmen. The trip appealed to our sense of adventure. The camels carried us far from Timbuktu into a romantic landscape of trackless desert wastes.

As night fell, we were brought to a Tuareg encampment. It turned out to be the tented home of our guide, a young Tuareg man who wore loose robes and a turban of deep blue cotton, wound around his head and neck, to protect him from the blasting rays of the sun. We slept under a vast and magnificent canopy of stars, our baggage stacked around us as a barricade against the camels, who had been known to tread upon sleeping humans.

We awoke to a clear and silent dawn, and wandered to the tents to join our guide and his family for breakfast. And here the romance began to shatter. The guide's young wife sat with her baby under a rough screen. The previous evening, in the dark, their shelter had appeared as a robust canvas tent. But it turned out to be a patchwork of plastic and hessian sacks. The young woman and her baby were besieged incessantly by large swarms of flies, which would land in waves upon her and her sleeping baby's face. The woman, clearly exhausted, perhaps by hunger or illness – we could not tell – listlessly swatted the flies away, but they would settle nonetheless on the baby's eyes and lips, in swarms so thick they appeared as a blanket on the poor child's face.

Shocked, my wife and I drank our tea and ate our bread in silence. The guide's father joined us. Talking to his son, he would with horrible frequency emit an awful hacking cough. As he coughed, he doubled over in pain, his throat broadcasting the most disgusting sounds of collecting phlegm and blood, which he would periodically spit onto the sand. He clearly had tuberculosis or some other serious respiratory disease. He was desperately thin, and appeared enfeebled to the point of death.

Conversing in broken French with the guide, we asked what was wrong. The young man answered that he didn't know. The old man had never seen a doctor. But, his son said, he had some drugs. He spoke to the old man, who pulled out a half-used packet of paracetamol, its use-by date long past. Perhaps, ventured the young man, we could give any drugs we might have. Of course we obliged and ended up handing over perhaps a couple of hundred dollars to the guide, in excessive payment for the trip. The old man had noticed my spectacles and exclaimed in delight when I handed them to him to try. I gave him these too (I had a spare pair).

We were appalled and upset by this encounter with desperate poverty. We were glad to return from the camel trip. After leaving Mali (to be honest, with some relief), we have not however had any further contact with the guide or his family. We give some money to charity on a regular basis, but it is not in truth very much, and certainly not enough to cause us any significant limits on our own consumption.

How should one respond to suffering? Consider two contrasting answers to this question. In a recent book, the philosopher Peter Singer uses an example to illustrate our obligation to others, including those far away who may be unknown to us[178]. A small girl is drowning in a lake in front of you and you are the only person who can rescue the child. You are however wearing expensive $400 shoes which will be ruined if you dive in to rescue the girl. Singer believes, of course, that the answer to such a dilemma is clear and accepted by almost everyone: you must save the child, but ruin the shoes.

Singer argues that in reality the crisis of the drowning child is presented to us constantly. Every minute, eighteen children die of hunger and preventable disease: 27,000 every day. It costs moreover far less than $400 to save them. Just as if the child were drowning directly in front of us, the moral imperative is clear and precise: we must act, even if there is a cost to ourselves, albeit a small one. Using calculations by economist Jeffrey Sachs and others, Singer suggests that if everyone in the rich world gave a mere one percent of their income, poverty and preventable disease in the world could be effectively eradicated. Singer has set up a website where individuals can make such pledges*. Singer reportedly donates twenty-five percent of his own income to charity.

At the other end of the moral spectrum, 19th-century German *über*-anarchist Max Stirner believed that the idea of morality is basically absurd and manufactured by those who cloak their selfish purposes in pseudo-universal principles which have no other origin. There is no such thing as society (as Margaret Thatcher too once famously observed). It is instead the individual and their own desires which matter. Thus, the individual is required to do nothing but follow their own wishes to the fullest, wherever this may lead. To do anything else is to act falsely and to invite falseness from others in response, thus risking an order – or rather disorder – based on dishonest and manufactured ideas.

Stirner's ideas imply that we have no obligation to dive in to save the child in Singer's thought experiment. Almost everyone would find this appalling. Yet, as Singer has observed, this is what we consistently do. Very few individuals give even one percent of their income to those worse-off than them. Several thousand people have made such pledges at Singer's website, but of course this is but a tiny drop in the bucket. Most rich governments have failed to fulfill their own oft-repeated pledges to commit 0.7 percent of their GDP to development aid. The funds required to meet the UN's "Millennium Development Goals", established in 2000 as achievable targets to reduce poverty and disease, have not been provided, including by the G8, G20, and UN General Assembly, which have, on repeated occasions, promised all efforts to do so.

So what's the flaw with Singer's reasoning? Why are we unconvinced to help the distant poor? Are we inherently selfish, more

---

* www.thelifeyoucansave.com

Max Stirner than Peter Singer? It is easy for a moralist to say that the needs of a Somali woman dying in childbirth should be as compelling to us as if she were our sister. But, as Singer has disappointingly discovered, such reasoning has little lasting impact.

If a child drowns before us, how tiny would be the minority who refused to act because they didn't want to get their expensive shoes wet, and what would the majority do to that person once they found out? Somehow we need to find a way to stimulate the emotional connection that evokes compassion, an emotion that, unlike moral rules, seems shared among humanity (with some sociopathic exceptions). How is compassion between people generated? One clear and straightforward answer presents itself: the encounter.

Missing in the reasoning of Singer is any sense of what Stirner by contrast believed necessary, intrinsic and inevitable – engagement. Stirner firmly rejected any *a priori* assumption of what such engagement might produce, least of all that it should result in an obligation to render help to others. But it makes sense that engagement produces a different kind of reaction, and a different conversation, than mere knowledge. It is clearly not enough to know that people "out there" are suffering. But locate oneself next to that suffering, as my wife and I found in the Malian desert, and the reaction becomes entirely different, even though the facts remain exactly the same.

Thus, 19th-century Stirner may paradoxically provide a truer guide to action in the connected 21st century than contemporary philosophers who, with great humanity, urge that we accept the obligation to rescue the drowning child. For it is engagement – or rather its absence – that may precisely explain why the Singers, and the proponents of the UN Millennium Development Goals, or the 0.7 percent goal, or the Bonos or Bobs have failed to convince those who have so much, to hand over even a little bit, and make a huge life-saving difference, to the billions who have so desperately little.

And from this, one conclusion stands out. States, borders and indeed institutions in general must by their very nature limit our engagement with one another; they channel, frame, render detached and sometimes obstruct the vast mêlée of human interaction. And by limiting that engagement, somewhere along the way our compassion is eviscerated. The requirement for engagement, as demanded too by the cosmopolitan criterion (above), is reinforced.

The 21st century offers engagement at levels unprecedented in human history. As Kwame Anthony Appiah observes in his elegant essay on cosmopolitanism* a stroller along New York's Fifth Avenue will pass more nationalities in half an hour than an ancient Roman would have encountered in a lifetime. The multi-hued society of America, Britain, Europe and more or less everywhere, increasingly, offers commensurately varied chances for encounters with the hitherto-distant Other, be they Somali, Kyrgyz, Malay or Tongan. Abroad is more and more located right here. At least four hundred million people now live in countries not of their birth. And these are just the first-generation immigrants; add a second and third generation and the proportion grows much higher. Over two million of London's seven and a half million inhabitants were born overseas. Heterogeneity will become routine. Whether we like it or not, we shall have to engage.

The sharp and unprecedented increases in immigration in almost all developed countries have triggered anguished debates in Europe and the US. In Switzerland, a popular referendum agreed a ban on mosque-building, although there were very few mosques already. In the Netherlands, the 2010 general election saw a significant swing to the far-right anti-immigration party of Geert Wilders. In the US, Arizona agreed a law allowing police to stop anyone merely on the suspicion of being an illegal immigrant.

And at first sight, it appears that fears of the effect of an influx of outsiders on established stable societies are well-placed. Robert

---

* *Cosmopolitanism: Ethics in a World of Strangers.*

Putnam has found that the more mixed a society, the lower its indices of "social capital" – trust, altruism, associations, active cooperation – and the higher its indices of social fragmentation – crime, for instance[179]. But crucially, he found that these reductions in social solidarity and "social capital" were *short term* effects. At first, it appears, local societies "hunker down"; trust declines, even within members of the same race or ethnic group. People retreat into privacy.

However, in the longer run, the outcomes are more positive. New forms of association and social solidarity emerge. In more hybrid societies, there is more creativity – as measured, for instance, by the number of Nobel prizes. Immigration is associated with more rapid economic growth, although short-term effects should not be overlooked, particularly on the lowest paid, who tend to feel first the effects of more intensified competition for jobs from immigrants. The evidence suggests that immigration from the global South to the global North greatly enhances development in the South, partly because of the flow of remittances from new immigrants to their families "back home" but also because of the transfer of technology and new ideas through immigrant networks. This effect is reportedly so powerful that it may offset the "brain drain" costs to the southern countries sending the migrants. Putnam cites evidence of yet greater positive effect, including a World Bank study that estimates that increasing annual northward immigration by only three percentage points might produce net benefits greater than meeting all national (US) targets for development assistance *plus* cancelling all Third World debt *plus* abolishing all barriers to Third World trade.

A further reason to address those suffering the most is simply this: here, you can make the most difference.

6. Consult and negotiate

One of the many deficits of the single-issue campaigns that today offer false promise of political effects is that they offer no negotiation with those most affected, or those who might oppose. They therefore offer no real prospect of lasting effect. Discussion with those affected is not a virtuous addendum to any campaign, it is in fact essential for success.

When I was responsible for sanctions policy on Iraq at the UK Mission to the United Nations, we were often approached by campaigning NGOs who wanted us to alter our policies, and lift or amend sanctions in order to end the humanitarian suffering in Iraq. They were of course right, but that didn't mean that they were effective.

In general, I avoided meeting these campaigners, well aware that I would be subjected to a rhetorical finger-wagging session. It was difficult for campaigners to find out who was dealing with Iraq in our mission, and we didn't make it easy for them (it's still very difficult, even though now the mission has the inevitable official website, as opaque as the smoked glass at the mission's entrance). Only rarely did the campaigners manage to identify me, and persuade me to meet them.

Such meetings were tedious and predictable. Invariably, the campaigners would march into my office, then lecture me about the immorality of what my government was doing, demanding change – but rarely specifying in any detail what that change should be: just change! Discussion would be tense and confrontational; the meetings would end with much relief, for me at least. I sensed too that the objective for the campaigners was often the fact of the meeting, which they could now parade as effective action on their part: the meeting alone amounting to a victory. Of course, it was not.

No doubt such lobbying made them feel better. But the effect on me of course was to make me more determined to avoid such encounters in future. Thanks to the superficiality of the campaigners' arguments, I was able easily to dismiss them. They forgot that I worked on Iraq full-time every day, and was steeped in the arguments and data to justify and defend our policies.

Two academics from Notre Dame University in Indiana used a

different approach. They approached the individual officials involved in the British and US governments, asking to collect information about our policies. They were polite and patient. They came to meet me several times. After several meetings, they offered a detailed set of proposals to change our policy, ideas that addressed our concerns to limit Iraq's potential to rearm while minimising the potential negative humanitarian effects of sanctions. The US State Department held a discussion meeting with many officials concerned to meet the academics and hear their proposals. Eventually, their ideas were adopted as British-American policy and led to a major amendment of sanctions policy, that was put into place in 2002*.

It was too late, and such a policy should have been enacted from the beginning of comprehensive sanctions on Iraq in 1990. But the point is clear.

Negotiation should ideally be direct, not through intermediaries. When my wife and I bought our apartment in New York City, we were represented in the negotiations by our real-estate agent and eventually by a lawyer. The negotiations quickly deteriorated. Every move by the seller was scrutinised for deviousness, every motive and communication was immediately placed under suspicion. When the seller sought to delay the sale after we had agreed a price, this was seized upon as a sign of "bad faith". Lawyers reported antagonistic exchanges. As stalemate beckoned, we proposed a meeting with the sellers. Tense and anticipating a conflict, we arrived at the apartment, to find – needless to say – a perfectly affable couple who merely wanted to stay in the apartment for a few weeks before their new home was ready. For them the alternative was taking their small children to live in a hotel.

---

* The new sanctions policy altered controls on exports to Iraq so that everything was permitted except goods that appeared on a "control list" of items that might be used for weapons manufacture. Previously, nothing could be exported except goods which were expressly permitted, case-by-case, by the UN sanctions committee (with some exceptions).

7. "Big picture, small deeds"

The innovation company ?What If! offers this maxim as a way to overcome the inertia that too often stymies change. ?What If! trains clients in how to be innovative but found that sometimes, though inspired by their training away-day, their trainees would still fail to implement the techniques they had learned. It was simply too overwhelming to change the prevailing culture of their everyday workplace. To counter this problem, ?What If! propose a simple philosophy: keep in mind the overall change you wish to achieve, but act a little every day to make it reality.

Though transposed to the corporate world, this technique echoes the "small steps" proposed by Mahatma Gandhi to achieve profound and enduring change. There is an ancient Chinese proverb to the same effect (the internet tells me): "It is better to take many small steps in the right direction than a great leap forward then stumble backwards", sage advice that Mao Tse-Tung clearly ignored in forcing China's "Great Leap Forward" in the 1960s, a disastrously sudden and poorly designed series of "reforms" that forced peasants from their land and led to the starvation and death of perhaps more than thirty million, the greatest loss of life of its own population directly caused by any government in history. Perhaps recognising this catastrophe, Mao's successor Deng Xiaoping proposed a more pragmatic method of change: "crossing the river by feeling the stones".

This metaphor is compelling and offers a more pragmatic approach: stones are palpable, material, solid. The steps of any strategy should be concrete; not rhetorical but practical. internet campaigns clearly fail this criterion; volunteering at a local school does not. Mahatma Gandhi distilled the epic struggle against British colonial rule into a simple act that anyone could practise: making salt.

And the goal must be epic. The spirit soars at the momentous challenge, not the banal. Break that challenge down into small, practical, daily tasks, and get to work. Though the steps towards it may be humble, find a goal that is great: end poverty, prevent war, save the planet. Locate your objective, grasp your flag, then march deliberately towards the enemy. If you do so with courage and conviction, others will surely follow.

8. Use non-violence

Alexander Berkman was an anarchist who passionately detested the widespread exploitation and abuse of workers in industrial America of the late 19th century. An immigrant from Russia, he was influenced by anarchist thinkers and groups in New York City, where he became a close friend of the famous anarchist Emma Goldman. As retailed by Goldman in her autobiography *My Life*, and Berkman in his (*Prison Memoirs of an Anarchist*), both were deeply affected by the Haymarket affair or massacre, as it is sometimes known: the name of the event an indicator, as it often is, of the prejudices of the namer.

On 4 May 1886, at the Haymarket Square in Chicago, at a rally in support of striking workers, an unknown person threw a bomb at police as they dispersed the gathering. The bomb blast and ensuing gunfire resulted in the deaths of eight police officers and an unknown number of civilians. In the trial that followed, eight anarchists were tried for murder despite paltry evidence against them. Four were put to death, and one committed suicide in prison. The judge declared, "Not because you have caused the Haymarket bomb, but because you are anarchists, you are on trial". To this day, debate continues about the true identity of the bomber.

It is clear from both Goldman's and Berkman's memoirs that they were radicalised by what they saw as a profound injustice. Both came to believe that only dramatic, and if necessary violent, acts – the *attentat* – would galvanise the working population to rise up against a deeply unjust system. The opportunity for such an act was soon to present itself.

In June 1892, workers at a steel plant in Homestead, Pennsylvania, were locked out after pay negotiations failed between the Carnegie

Steel Company and the Amalgamated Association of Iron and Steel Workers. The result was one of the first organised strikes in American labour history. Andrew Carnegie had placed his factories, and indeed later his industrial empire, under the control of Henry Clay Frick. Carnegie publicly supported the rights of workers to join unions and employ collective bargaining. Privately, however, he encouraged Frick to break the strike, and with it, the union.

Frick locked the union workers out and placed barbed-wire fences, searchlights and watchtowers around the factory. He hired non-union workers to take the strikers' jobs and get the factory going again, but they were unable to break through the union's picket lines. So Frick hired three hundred armed guards from the Pinkerton Detective Agency to break the picket lines. When the Pinkerton guards arrived at the factory on the morning of 6 July, a gunfight broke out. Nine union workers and seven guards were killed during the fight, which lasted twelve hours.

There was widespread outrage at Frick's actions and the bloody attack of the "Pinkertons". Berkman and Goldman decided to assassinate Frick. This was the opportunity for the violent *attentat* to rouse the working class to revolt. There was no viler capitalist than Frick: for a while he was known as "America's most hated man". In his memoir, Berkman recounts his romantic fascination with the extreme act:

> Could anything be nobler than to die for a grand, a sublime Cause [*sic*]? Why, the very life of a true revolutionist has no other purpose, no significance whatever, save to sacrifice it on the altar of the beloved People.

Berkman's execution of the plan however was amateurish. His plan was to assassinate Frick and commit suicide afterwards; Goldman's rôle was to explain Berkman's motives after his death. First, Berkman tried to make a bomb, but he failed. Berkman and Goldman then pooled their meagre savings to buy a handgun, and a suit for Berkman to wear for the assassination attempt.

On 23 July 1892, Berkman entered Frick's office armed with a gun and a sharpened steel file. Frick dived under a chair and began to yell. Berkman shot Frick three times, then grappled with him and stabbed him in the leg. Others in the office came to Frick's rescue and beat Berkman unconscious. He was convicted of attempted murder and given a 22-year prison sentence. Frick survived the attack.

As he later related in his prison memoir, Berkman encountered a Homestead striker soon after his imprisonment. Berkman immediately romanticises the man as the embodiment of the workers' struggle. He is enthralled to meet an actual striker, a true-blooded member of the working classes. Here at last Berkman would find his vindication. But the meeting produces nothing but bitter disappointment. The striker decries Berkman's assassination attempt. "We are law-abiding people", he says, adding that the workers don't want anything to do with the "anachrists" as he misnames them.

Other workers on whose behalf Berkman attempted the *attentat* were not impressed either. There was no worker uprising as a result of Berkman's effort; his attack was widely condemned, including by unions, workers and even other anarchists. Negative publicity from the attempted assassination resulted in the collapse of the Homestead strike. Two thousand five hundred men lost their jobs, and most of the workers who stayed had their wages halved.

In 1910, Frick purchased an entire city block in New York at Fifth Avenue and 70th Street to construct a huge mansion, to serve as his home and to house his enormous collection of art and artefacts. A heavy, stone building, built to a massive size, "the Frick", as it is widely known, contains many magnificent objects and paintings. One of them is Holbein's exquisite portrait of Sir Thomas More, who is famed for his principled refusal to recant his Catholic faith after the English monarch, King Henry VIII, had broken with

Rome, and established the Church of England, in order to divorce his wife. More is also known as the author of *Utopia*, the fictional depiction of a perfect society.

There is no memorial to Alexander Berkman.

If not violence, then what? All too often, the debate is framed as violence or nothing; pacifism as mere inactivity. As the world contemplated how to respond to Colonel Gadhaffi's brutal repression of unrest in Libya, media commentators dwelt on the debate over the imposition of No Fly Zones or other forms of military intervention, ignoring the many various non-military but nonetheless coercive measures available: these were complicated, and thus ill suited to the Punch and Judy requirements of soundbite debate[180]. The whole framing of such debates suggests that violence is strong, the absence of violence weak. Pacifism is invariably portrayed as a kind of "do nothing" philosophy.

Non-violence resolves this problem. Non-violent methods are not doing nothing. Instead, they are forceful methods that can be highly effective but avoid injury and bloodshed, while gaining moral authority from the rejection of violence.

To get down to specifics, non-violent action can take many different forms. In his essential and concise essay "From Dictatorship to Democracy", Gene Sharp lists no fewer than 198 different non-violent methods*, but here are three:

Boycott – The word *boycott* entered the English language thanks to Captain Charles Boycott, the land agent of an absentee landlord in Ireland. In 1880, harvests had been poor so the landlord offered his tenants a ten percent reduction in their rents. The tenants demanded a twenty-five percent reduction, but were refused. Boycott then attempted to evict eleven tenants from the land. The Irish nationalist Charles Stewart Parnell proposed that ostracism was more

---

* I also recommend Mark Kurlansky's *Non-violence: The History of a Dangerous Idea*.

powerful than violence: greedy landlords and land agents like Boycott should be made pariahs. Despite the short-term economic hardship they incurred, Boycott's workers stopped work in the fields and stables, as well as in his house. Local businessmen ceased trading with him, and the local postman refused to deliver mail. Boycott soon found himself isolated, and unable to hire anyone to harvest the crops. Eventually fifty outsiders volunteered to do the work, but they had to be escorted by one thousand policemen and soldiers, despite the fact that local leaders had said that there would be no violence, and none in fact materialised. This protection ended up costing far more than the harvest was worth. After the harvest, the "boycott" was successfully continued.

Gandhi organised a boycott of British goods. In Montgomery, Alabama, African-Americans boycotted segregated buses. The National Negro Convention boycotted slave-produced goods in 1830. Today boycotts are even easier to organise, thanks to the internet. The Dutch bank ING was forced to cancel bonuses for its senior staff after thousands of its customers threatened to withdraw their deposits, and thus risk a run on the bank. A Facebook and Twitter boycott campaign erupted after news emerged that the chief executive was to be awarded a £1 million bonus despite the bank having received €10bn in state aid to keep afloat, having frozen pensions and given staff only a one percent pay rise. Dutch politicians later voted for a hundred percent retrospective tax on all bonuses paid to executives at institutions that had received state aid as a result of the financial crisis[181].

Isolate – The withdrawal of social approval for individuals is distressing to those subjected to it. Public shaming is an under-utilised tool. To politicians and public figures who bask in public attention, its denial can be painful indeed. But it is today more available with the global panopticon of the internet, where many acts are now public.

In New York City, a group of women were fed up with the

harassment they routinely faced on public subways or the street, ranging from unwelcome sexual comments to groping and stalking. Frustrated with cultural attitudes that suggested such abuse was an inevitable price of being a woman, they founded a group to fight back, called "I holla back" (www.ihollaback.org). Emily May founded Hollaback with friends five years ago. Today it has chapters in six American cities, along with others in Britain, Canada and Australia. The group has recently developed an iPhone application to allow women immediately to log and report such incidents, and, if possible, photograph the perpetrators. The aim is to produce a comprehensive picture – and identify "hotspots" – of such harassment, citywide and even nationwide. Reports will be forwarded to police for action, including particular zones of repeated activity. But there are obvious obstacles for the police to press convictions – they cannot solve the problem alone. By identifying and exhibiting the photographs of perpetrators, the group also hopes to shame the men who carry out the abuse, and create new cultural attitudes to replace the old: to render harassment socially unacceptable[182].

In a more international context, a white farmer in newly independent Zimbabwe once told me that the economic and political isolation of white minority-dominated Rhodesia may not have undermined the economy sufficiently to force the Rhodesian government to give up its apartheid practices. We could survive economically, she told me, but once we were under international sanctions, she said, we knew one thing with certainty – that white minority rule could not last for ever.

Sabotage – This method is to be used only in the most extreme circumstances of gross injustice and repression, such as slavery or killing, and when other non-violent methods have failed. A recent illustration of the inherent risks and ambiguous consequences of sabotage, even of the non-violent kind, is the story of the "Stuxnet" computer worm, which appears to have been deliberately designed to interfere with Iran's nuclear programme. The worm was highly sophisticated, suggesting that states (perhaps Israel or the United States) were behind its creation. Concealing itself in the operating system of computers that control industrial mechanisms, Stuxnet reportedly works by speeding up the gas centrifuges used to enrich uranium so that the centrifuges are damaged or destroyed. All the while, the control systems continue to indicate that everything is normal. The effects of Stuxnet are not clear, and Iran has admitted to only limited damage from the virus. Illustrating the dangers of using such techniques however, there is now debate that the way has been cleared for others to use similar devices – which are effectively sabotage, albeit by the most modern methods. In effect, a new front has been opened in conflict, with few rules to govern it. As one journalist put it: "we have crossed a threshold and there is no turning back"[183]. There are now belated calls for new international agreements to prohibit such cyberwarfare, while others comment that enforcement of such rules would in any case be all but impossible, given the intrinsic anonymity and complexity of the web. If you are going to use these tools, it would be wise to ensure that they cannot then be turned against you. Hence the requirement to use non-violent sabotage only *in extremis*.

But for all the drawbacks of sabotage, it has one signal and perhaps over-riding virtue: it doesn't kill people.

In Wim Wenders's film *Wings of Desire* an old man is in a library in Berlin contemplating wartime photographs of dead children. He is very elderly and perhaps dying. He thinks to himself, "My heroes are no longer warriors and kings, but the things of peace . . . But so far no one has succeeded in singing an epic of peace. What is it about peace that its inspiration is not enduring? Why is its story so hard to tell?"

9. Kill the king

Chess may be useless as a metaphor for international relations but it carries one very important lesson. The only point of the game is to take the opponent's king. All other moves, and elegant plays with bishop or pawns, are but preliminary to this object. Do not be satisfied with process, but only with results. A campaign to end genocide, richly adorned with expensive video and glamorous celebrities, is worth nothing if it doesn't save a single life. Don't campaign for others to perform the action required to achieve change: do it yourself. Sending a text message or signing an internet petition is likely to achieve nothing, given that so little went into it.

The measure of any political action is not how many hits you get on the campaign website, how many followers you have on Twitter, or supporters on your Facebook page. The measure is effects in the real world on the thing you are trying to change: are there fewer nuclear weapons, has the dictator been overthrown, is one child saved from starvation?

Alexander the Great always aimed his forces at his enemy's strongest point. When that fell, the enemy collapsed. Kill the king! ("But remember: once the game is over, the king and pawn go back in the same box."*)

Individually, these principles are unexceptionable. Who can object to non-violent, step-by-step action, negotiated with those affected, and designed to address those in most suffering? But taken together, these principles in fact amount to a radically different form of political action from the contemporary cultural model which seems by contrast to amount to very little: vote for the government, maybe campaign a little to ask others to do things you want, and, if you're directly concerned, perhaps lobby government. The principles suggested above offer a rather more vigorous, directed but above all effective, indeed transformative, course of action. This is perhaps why there is such establishment hostility to these methods, and indeed to the word "anarchism", including the very peaceful and collaborative form proposed here: the employment of these methods will actually change things, including by changing the way that

---

* I am grateful to Twitter for this exquisite piece of wisdom.

things change. Those who benefit from the current *status quo* don't want you to know that.

One person following these principles will not cause a global revolution, though it may revolutionise their own lives. But the action of one may stimulate others. And if many adopt these principles, a revolution – a leaderless revolution – will eventually become manifest.

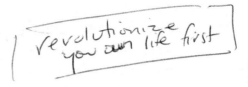

9

CONCLUSION: A VISION OF THE HUMAN

IN TOLSTOY'S *WAR AND PEACE*, SOME OF THE GREATEST scenes are those depicting the battles of the Franco/Russian wars that form the spine of Tolstoy's story. Cannonballs from Napoleon's artillery whizz overhead, cavalry horses rear and flare at fusillades of musket fire, men quiver with fear and red flows their blood.

In one scene during the Battle of Austerlitz, the Russian troops are taken by surprise by advancing French columns that suddenly emerge from the engulfing fog. As the French fire scatters them, the Russian front collapses and men flee in disarray. Weeping with anger and shame as he contemplates imminent defeat, Prince Andrew picks up a standard that a retreating officer has let fall. Heedless of the danger and the bullets cracking all around him, he gives a cry "piercing as a child's" and runs forward[184].

At first alone, his singular action is enough to rally the disordered infantrymen around him. Suddenly, one soldier moves and then another and soon the whole battalion runs forward shouting "Hurrah!" and overtakes him. Surrounded by charging troops, Prince Andrew races onward, now just twenty paces from the French guns, so close that he sees the fear and anger on the gunners' faces. Prince Andrew is struck down; others seize the flag to maintain the advance.

The battle is however lost. Later, Prince Andrew, now captured, lies gravely wounded in a French dressing station. Napoleon visits the injured Russians. Close to death, Prince Andrew is unmoved by the sight of his erstwhile hero. Looking into Napoleon's eyes,

> Prince Andrew thought of the insignificance of greatness, the unimportance of life which no one could understand, and the still greater unimportance of death, the meaning of which no one alive could understand or explain.

Tolstoy's battle scenes are of the microcosmic actions upon which pivot victory or defeat. These actions are not the function of the decisions of generals or emperors; they are the contingent decisions of individual officers and soldiers, like the courageous if ultimately futile charge of Prince Andrew. In an earlier chapter, the Battle of Schön Grabern is turned by the decision of one man, Timókhin, to charge the French lines, armed only with a sword. Such actions, almost random in appearance, are for Tolstoy what matters, not grand strategy or great men.

In his seminal essay *The Hedgehog and the Fox*, Isaiah Berlin analysed Tolstoy's view of history. *War and Peace*, according to Berlin, illustrates Tolstoy's scepticism of an account that suggested that events were under the control of leaders, states or governments. Such history, Tolstoy believed, accounted for not more than 0.001 percent of human affairs; it was moreover basically false. At Austerlitz, the Russian czar and his generals are described standing on a hilltop observing their troops descend into the thick fog enveloping the valley beneath them. It is a figurative illustration of their true knowledge, Tolstoy suggests. The chief Russian general, Kutúzov, enjoys heroic stature in Russian history, but Tolstoy portrays him groaning helplessly as his troops are attacked by surprise. Only Prince Andrew is decisive in response to the emerging catastrophe, and his response is not to issue orders but to seize the fallen flag and advance.

In Tolstoy's descriptions, real life was far too complex and contingent to be controlled by those at the summit of the pyramid. In fact, they could not be expected to understand it at all, because they were not part of it or close enough to witness it. Those who claimed such understanding were either naïve or were claiming knowledge for some other purpose – to wield power, for instance. In fact, as *War and Peace* shows, it is those at the base of the pyramid who make history, even if they do not know it.

This chimes with our own intuition. Battles are as life: the strange and inconstant mix of circumstance, random events and our own volition. Each is crucial; none is separable. The abstraction from this mix into a linear and polished narrative is inherently false. Equally false is any claim that human action is driven by a singular motive, such as the requirement to "maximise utility" as some economists would claim. Above all, life's events and decisions are microcosmic, even if in their totality they make up the whole world. Under scrutiny, any event, however great or small, is revealed as a fantastic and hugely complex mix of influence and causation, some inconsequential, some crucial. The closer one analyses any event, even one as familiar as one's own life, the more microcosmically complex its origins and consequences appear. There is no base, no bottom to these causes and effects, all are contingent upon others.

Tolstoy's hostility was directed against those who pretended that history was of great men and their decisions, a depiction he believed fundamentally inaccurate and dishonest. But it is not only historians who must reduce. Governments too are required to aggregate the world's incredible complexity into simple truths; to take the billions of actions and wishes of their populations and claim that they can be aggregated. This adduces no malign purpose to government; they have no alternative but to reduce in this way. They are required to do so in order to claim that they understand, in order that they can produce policies and decisions that offer to arbitrate the complexity.

The Hedgehog and the Fox is celebrated as a superb analysis of Tolstoy's writing and historical views, and a seminal work on politics and our understanding of the world. Oddly, however, Berlin does not explore how Tolstoy's writing, and the view of history intrinsic in it, informed the writer's politics, instead concentrating on the more mystical aspects of Tolstoy's thought demonstrated, for instance, in Prince Andrew's sickbed musings. For Tolstoy believed that all authority impeded the power of independent action by individuals – and that only the individual had any authentic understanding of their circumstance and how to change it. Tolstoy was an anarchist.

Tolstoy believed that it was those at the base of the pyramid – the foot-soldiers on the battlefields of Borodino or Austerlitz – who in fact made history. The "great men" and generals who claimed to understand it in fact had not a clue. For Tolstoy, it was ironic that historians looked to the generals and leaders for the decisions that determined history, rather than to the infantry. More ironic still was that the infantrymen did so too.

* * *

The dominating thought-systems of the 20th century hold only fragmentary clues to the necessary remedies today. Communism offered a spurious equality at the sacrifice of individual liberty. Capitalism offers liberty at the expense of social justice, harmony and that essential sense of individual or shared meaning.

But both Left and Right do however offer hints of a new and stronger philosophy. The greatest strength of the Right has been its appeal to individual enterprise and self-expression, freed of the deadening burden of government. That of the Left is its recognition that we are not separated from one another, that community embraces and succours all, opposing injustice, inequality and a merely selfish and ultimately divisive individualism. We are all better off together. Both strands evoke fundamental truths of the human condition.

But both the economic theory underlying capitalism and communist orthodoxy offer a very limited and ultimately negative view of the human. In neo-classical economic theory, it is claimed without evidence that people are basically self-seeking, that they want above all the satisfaction of their material desires: what economists call "maximising utility". The ultimate objective of mankind is economic growth, and that is maximised only through raw, and lightly regulated, competition. If the rewards of this system are spread unevenly, that is a necessary price. Others on the planet are to be regarded as either customers, competitors or factors of production. Effects upon the planet itself are mere "externalities" to the model, with no reckoning of the cost – at least for now. Nowhere in this analysis appear factors such as human cooperation, love, trust, compassion or hatred, curiosity or beauty. Nowhere appears the concept of meaning. What cannot be measured is ignored. But the trouble is that once our basic needs for shelter and food have been met, these factors may be the most important of all.

In Marxist theory the proletariat should eventually be freed of all burdens, including of government. But in practice all communist systems rapidly established and maintained huge bureaucracies, with their privileged élites, to instruct the people on their best interests. Never were they to be asked what these might be. Those who offered a dissenting voice were repressed, often with great cruelty. In suppressing the anarchists of the Spanish republic, or the Bolsheviks of the Kronstadt rebellion in 1921, the Communists showed their true colours. Communism could never mean freedom from authority. *That* revolution would never be permitted. The people, in short, were not to be trusted.

The methods discussed here instead imply a different view of mankind. That people can be trusted successfully to manage their own affairs, to negotiate with one another, to regulate their own societies from the bottom up – by moral rules, rather than coercion and punishment. That there is more available than the ugliness, conflict and emptiness of contemporary society.

Cynics will argue that such trust is misplaced, and that conflict is inevitable. But the evidence from the few occasions when people have been given true agency over their affairs suggests rather the opposite: respect, consensus, or at worst an acceptance of difference. If all authority disappeared today, our current condition of mistrust and fear would guarantee the "war of all against all". But the practices offered here would, if implemented gradually, build something never experienced before, something extraordinary and beautiful – a new society, governed by itself.

By contrast, the existence of government reminds us – as government itself must remind us repeatedly – that other people are not to be trusted. Hierarchical forms of organisation, so prevalent in the commercial realm as well as government, encourage the worst arrogance in the bosses, and disaffection and alienation amongst everyone else. All for what? What is the point of all this production, competition and consumption? The vapid management-speak of business culture tells its own story of the inauthenticity and boredom of the contemporary workplace. Actresses on billboards pretend that bottled water can bring spiritual fulfilment. The desperate methods of advertisers to ensnare the dazed consumer, now infiltrating their tedious wares into so-called "entertainment"*, reveal not only their own cynicism but the hollowness of the whole venture. Beyond the material, capitalism has no point. And a point is what everyone craves.

No government, however well-intentioned, can provide it. No product can do so either. There is no choice but to find it yourself. It can take a while to realise this.

* * *

---

* As we become resistant to "product placement", several TV channels are working with major advertisers like Coke to "build content", i.e., produce programming entirely oriented around their products.

My journey to anarchism began with a profound belief in government. I was brought up to believe that enlightened government was a force for good in the world. Less nobly, I was also excited by the élite status and power of government, especially the diplomatic corps. Various members of my family had tried to become diplomats. I was determined to be the one to succeed. I wanted to be the one speaking for Britain. I wanted to be the one ordering the world, shifting the chess pieces around the board, wisely but also humanely (I think I would have made a good colonialist). Nobility of purpose and snob appeal made for a bewitching combination.

And indeed such self-regard was only encouraged in my profession. Small groups of us would decide policy for our whole country. Other countries deferred to us, the designated exponents of our state. There are still places in the world where to be a British diplomat is to be special indeed.

Once I travelled to Moscow with a friend. We were last off the plane and observed with sinking hearts the long queue of other passengers waiting at the single immigration desk, where a single surly official slowly flicked through their passports. I flashed my diplomatic passport at a nearby guard. He sprang to attention and yelled "Diplomati! Diplomati!". A squad of other guards suddenly emerged from a side door and trotted to an empty booth. My friend and I were ushered past the long line of hundreds of our, now very envious, fellow passengers. Our passports were quickly stamped. The guard accompanied us to the front of the queue for taxis.

Above all, working for government gave me an extraordinary feeling of control – that my decisions really mattered. And the more senior I became, the more this feeling grew. But it was in fact an illusion. For in reality, my decisions were framed by others. My views were confined to the limited range defined by my seniors as "realistic" or "sensible" – consonant with Britain's narrowly defined "interests", and this was the same whatever the political complexion of the government of the day.

At first, I thought I could help enlarge this space of possible decision, and push at its boundaries. But over time it was easier just to romp about in that small clump of trees, pretending that was in fact the whole forest. The limits of what was politically available came to define the limits of my thought. Since there was no point in thinking of what would not be permitted, I slowly learned not to bother. My view of the world began more and more to look like the view of everyone else in the Foreign Office. My letters, telegrams and speeches – I was for a while speechwriter to the Foreign Secretary – became just like all the rest. Articulate, well-crafted, even impressive, but utterly conventional. And oddly enough as I became more senior, I did not enjoy greater space to express my views; there was in fact less. The higher my diplomatic rank, the more important it became that my personal views should not deviate from the official line. I looked at my ambassador for his example: nothing he said, privately or publicly, differed from policy. He was consistent. He was the complete diplomat. He was professional. And he never questioned anything.

It was fun to be a British diplomat in New York City, in what was to prove my last posting, at least for a while. Girls were impressed when I told them my profession. I was invited to high-end parties with guest lists and velvet ropes: I played poker in huge penthouses overlooking Central Park. I worked hard, and drank Martinis at the end of the week.

But things began to fall apart in New York. My work, defending sanctions on Iraq and liaising with the weapons inspectors, was frontline diplomacy of the most gruelling kind. Late-night negotiations, aggressive diplomatic confrontations, long detailed telegrams that had to be carefully drafted before going home, sometimes as late as five in the morning. At first I thought the controversy of my work was exciting. Television crews would run after me inside the UN building. Journalists would take me to ice-hockey matches to try to be my "friend" and source on some of the most important international negotiations of the time. Other diplomats treated me to expensive lunches, the better to learn secrets from the inside track, which I would judiciously dispense over our espressos. I made special time for the beautiful Swedish Middle East expert. I dated a gorgeous member of the Venezuelan delegation.

But my weekend "unwinding" in downtown bars often began on a Tuesday night. I began to suffer from a depression that Upper West Side psychotherapists could not shift. I resorted to leaving post-it notes around my apartment telling myself, pathetically, to keep going. I started to hate my $5,000-a-month apartment with its expansive views of downtown Manhattan, that I couldn't decorate without official approval. My work felt stale and empty, though it concerned dramatic issues of war and peace. My relationships felt phoney and inauthentic. Hitting my mid-thirties, I wondered if I would ever find true love. I doubted it, as long as I hated myself.

One September morning around this time, I joined my ambassador in his Rolls-Royce to travel to a meeting at the UN. The driver said matter-of-factly, an aircraft has hit the World Trade Center. At the meeting, the news filtered in on slips of paper passed from hand to hand. Outside the conference room, diplomats were gathered around a television watching images of the burning towers. My ambassador and I returned to the mission, where he called the staff together to send us home. One colleague wandered lost along the corridor towards me, her face stricken, catching my eye in mutual acknowledgement of pure horror.

I took my usual path home down 2nd Avenue. In the other direction came a stream of people. Dressed mostly in business and work clothes, some were distraught, some held one another, some were coated in ash. My apartment faced downtown; hitherto the towers had been the centrepiece of the view from my window. Now, their place had been taken by a huge dark column of thick and filthy smoke. I stared at it, bewildered, for a long time, the television chattering unwatched in the corner.

That night, the city downtown was mostly deserted. I passed St Vincent's hospital in the West Village. A crowd of perhaps two hundred people had gathered to watch ambulances arrive. There was silence under the klieg lights that the hospital – or was it TV crews – had erected. Doctors and nurses stood expectant at the hospital entrance. The broad avenue, normally bustling with traffic, was closed below 14th Street and now was empty. But there were no arriving ambulances to be seen. It turned out that only a few of the victims had been injured in the disaster. Most had been killed outright.

The attacks transported the city into another dimension. It was as if something had been rent open that had hitherto been closed. In the days that followed, there was a certain hush about the streets; people went more quietly about their business. Strangers would catch one's eyes on the street and smile with consolation.

I lived next to Union Square, which quickly became the centre of collective grieving. It was the southernmost point before the controlled zone south of 14th Street where vehicles could not freely enter. Forests of candles lit the evenings. I could hear soft singing lilting upwards from the gathered crowds. With a friend, I watched the huge removal trucks lumber northwards up the West Side Highway, heavy with their grim cargo of rubble. People cheered the firemen, ambulance men, policemen and pretty much anyone who was travelling to and from the site of the disaster. It was a few days before "Ground Zero" became the approved appellation.

Some nights I had to close my windows to stop the acrid smell of the still-burning pyre downtown from entering my apartment. Ash collected on the window ledges. For several mornings afterwards, I raised my blinds and, confronted with the vista of smoke and its portent of death, briefly wept before collecting myself for the day. One afternoon at the office, I spent an hour watching F-15 fighters just like the ones from the poster on my childhood bedroom wall circling the city. This sign from an innocent past seemed a comfort in those jittery days. But in another way they were a symbol of the change to come.

For in the days that followed, the meaning of the disaster

seemed to change. At first, it felt profoundly human: about real and individual people, a city in trauma, the ever-present smell of smoke in the air. Then, as the days passed, I had the sense of the disaster being transformed, of governments claiming the right to interpret what it meant, what it was all "about". I remember a colleague from the embassy in Washington calling me to discuss what he called "9/11", as it had come to be known in that distant city. Until that point I had not heard this expression – people in New York tended simply to call the catastrophe "it" as everyone knew what "it" was: we talked about nothing else. I ushered at a remembrance service for families of British victims at St Patrick's Cathedral. The bereaved were kept standing in the rain outside whilst officious and rude staff from the Prime Minister's office bustled about inside organis-ing seating plans for the VIPs and barking at the local staff.

Immediately after the attacks, I had been overwhelmed by the compassion manifest on the streets of New York. When I had watched the people cheering the fire trucks and police cars on the West Side Highway on 12 September, some of them were waving flags. I was very moved by this sight, which seemed to me to be heartfelt, a sign of solidarity, not nationalism. Two weekends after it happened, I went to a Mets baseball game with a friend and felt my blood rise and tears spring to my eyes when the spectators stood to sing "America the Beautiful". The British consulate in New York distributed lapel pins of the Stars and Stripes and Union Jack entwined together. I wore mine to express my heartfelt solidarity with the city and, by extension, the country. Spotting my flags pin, people would smile on the subway.

But then something began to change. Amongst the crowds in Union Square, small groups began to appear, often young men, who would gather to argue, some that it was "all the Muslims' fault", some that it was not. Political chanting replaced the singing. Preachers from Texas set up microphones to tell us loudly what they thought about "9/11". I began to avoid Union Square.

With the arrival of the presidents and politicians, one began to hear talk of revenge, not from ordinary people but from leader writers and commentators. Posters torn from newspapers appeared in shop windows: Osama "Wanted Dead or Alive", except that the "Alive" was invariably crossed out. Cars, often with out-of-state registration plates, began to carry ostentatious flags, plastered to the bumper or fluttering from a window. The symbolism of the flag itself began to change. I took off my two-flagged pin.

One woman I met soon after the attacks had been buried by rubble from the falling towers. She said that she had no desire for others to suffer as she had. But suffer they would. That terrible night I had met a friend in a bar. "Governments will return" I said, not really knowing what I meant. But I was right. Their credibility as our guardians challenged, it was essential to governments to reassert their authority, by whatever means necessary.

Presciently, Tony Blair's foreign-policy adviser had suggested I insert almost those very words into the resolution we negotiated at the UN Security Council the morning after the attacks. His proposal was to include the loaded terms "all necessary means" – in other words, that the US and UK would be legally authorised to use military force in response to the attacks – anywhere. I proposed this to the US delegation (as British diplomats always first do), but they demurred. I remember their eyes glassy with shock. I had the impression that they – like Washington – were overwhelmed and could not take anything in. Such was the atmosphere of sympathy for the US at the Council that horrified day, I think we could have agreed anything, and even the language Number Ten had suggested. History might have been rather different if we had. For the only time in the Council's history, the diplomats stood in silence at the adoption of the resolution.

I was to play a small part in the ensuing campaigns. I delivered Britain's letter to the UN claiming our legal right of self-defence under the UN charter to invade Afghanistan, whose Taliban government had given shelter to the 9/11 attackers. Later, I was briefly to serve in Kabul soon after the fall of the Taliban.

Meanwhile, I continued to work on Iraq, but with intensified tempo, aware that the mood was shifting in Washington towards war. You could somehow sense it, like an awful momentum – the angry relation at Christmas dinner you can tell is going to "lose it" sooner or later. One country was not enough – it was almost too easy: another must be sacrificed.

Reports from the British embassy in Washington began to record the claims of the "neo-cons" that Saddam was a threat, that he was collaborating with Al Qaeda. Naïvely, I thought, These will never be believed! It's rubbish! But from London too, I was asked to review early drafts of what became the infamous Number Ten WMD dossier, with its exaggerated claims of weapons stocks and capabilities for which we had no proof and scant intelligence. One day perhaps, the publication of my reply to London will vindicate my memory that I questioned these claims – I hope. I failed to see what was coming. I told my friends who asked, Britain does not want to go to war with Iraq. We want to contain Iraq through inspections. Idiotically, I kept saying this until practically the day of the invasion, by which time I had left the mission to take a year-long sabbatical at a university in New York. I said this because this is what I had been instructed to say for the previous four years. This was British policy. I simply couldn't believe that my ministers and colleagues could participate in such a farrago. I am still recovering from the shock today.

I contemplated resigning. I knew that the claims of imminent Iraqi threat were a travesty of what little intelligence we had. I drafted several resignation letters to the head of my ministry. All very measured and regretful, none was ever sent. I was too afraid. Somehow I sensed that sticking my hand up at this moment would lead to my destruction. At the least, I feared, I would be publicly ridiculed and belittled.

I was right, though the victim would not be me but my friend and colleague, David Kelly. His tragic story – hounded by government and press to his lonely suicide – is now well-known. But for me his ghastly death struck very close to home, for I too but with less expertise had been telling the press very much "off the record" that the government's claims were nonsense. He and I had discussed the detail of this exaggeration at what was to be our last meeting, at a diner on 6th Avenue, after he had generously given a talk on weapons inspections at my university.

He was caught out after speaking to an irresponsible journalist, and exposed in a disgraceful macho face-off between Tony Blair's advisers and the head of the BBC. Blair's press spokesmen duly traduced this loyal and humble man, who had been Britain's most authoritative expert on biological weapons and indeed our most cogent analyst of the whole messy WMD picture. Blair's press aides claimed that David was merely a "mid-level" official unacquainted with the "full picture". In fact, the government – and I – had relied upon him heavily. He had been our principal briefer on the WMD intelligence assessment to the UN Security Council, whose members I invited to the British mission to hear him. Now the government, to whose service he had devoted his life, was happy to rubbish and humiliate him in order to distract attention from its own mendacity.

I was appalled. On the train to David's funeral, I asked the small group of Foreign Office and Ministry of Defence colleagues whether any one of us had believed the government's claims about Iraq. No one spoke.

Eventually I did resign, but in no heroic manner. The British government had, under pressure, at last convened an inquiry into the use of intelligence in the run-up to the war. While on secondment to the UN in Kosovo, I had submitted detailed written testimony with the request that it be kept secret, for fear that my authorship would damage my successful career in the Foreign Ministry – I was due to head a department on my return to London. That testimony said what I knew: that the WMD claims were grossly exaggerated, that available alternatives to war had been ignored, and that in terms of the many resolutions I had helped negotiate on

Iraq weapons inspections, the war was manifestly illegal. I remember very clearly the moment when I pressed the "send" button on my clunky UN computer. A few days later, I sent another letter, this time to my Foreign Secretary, enclosing my evidence as the reason for my resignation. He never replied.

At first this breach felt like a disaster. Aside from my youthful – and thwarted – desire to be a fighter pilot, I had only ever wanted to be a diplomat. I thought that there was no way to practise this craft outside government, and the waste and incompetence of the UN in Kosovo had dissuaded me of that alternative. I felt bereft of my sense of identity. I had been a diplomat, and now I was nothing.

But in truth that awful parting turned out to be a liberation. My wife suggested I advise the Kosovo government on the diplomatic process concerning its future, a process from which it had been largely excluded – a subject, not an actor, in its own future. Over a glass of the local *raki*, the Kosovo Prime Minister agreed my suggestion when I returned to Pristina a few weeks later. The non-profit diplomatic advisory group Independent Diplomat was born. Today, nearly seven years later, Independent Diplomat is advising countries, governments and legitimate political actors in conflicts – and other diplomatic processes – all over the world. It enjoys an excellent team of experts in diplomacy – not always diplomats – across five offices in the major diplomatic centres.

My painful departure from government service however also marked the start of a deeper examination. I reviewed my professional life as a diplomat, and I felt little pride in what I saw. I remain deeply ashamed of the inhumane decisions I was part of in effecting economic sanctions on Iraq. But this was not my only regret.

There was another issue which at the time I had regarded as trivial and unimportant. I had written a telegram from New York saying that the UK had "no dog in the fight" in involving itself in the long-standing dispute over the Western Sahara. This country had been occupied by Morocco in 1975. Its indigenous people had fled to refugee camps in the Algerian Sahara, where they remain to this day. Inside the territory, the Saharawis suffer repression and violence from the Moroccan occupiers. With the privilege of distance, ignorance and moral unaccountability, my telegram had eloquently explained why Britain's "interest" was in its economic trade with Morocco, not with 150,000 refugees who had been denied their legal right, which Britain claimed to support, of self-determination.

This is what I had become. I had lost all the moral bearings that mattered to me. I had lost the sense of political justice that had fired me in student debates at university, that inspired me to collect signatures from my colleagues at a summer job to send a letter of protest to the Chinese embassy after the massacres at Tiananmen Square. I was de-natured; I had lost any real sense of what I stood for. I was – literally – de-moralised by my work for government.

So it was that I began to examine my life, and with it the rôle of government in today's world. I had wasted many months of my sabbatical reading irrelevant and outdated political philosophy. Instead, I began to record events of the real world, today. These were the outputs of the political system. What did they amount to, really? How did they measure up to the reassuring claims of governments and international institutions? This exercise continues to consume me. I had once helped write those claims, in speeches for my ministers and statements at the UN. I had once even written a statement for the US Secretary of State (a long story). Looking back, I saw that I had never examined the grounds for these claims, never once questioned, but always assumed.

At the same time, I began to rediscover the passions of my youth. My disgust at the rampant injustice of our economic order, society's indifference to the suffering of others, and the sheer ugliness and crassness of contemporary culture. I went back to the economics courses I had studied at university, and quickly saw the gross and obvious deficits in that very limited set of theories. I learned about new theories, including behavioural economics and complexity theory, both of which shed a brighter light on humanity's conduct, but which remain limited by their own terms and models, and inevitably insufficient to comprehend the full – and true – picture.

I wondered why Britain refused to lift a finger to help the Saharawis, even though the ministers and officials concerned were decent people (most of them, anyway). I knew them, some of them were my friends. They would stop to save an injured child on the street. But transport that child to the realm of "foreign policy" and she is ignored, rendered irrelevant, inconvenient to the dominating calculus of what matters to states, not people. I watched my country and America's "global War on Terror" with a dawning realisation that our strategy was doomed to render the problem not better, but worse. Darker still, I saw how our side, we who had preened ourselves at places like the UN for our democracy and adherence to law, were prepared to cast principle aside when it suited us. Though allegedly outlawed by international treaty, it appears still that states – even the good guys – can forgive themselves torture, murder and the massed death of innocent civilians.

I listened to friends and acquaintances demand better, but with a sinking heart as they described their methods. Once, I had written the stock replies to "letters from the public", the lowliest task for a junior civil servant. I had barely heard the shouts of demonstrators on the streets below my office in New York as they protested the damage done by sanctions on Iraq. I had sighed from tedium with colleagues as we drafted simplistic replies to questions posed to our ministers in parliament. It was tedious because it was so easy. The questions were so stupid. No one – and I mean no one – knew as much as we did. We claimed not only a monopoly on morality, but also on knowledge. The supposedly democratic forces marshalled to check and balance our policies were pathetically feeble.

So I began to wonder what would work better. What might actually *deliver* the change I sought. I was tired and bored of campaigning for it; I had lost all hope that such methods could be effective. I wanted something that might, at least might, work.

And in its own unexpected way, Independent Diplomat provided a kind of answer, one which became clearer to me as I read and researched anarchists of the past, and the small bright moments of history when anarchism was tried, when states and their armies had not dominated human affairs. Independent Diplomat does things; it doesn't ask others to do them. With practical tools and ideas every day, we work to repair the disadvantage suffered by the peoples we advise. It is often not enough, and the work is often daunting, but sometimes it works, and just the doing of it is infinitely more satisfying and fulfilling than the best day I ever had as a formal diplomat inside the system.

The system can be altered. When I first set up Independent Diplomat, I had thought that at best it might serve as an expert guide to a fixed and permanent system for our clients, the countries and peoples trying to find their way through a grotesquely inefficient and over-complicated machinery. Cheesily, I chose a compass for our logo.

But, to my surprise, we've discovered that not only can we navigate that system; we can change it – just by acting differently, by doing diplomacy differently from the way it's been done until now.

We've found that by our mere existence we're sending out a signal that business as usual in diplomacy is not OK, and needs reform. Though we are a private organisation working outside the public gaze, our influence appears to be greater than our tiny scale. We've found that when they encounter our alternative approach to diplomacy, many diplomats immediately declare that they hate the system as much as we do. They inform upon it, they work with us secretly to change it. Every week we receive applications from serving diplomats who want to abandon a system in which they have lost faith. And perhaps most profoundly, we've discovered the immense power of not accepting things as they are – the *status quo*.

Our clients, many of them marginalised and disempowered

political actors, would often meekly accept the form and the manner of their treatment by the more important players and the institutions that serve them, like the EU and UN. They were often simply thankful to be on the agenda, and would gratefully accede to whatever crummy treatment was meted out to them, while hating those that were doing the meting-out: the classic behaviour of disempowered people.

Independent Diplomat encouraged our clients to start demanding better treatment, that their concerns be taken as seriously as anyone else's: to assert their demands, rather than passively await the verdict of the powerful.

One of our clients was the elected government of South Sudan. To end Sudan's long civil war, the people of that region had been given the right to vote on its secession. The UN, being a body of states, decided to hold a meeting on the future of Sudan, including that vote on South's self-determination. The UN invited the government of Sudan, but not the government of the Southerners, even though they were deeply and intimately concerned with the substance of the meeting. Thirty-four other countries were invited, but not the elected representatives of the people whose fate was most directly at stake.

Our clients did not even know about the meeting. The UN had sent its invitation to the Sudanese capital Khartoum, mistakenly assuming that the national government would include the Southerners*. They had not bothered to inform them. The Southern government's reaction was at first surly – this was typical of the treatment they expected from the UN; they could go to hell. Independent Diplomat encouraged them to protest, and to get

---

* Under the 2005 Comprehensive Peace Agreement in Sudan, the government of Sudan was in theory one of "national unity" between the National Congress Party (the Northerners) and the Sudan People's Liberation Movement (the South). In practice, it was united only in name; totally dominated by the NCP, there was very little actual cooperation or communication between these two parties.

sympathetic allies at the UN to do the same. As a result, the President of South Sudan was eventually invited to attend the meeting, where he was able to present his views on the desires of his people to the thirty-four countries assembled, including President Barack Obama. A precedent had moreover been established. When a couple of months later a formal meeting of the UN Security Council was organised to discuss Sudan, with the Foreign Ministers of the Council members – William Hague, Hillary Clinton – in attendance, a formal invitation from the Council's president was issued to the government of South Sudan, this time without any chivvying from us. By pressing their demands politely but with persistence our client changed the way that the UN dealt with their country. The system had been altered.

These are of course but small steps. Independent Diplomat has not yet pulled off the wholesale reform of the world's diplomatic system, and won't on its own. As discussed earlier, this would require a deeper reform, including of the way ordinary people consider their rôles and that of their governments in deciding their futures.

But there was one last lesson that Independent Diplomat was to teach me; perhaps there will be others in the future. And this was perhaps the most important of all, to me at least. I had decided to start this venture primarily because I loved diplomacy and didn't want my resignation from the British Foreign Office to end my involvement in international relations. When I had left the diplomatic corps, however righteous my reasons, it felt in some way that I was having to settle for second best. Perhaps this was a result of the deep-seated élitism that the foreign service had instilled within me, and that I had relished, snob that I am.

And at first, it did indeed feel like a second-class experience. I had been used to flying business class, and now I was crammed back in the economy cabin with all the other plebs (this was one direct and uncomfortable consequence of leaving the Foreign Office). I acutely remember the first day that I returned to the UN Security Council, more than two years after leaving it as a British delegate, but this time as a member of the delegation of the Kosovo Prime Minister, to watch his country being debated by others. I had been used to the deference and access shown to delegates of the "Permanent Five" countries, the closed circle that runs the UN. Even the security guards had known my name, and nodded and smiled like doormen when I passed.

When I returned with the Kosovars, some of the guards pretended not to know me. Suddenly, I was at the back of the queue at the velvet rope, no longer "on the list". When I had been a British diplomat at the Council, I had the run of the place, slipping texts to my colleagues, and using the Secretariat offices around the Council as my own. This time, when we were finally allowed in, we were guided to the seats where non-Council UN members had to sit, far away from the Council's U-shaped table where the action was. We were spectators not players. I hated it.

I still hate the second-class treatment, and still prefer to fly business class if I can (who doesn't?). But I have gained something more valuable in return. There is no greater satisfaction than fighting for a cause you believe in. Instead of a formal diplomatic passport, I enjoy the extraordinary privilege of working till late at night with a man who has spent most of his life as a guerrilla commander in the African bush, as he prepares his country's first ever statement to the gathered states at the UN. No longer do I tell him what he should do, as once I had as a British diplomat. Instead, he sees me as an ally and confidant. Words like fulfilment and satisfaction capture these experiences. Not once do I wonder if I'm doing the right thing with my life. I know that I am. My blood rises at the fight; my heart is in it, without reservation.

I have been extraordinarily lucky to find this one essential element of a satisfactory life (there are of course others, no less difficult to locate). And I've realised too that this good fortune had very little to do with my own wisdom or virtue: a humbling reminder, if one were needed, of the importance of chance and the choices of others as well as one's own in life's journey. If it hadn't been for the Iraq war, I would probably still be in one of Her Majesty's embassies, wondering what the hell I was doing with my life, having fruitless arguments with "London", drinking too much and popping anti-depressants. If it hadn't been for the advice and patience of my long-suffering wife, I would probably not have had the gumption or self-confidence to set up Independent Diplomat and instead I would have run frightened into a job at some other ossified institution, because I didn't know how to run anything on my own, and didn't believe that I could. And if it wasn't for the drive and intelligence of my colleagues who've joined Independent Diplomat, and the extraordinary help of mentors and advisers with ten times my experience, it would have remained a very minor operation, fumbling around at the edges. It has succeeded partly because others believe in its ambitions as much as I do. It has become bigger and more important than me.

The lessons from this experience barely need spelling out. The satisfactions of mapping and walking one's own political journey are manifold. But they come to pass thanks to the succour and wisdom of others.

It is not all roses. I still miss the tiled corridors of the Foreign Office. I miss my index-linked pension (a lot). I worry about the future. With no institution to frame my choices, or to approve or excuse my statements, I live with a continual anxiety of mistakes. That anxiety is with me as I write these words.

To choose a life freed of restraint, but also security, is to choose fear as a constant companion. While partners and friends may give vital encouragement, the battle against fear is one that must be fought, ultimately, alone. And in truth I do not think it is ever fully won*. In my wallet I keep a poem by W.H. Auden, another Briton

---

* In the film *A Place Called Chiapas*, a priest who fights for the rights of landless *campesinos* against often-violent big landowners puts this rather more eloquently than I can, and in more religious terms than I would choose. After his house was attacked by thugs throwing firebombs, Father Noriberto Cruz Verain commented, "They threw Molotov cocktails into my house. I'm not

who moved to America, who once lived a few yards from where I now write.

W.H. Auden

> The sense of danger must not disappear:
> The way is certainly both short and steep,
> However gradual it looks from here;
> Look if you like, but you will have to leap.

He concludes:

> A solitude ten thousand fathoms deep
> Sustains the bed on which we lie, my dear;
> Although I love you, you will have to leap;
> Our dream of safety has to disappear.

Too Pithy.

The first step has to be taken. And after that another. And eventually something odd may become apparent. The fear that once appeared an enemy, an impediment, has metamorphosed into something else: an ally. For it is fear that provides the jolt of electricity that fires action; it is fear that makes the colours of a bright day the more vivid, the clutch of a child the more moving. Now, if I do not feel fearful, I suspect that I am not going far enough. Fear is not an addiction, but it is somehow a test: if it is absent, then something is wrong.

Objections to anarchism are continually nourished by those who play upon our fears, above all of each other. Quoting Yeats, whose poem began this book, commentators suggest, "Things fall apart, the centre cannot hold", mere anarchy unloosing a "blood-dimmed tide". Yeats's vision is the stuff of nightmares:

---

saying we weren't afraid. We're all afraid, but we can't let it paralyse us. Jesus was afraid, not paralysed. Jesus inspires us not to be afraid. The fear that paralyses is the fear we should be most afraid of. Terror makes you stand still. But when fear makes you think and makes you walk, you realise it's a step. It's the way to achieve something better."

a shape with lion body and the head of a man, a gaze blank and
pitiless as the sun . . . The darkness drops again.

Auden had mixed feelings about Yeats. He admired his poetry
but abhorred his world view, such as the apocalypse laid out in *The
Second Coming*[185]. In his elegy upon Yeats's death, *In Memory of
W.B. Yeats*, Auden exhorts his readers not merely to read poetry but
to think and to act, "for poetry makes nothing happen". Poetry was
not mere fancy and literary adornment, but profoundly political.
Auden laid responsibility at the reader's feet: poetry is only as effective as the readers make it.

Just as Yeats proffered a nightmare vision of monsters with pitiless gazes, movies abound with zombie armies who rattle the gates of
our safety. Television offers ceaseless stories of vicious crime, true
and imagined, but invariably served up salaciously, spine-shivering
and erotic all at once. The effects are unmistakable. These devices
should be seen for what they are: political statements, whether inten-
tional or subconscious. With less guile and sometimes deceit,
politicians decry threats that do not threaten, the better to justify
their own existence: only they and their cohorts can protect us.

This book is not proposing a revolution against government,
but one in our own attitudes. The individual is the most effective
agent in altering their immediate circumstances. Thus, they are
the most effective agent, when acting collectively, in effecting
global change, in anything. Moreover, action opens a possibility
that is strange and unfamiliar: a world without limits; to realise at
last fully what one is, what we are as humans. But this will not
come about of its own accord. This is not an immutable or logical
force that we can simply observe, and idly comment upon. It
requires summoning up our own dark forces, our fear, our hunger,
our ideals: it requires action.

The alternatives are grim to contemplate. The slow but inevitable decline in state power can be arrested, but only by government
acquiring more power, thereby constraining our own freedom, and

exacerbating many of the pernicious trends already here identified. The growing sense of disorder will with equal certainty attract those who offer to calm the stormy waters, proclaiming order and certainty in place of chaos.

Twenty-first-century fascism probably won't look much like 20th-century fascism. We are too inoculated against the crude semiotics of the swastika and black shirts and the devastating violence of the Holocaust. It will come in a different form, cleverly argued and convincingly presented. Instead of gatherings in Munich beer halls, it may start on a website, for technology is indifferent to democrats or fascists. Indeed, jihadist terrorists share with 20th-century European fascists their absolutism and willingness to sacrifice innocent life in the construction of a greater society – and they are not alone in this inhuman calculus. Meanwhile, a new breed rises of far-right politicians in Europe and America, with smart suits and polished television manners. As the disorder grows, so too, with inevitability, will emerge those who promise to tame it with authoritarianism and, in parallel but admitted only *sotto voce,* coercion.

The choice will become clearer: to cede our voice to those louder, to watch while governments, corporations and criminal networks joust for control, or to join battle for agency over affairs that are rightfully our own.

There is no easy answer to the problems that confront humanity in the 21st century; it would be foolish to place our faith in one form of management – government – to solve them. Whether environmental degradation, incipient political violence, economic volatility or a host of other dangers, the evidence is stark of government's waning competence. If others are not to exploit this instability, there is but one alternative: to step in ourselves.

The greatest paradox faced by any proponent of an anarchist approach to life is this. Anarchism rejects authority, it rejects hierarchical institutions; it rejects the state. The goal cannot be defined neatly, as a concrete system or a state of affairs. It is instead a method, a process, a means – which is itself an end. And by its nature, no one can define where that process may lead. Critics can paint that blank canvas with nightmares; I can suggest instead a future of cooperation, justice, mutual understanding and a deeper sense of purpose upon this crowded planet. If this path is taken, a vista of possibility may open up, beyond the dull limits of the ideas that today dominate our conception of society and ourselves. The limits are of conventional thought; the possibility is of us, ourselves: the human.

Our dream of safety has to disappear.

ACKNOWLEDGEMENTS

Over a dozen people helped with the research for the book over a period of years. I would like particularly to thank Tait Foster, who gave me a great deal of excellent, prompt and accurate research help.

There were many others who read the book, listened to its ideas and provided suggestions and helpful criticism. Many people therefore should share the credit for the book, and I thank them sincerely, while all errors of course remain my own. They include:

Rob Akam, Ardian Arifaj, Lyle Berman, Lili Birnbaum, John Brademas, Jake Camara, Royston Coppenger, David Cornwell, Neill Denny, Anna Dupont, Mark Earls, Susanna Emmet, Nick Fraser, Karl French, Sasha Frère-Jones, Katie Genereux, Ed Harriman, Arya Iranpour, Ian Irvine, Mladen Joksic, Tina Kraja, Jordan Kyle, Alnoor Ladha, Horatia Lawson, Ann Lee, Neil Levine, Andrew Lewis, Professor Catherine Lu, Joshua Marston, Catherine Martin, Charlotte Meyer, Professor Laila Parsons, Vincent Pouliot, Jesse Rosenthal, Catherine Ross, Clementine Ross, Ivo Ross, Karmen Ross, Oliver Ross, Paddy (Alan) Ross, Victoria (Tori) Rowan, Jeffrey Rubin, Iain Scollay, Imran Shafi, Angharad Thain, Inigo Thomas, Professor Rob Wisnovsky and last, and by no means least, Melissa Withers (thanks to whom there will one day be participatory democracy in Providence, Rhode Island).

I want to thank my colleagues at, and the board members of, Independent Diplomat, and Whitney Ellsworth in particular, who have been very patient in tolerating the preparation of this book, and the voluble expression of its ideas, sometimes in very primitive form. I am profoundly grateful to my wife, Karmen, who has accompanied me in the long journey of this book, and remains, as ever, my chief inspiration and most acute critic. More than anyone, she has helped me cut through the woolliness and hypocrisies of political convention, including most particularly my own, to the necessary truths of injustice.

I am especially grateful for the support, patience and advice of my editor at Simon & Schuster, Mike Jones, and of my agents in the UK and US, respectively Jonny Geller at Curtis Brown and George Lucas at Inkwell Management. Without their help and encouragement, including in some dark days, this book would not have come into being.

Carne Ross
New York City, April 2011

You will find further discussion of this book and other topics, particularly foreign policy, at my personal website, www.carneross. com and by following me on Twitter - @carneross.

You can see more about Independent Diplomat at www. Independentdiplomat.org. Independent Diplomat is a non-profit diplomatic advisory group, and a registered charity in the UK.

ENDNOTES

1   See *The Economist*, 7 October 2010: "The Flash Crash: Autopsy"
2   Alex Evans at Chatham House
3   *The Observer*, 7 March 2010, "Food and water driving 21st-century African land grab"
4   *The Economist*, "Immeasurable loss" 12 November 2008
5   As reported in *Financial Times*, 9 November 2010
6   State Department Assistant Secretary for human rights Mike Posner reported in the *New York Times*, 14 December 2009 "Clinton defends human rights approach"
7   *Foreign Policy* website, Turtle Bay, "UN takes stock of its diminished influence" by Colum Lynch, 13 September 2010
8   "Future shock: Welcome to the new Middle Ages" Parag Khanna, *Financial Times*, 29 December 2010
9   Timothy Garton Ash, "Timothy Garton Ash in Davos: Illiberal capitalism and new world disorder" article emailed to his listserve, 28 January 2011
10 *The Economist*, 16 December 2010 "Climate Change diplomacy: Back from the Brink"
11 *The Economist*, 6 May 2010 "As jobs fade away"
12 Bob Diamond, the chief executive of Barclays Bank said, "There was a period of remorse and apology; that period needs to be over". His expected bonus that year was over £3 million.
13 Source: Joseph Rowntree Foundation
14 Source: *Financial Times*, "China to alter taxes in attempt to cut wealth gap", 20 April 2011

15   See *Financial Times*, 23 December 2010, "India's boom fails to feed the hungry"

16   *The Economist*, 6 May 2010

17   AFP, "Al-Qaeda vows to continue parcel bomb attacks", 20 November 2010

18   Source: *The Gun* by C.J. Chivers, Simon & Schuster, 2010

19   Source: *Small Arms Survey*, Graduate Institute of International and Development Studies, Geneva

20   *Open Democracy*, 27 September 2010, "From Helmand to Merseyside: Unmanned drones and the militarization of UK policing" by Steve Graham

21   See "Monitoring America" and "Top Secret America", *Washington Post* projects published in 2010 by Dana Priest and William M. Arkin

22   BBC website report, "Life in UK 'has become lonelier'" on Mark Easton's blog

23   *Loneliness: Human Nature and the Need for Social Connection*, John T. Cacioppo & William Patrick, Norton 2008

24   See BBC website "Iraq warns of more suicide missions" 29 March 2003

25   Dexter Filkins, *The Forever War*, Vintage Books, 2008

26   BBC website 5 April 2003: http://news.bbc.co.uk/2/hi/middle_east/2917107.stm

27   See, for example, Robert Pape, "Suicide Terrorism and Democracy", Cato Institute, *Policy Analysis*, 1 November 2006 and other similar such arguments by Pape

28   See, for instance, Assaf Moghadam "Motives for Martyrdom: Al Qaida, Salafi Jihad, and the Spread of Suicide Attacks", *International Security* 33:3, 2009

29   The PKK in Turkey fights for a Kurdish homeland

30   See Max Hastings, *Retribution: The Battle for Japan 1944–45*, Vintage, 2009

31   See *Financial Times*, "Setback for US mortgage sector", 30 April 2010, quoting a study of the same date by the Kellogg School of Management at Northwestern University

32   "A framework for pro-environmental behaviours", 2008, Department for Environment, Food and Rural Affairs (DEFRA); http://www.defra.gov.uk/evidence/social/behaviour/pdf/behaviours-jan08-report.pdf

33   "The spreading of disorder", Kees Keizer, Siegwart Lindenberg, Linda

Steg, Faculty of Behavioral and Social Sciences, University of Groningen, Netherlands; published in *Science Express*, 20 November 2008

34 Source: *New York Times*, "From footnote to fame in civil rights history" by Brooks Barnes, 26 November 2009

35 Philip Hoose, *Claudette Colvin: Twice Toward Justice*, Farrar, Straus & Giroux, 2009

36 David J. Garrow, a biographer of Dr King, quoted in *New York Times*, 26 November 2009

37 For a useful summary of Watts's research on this, see "Is the Tipping Point toast?" by Clive Thompson, *Fast Company*, 28 January 2008. Watts's papers in *Nature* and several other publications are also relevant

38 The picture is on-line at http://www.nytimes.com/interactive/2008/08/28/us/politics/20080828_OBAMA_PANO.html?scp=2&sq=obama%20denver%20speech&st=cse

39 Source: OpenSecrets.org

40 National Public Radio, *Morning Edition* 9 February 2009

41 Robert Putnam, *Bowling Alone: The Collapse and Revival of American Community*, Simon & Schuster 2001

42 Horst Schlämmer, a mock politician played by a well-known German comedian

43 *New York Times*, 20 August 2009, "Before election, not a voter was stirring"

44 Source: Opensecrets.org

45 Source: *Washington Post*, 22 June 2005, "The Road to Riches is called K Street"

46 Source: European Parliament

47 *Financial Times*, "A Field to Level", 10 February 2010

48 Source: *Spinwatch* (www.Spinwatch.org), "How BP drafted Brussels' climate legislation" 15 December 2010

49 *Financial Times*, "Europe's Hidden Billions" 2 December 2010; see more at www.ft.com/eu-funds

50 This trend is well-documented in many democratic systems. See, for instance, Peter Mair and Ingrid van Biezen, "Party Membership in twenty European democracies: 1980–2000", *Party Politics* (January 2001), Robert Putnam, "Democracies in flux: the evolution of social capital in contemporary society", OUP 2002, and most recently Paul Whiteley, "Is the Party over? – the decline of Party activism and membership across the democratic world", paper at University of Manchester conference, April 2009

51 Source: worldpublicopinion.org, whose survey "World Public

Opinion on Democracy", a twenty-country global public-opinion poll on democracy and governance, conducted by worldpublicopinion.org and its network of public-opinion research organisations, found that in every nation polled publics support the principles of democracy. At the same time, in nearly every nation majorities are dissatisfied with how responsive their government is to the will of the people. For a more detailed analysis, see: http://www.worldpublicopinion.org/pipa/articles/home_page/482.php?lb=hmpg1&pnt=482&nid=&id=

52   Turnout to elect Kennedy was 62.8 percent; Clinton in 1996 was 48.9 percent

53   *New York Times*, 23 June 2010, "Cuomo accepts millions from the interests he assails"

54   Senator Fritz Hollings, interviewed on PBS *NewsHour*

55   Source: Center for Responsive Politics

56   See the *New York Times*, 27 December 2008, "City of Immigrants Fills Jail Cells with Its Own" by Nina Bernstein

57   Source: BBC news

58   One of the clients of the Gabriel Company, headed by Edward Gabriel, former US Ambassador to Morocco is, of course, Morocco (source: US Department of Justice, Foreign Agents Registration Act (FARA) listings)

59   See the *New York Times*, 23 December 2010, "American lobbyists work for Ivorian leader"

60   See www.opensecrets.org for more details, in particular for up-to-date data on corporate donations

61   Source: the Electoral Commission

62   *New York Times*, 23 December 2010, "US approved trade with blacklisted nations"

63   Source: *New York Times*, 6 November 2010 "While warning about fat, US pushes cheese sales"

64   Source: *Private Eye*, 18 March 2011

65   *Financial Times*, 25 June 2009 "Obama pulls no punches in fight to push through reforms"

66   *New York Times*, 7 November 2008, "Some philanthropists are no longer content to work quietly"

67   Source: Urban Institute, National Center for Charitable Statistics

68   Jordan, Grant and W. Maloney, "The Rise of Protest Business in Britain", *Private Groups and Public Life,* ed. J. van Deth. New York: Routledge, 1997

69 *New York Times*, 17 November 2008, "At National Review, a Threat to Its Reputation for Erudition"

70 *New York Times*, 19 March 2009, "The Daily Me"

71 *The Economist*, 19 June 2008 "The Big Sort"

72 I was the Strategy Coordinator at the UN Mission in Kosovo (UNMIK) from 2003–4

73 Source: Human Rights Watch

74 Fareed Zakaria, "What America has lost: It's clear we over-reacted to 9/11" *Newsweek*, 4 September 2010

75 *A Paradise Built in Hell: The Extraordinary Communities That Arise in Disaster* by Rebecca Solnit, Viking, 2009

76 *Financial Times*, 4 January 2010, letter from Professor Robert H. Wade

77 See "From behind bars, Madoff spins his story", *Financial Times*, 8 April 2011

78 SEC, Office of Inspector-General Report, case number OIG-509; http://www.sec.gov/spotlight/secpostmadoffreforms/oig-509-exec-summary.pdf

79 See, for instance, *New York Times*, 3 September 2009, "Report details how Madoff's web ensnared S.E.C."

80 See *Financial Times* 28 May 2010, "Chief regulator resigns after strong criticism"

81 http://online.wsj.com/public/resources/documents/Markopolos Testimony20090203.pdf

82 The full name of the bill is the Wall Street Reform and Consumer Protection Act of 2009

83 *Financial Times*, 10 November 2010, "Wall Street to sidestep Volcker rule"

84 See letter to *Financial Times*, 9 November 2010, from Professor Anat Admati of Stanford University and nineteen others, "Healthy banking system is the goal, not profitable banks"

85 *Financial Times*, "We have failed to muffle the banks" by Clive Crook, 12 September 2010

86 "Dimon warns of bank 'nail in coffin'", *Financial Times*, 30 March 2011

87 See *New York Times*, "The Bipartisanship Racket", 19 December 2010

88 See *Wired* magazine, "Why Craig's List is such a mess" by Gary Wolf, 24 August 2009

89 Mark Pesce at the Personal Democracy Forum, New York City, 2008

90   The Business and Human Rights Council is one example

91   Sourcemap: www.sourcemap.org

92   See "From behind bars, Madoff spins his story", *Financial Times*, 8 April 2011

93   See "From behind bars, Madoff spins his story", *Financial Times*, 8 April 2011

94   That NGO is International Crisis Group, whose local researcher, Ardian Arifaj, contributed to the preparation of this section; see the full Crisis Group report on the 2004 violence at their website, www.crisisgroup.org

95   Eight Serbs and 11 Albanians were killed in the violence. Source: International Crisis Group

96   Samantha Power in a video presentation of the International Crisis Group

97   Kosovo became a state on 17 February 2008. Independent Diplomat has advised various of Kosovo's governments and the multi-party negotiating team in this process

98   Source: Anthony Beevor, *The Battle for Spain: The Spanish Civil War 1936–1939*, Weidenfeld & Nicolson 2006

99   www.notonourwatchproject.org

100   1-800-GENOCIDE

101   *Los Angeles Times*, "Is the Darfur bloodshed genocide? Opinions differ" by Edmund Sanders, 4 May 2009

102   Rob Crilly has made this accusation in his book *Saving Darfur: Everyone's Favourite African War*; see also: http://news.bbc.co.uk/go/pr/fr/-/2/hi/africa/8501526.stm

103   The laughably named lordsoftheblog.net

104   *Financial Times*, 14 September 2010, "Chinese communist party opens online forum", including quote from Russell Leigh Moses, a Beijing-based political analyst

105   *New York Times*, "Athens on the Net" 13 September 2009

106   www.seeclickfix.com

107   BBC News website

108   "Sudan's government crushed protests by embracing internet" by Alan Boswell, McClatchy Newspapers (syndicated), 7 April 2011

109   *New York Times*, "China's Censors tackle and trip over the internet" 7 April 2010

110   "The booming business of internet censorship" by Jillian C. York, opinion piece on Al Jazeera English website, 29 March 2011

111 See an excellent article in the *New York Times*, "Google's Gatekeepers" by Jeffrey Rosen, 30 November 2008

112 *New York Times*, "Google's Gatekeepers" by Jeffrey Rosen, 30 November 2008

113 At the Personal Democracy Forum, New York City, 2010

114 *New York Times*, "Google's Gatekeepers" by Jeffrey Rosen, 30 November 2008

115 *New York Times*, 19 March 2009, "The Daily Me"

116 *Financial Times*, 6 October 2010, "US warns of terror groups' western recruits"

117 See report by International Institute for Strategic Studies, October 2010

118 Dave Grossman, *On Killing* (1995)

119 "Military robots and the laws of war", P.W. Singer, *The New Atlantis*, Winter 09 edition

120 *New York Times*, "In new military, data overload can be deadly" 17 January 2011

121 See www.americaspeaks.org: "Unified New Orleans Plan"; this site also has many other examples of deliberative democracy in action

122 Sources: Wikipedia; *Le Monde Diplomatique* (English edition), October 1998, "Participative Democracy in Porto Alegre"

123 See, for instance, www.participatorybudgeting.org.uk

124 See in particular "Ten years on: the case for participatory budgeting; A review of the outcomes delivered via PB projects in the UK", PB Unit, June 2010

125 *Going to Extremes: how like minds unite and divide*, OUP 2009; Sunstein is now an adviser to the Obama White House

126 *Financial Times*, "How to get a better informed European public", 3 June 2009

127 A senior Labour government minister, Peter Hain, for instance, chose *Homage* as "The book that changed his life" in the *New Statesman*

128 *Homage to Catalonia*, Harcourt, p. 104

129 Arendt coined the term, in describing Nazi Adolf Eichmann during his trial, "the banality of evil"

130 *Ordinary men: Reserve Police Battalion 101 and the final solution in Poland* (Harper Perennial, 1993) is the title of Christopher Browning's extraordinary book about Police Battalion 101

131 See, for instance, *Armageddon: The Battle for Germany 1944–45* by Max Hastings, *Among the Dead Cities* by A.C. Grayling

132   For instance, according to American historian J. Robert Lilly, there were around 3,500 rapes by American servicemen in France between June 1944 and the end of the war (source: BBC: http://news.bbc.co.uk/2/hi/europe/8084210.stm)

133   See also *New York Review of Books*, "The Bitter End" by Freeman Dyson, 28 April 2005

134   *New York Times*, 1 July 2008, "Decades later, still asking: would I pull that switch" by Benedict Carey

135   "Replicating Milgram: would people still obey today?" by Dr Jerry M. Burger, *American Psychologist*, January 2009

136   *Invisible War: The United States and the Iraq Sanctions*, Professor Joy Gordon, Harvard University Press, 2010

137   Source: International Maritime Bureau

138   *The Independent*, 28 September 2010, "Insurance firms plan private navy to take on Somali pirates"

139   See, for instance, *Financial Times*, "Wealthy countries fail to hit aid target" by Alan Beattie, 16 February 2010

140   Source: *Financial Times*, editorial "Millennium Goals", 21 September 2010

141   See *The Economist*, 29 July 2006

142   Full title *De la manière de négocier avec les souverains, de l'utilité des négotiations, du choix des ambassadeurs et des envoyés, et des qualités nécessaires pour réussir dans ces emplois*

143   Unpublished research by Independent Diplomat

144   See Robert Cooper, *The Breaking of Nations: Order and Chaos in the 21st Century*, Atlantic Monthly Press, 2004

145   By contrast, an excellent account of the review conference is here: *Open Democracy*, "NPT: Challenging the nuclear powers' fiefdom" by Rebecca Johnson, 15 June 2010: http://www.opendemocracy.net/5050/rebecca-johnson/npt-challenge-to-nuclear-powers-fiefdom

146   See *Moscow Times*, 30 March 2010, "An Illusory New START" by Alexander Golts

147   "Re-framing Nuclear De-Alert: Decreasing the operational readiness of US and Russian arsenals", EastWest Institute, 2009

148   Reported in *ScienceDaily*, 11 December 2006, reporting from the annual meeting of the American Geophysical Union in San Francisco, where twin papers on this topic by scientists from Rutgers University in New Jersey, the University of Colorado at Boulder and UCLA were announced

149 "Exoneration", 2008, referred to in "Al Qaeda's Nuclear Ambitions" by Rolf Mowatt-Larssen, *Foreign Policy*, 16 November 2010

150 See *The New Yorker*, "The Online Threat: Should we be worried about Cyber War?" by Seymour Hersh, 1 November 2010

151 See "Complexity and Collapse: Empires on the Edge of Chaos" by Niall Ferguson, *Foreign Affairs*, March/April 2010

152 Professor Page teaches complexity theory at the University of Michigan and presents the invaluable primer on complexity theory "Understanding Complexity" a DVD-based course from the Teaching Company

153 See www.commonsecurityclub.org

154 We've got time to help: http://wevegottimetohelp.blogspot.com/

155 Judith Brown, the eminent historian of Gandhi, reaches a more nuanced view of the Salt Satyagraha, and indeed Gandhi's movement of civil resistance, in her excellent essay, "Gandhi and Civil Resistance in India, 1917–47" in *Civil Resistance and Power Politics* edited by Adam Roberts and Timothy Garton Ash, Oxford University Press, 2009. The essay is well worth reading for those interested in judgements of the effectiveness of Gandhi's methods

156 *Guerrilla Warfare*, Ernesto "Che" Guevara, Penguin Books 1961

157 Bobby Sands had been imprisoned for terrorist activity, including possession of weapons. Other hunger strikers included convicted murderers

158 Ronan Bennett, also a former republican inmate at the Maze, formerly known as Long Kesh, writing in *The Guardian*, 22 October 2008

159 The POLISARIO Front, the political representatives of the Saharawi people, is a client of Independent Diplomat

160 Source: Nelson Santos, East Timor's Permanent Representative to the United Nations, in conversation with the author

161 Source: *The Red Flag: a history of communism*, David Priestland, Grove Press, 2009

162 *New York Daily News*, 30 November 2010 "Group of Bed-Stuy men, We make us better, escorts pedestrians in wake of robberies"

163 *Financial Times*, Guy Dinmore, "Naples fights to reclaim the Mafia badlands" 27 September 2010

164 See *Dreams from the Monster Factory: A Tale of Prison, Redemption and One Woman's Fight to Restore Justice to All* by Sunny Schwartz, with David Boodell, Scribner, 2009

165 *Fault Lines: How Hidden Fractures Still Threaten the World Economy*, Raghuram G. Rajan, Princeton University Press, 2010

166   Transcript and recording available at www.johnlewispartnership. co.uk

167   See *Financial Times*, 23 December 2010, "Case Study: How to cope with a slump in demand"

168   See *Financial Times*, "A less wonderful life for bankers" by Martin Sandbu (review of Kotlikoff's book), 22 March 2010

169   See Elinor Olstrom's excellent "meta-research" article: "A Behavioral Approach to the Rational Choice Theory of Collective Action: Presidential Address, American Political Science Association, 1997" *The American Political Science Review* 92(1): 1–22.

170   The Heritage Foundation published on 18 June 2009 an interesting but not comprehensive analysis of principles to observe in health-care cooperatives, "Healthcare cooperatives, doing it the right way" by Edmund Haislmaier, Dennis Smith and Nina Owcharenko, available at http://www.heritage.org/research/reports/2009/06/health-care-co-operatives-doing-it-the-right-way

171   www.ghc.org

172   ForestEthics

173   https://www.cdproject.net

174   *New York Times*, "Banks grow wary of environmental risks" 30 August 2010

175   See for instance the Business and Human Rights Resource Centre (www.business-humanrights.org), or www.climatecounts.org

176   This is a paraphrasing of what Bernard Henri-Lévy said during a discussion at the New York Public Library on 16 September 2008. It's possible that I recorded this statement incorrectly, in which case my apologies to the reader and "BHL"

177   If in doubt about this question, please consult my testimony to the Butler inquiry in 2004, and to the Chilcot inquiry in 2010, both available at relevant websites, or upon request

178   *The Life You Can Save, Acting Now to End World Poverty*, Random House, 2009

179   "*E Pluribus Unum*: Diversity and Community in the 21st Century", the 2006 Johan Skytte Prize Lecture, Robert D. Putnam, published in *Scandinavian Political Studies*, Vol. 30 – No. 2, 2007

180   You will find further discussion of these options on my personal website, www.carneross.com, and also in my opinion article "Let's Boycott, Isolate and Sabotage Gadhaffi" in the *Financial Times*, 10 March 2011

181   See *The Observer*, 27 March 2011, "Dutch bankers' bonuses axed by people power"

182   See "Helping women fight back against street harassment, seconds after it occurs", *New York Times*, 8 November 2010

183   See this invaluable article on Stuxnet in *Vanity Fair*, April 2011 edition, "A Declaration of Cyber-War"

184   Quotations from Leo Tolstoy, *War and Peace*, translated by Louise and Aylmer Maude, Macmillan, 1943

185   I am indebted for this analysis to Christopher Brown, whose excellent essay on this subject I found on the web: http://www.scribd. com/doc/8689109/Analysis-of-Audens-In-Memory-of-W-B-Yeats. See also Auden's prose essay on Yeats, "The Public vs Willam Butler Yeats", in *The Complete Works of W.H. Auden: Prose, Volume II, 1939–48*, Princeton University Press, 2002

INDEX

(CR in subentries denotes Carne Ross)